Copyright © 2012 Amy Shapiro and Jay Hickey
All rights reserved.

Copyright © 2012 by Amy Shapiro and Jay Hickey, All rights reserved.

No part of this book may be reproduced or transcribed in any form or by any means, electronic or mechanical, including photocopying or recording or by any information storage and retrieval system without written permission from the publisher, except in the case of brief quotations embodied in critical reviews and articles. Send requests and inquiries to Amy Shapiro at NewAgeSages.com

ISBN-13: 978-1477408247
ISBN-10: 147740824X

Editor: Amy Shapiro
Co-Owners: Amy Shapiro (aka Shapiro-Kaznocha) and John (Jay) Hickey
Cover design by Amy Shapiro
Published by Amy Shapiro, printed by CreateSpace, a DBA of On-Demand Publishing LLC, part of Amazon.com
Printed in the United States of America

For Isabel who IS a BELL Awakening All Seekers!

Isabel Hickey incarnated August 19, 1903, at 12:30 PM EST in Brookline, MA and grew to become known as *"Boston's Spiritual Sparkplug"* in the 1960s and 1970s, as a meditation teacher, healer, author, astrologer and director of Boston School of Astrology. A true New Age Sage, *Issie* uplifted thousands by her guidance, classes, seminars, retreats and book. She was honored in <u>Meetings with Remarkable Men and Women</u> under the category of *Spirit* in which she spoke of western mysticism, Christianity, astrology, the importance of positive attitude and the shifts of global vibrations that are unfolding today. Issie *graduated* June 17, 1980 at age 76 at Harmony Hill, her sanctuary, having lived her belief, that peace comes from one's heart and Higher Self, ***never mind!***

CONTENTS

	PREFACE	i
1	NEVER MIND	3
2	THE TWENTIES AND THIRTIES	11
3	THE PERSONAL YEARS – 1921 to 1933	17
4	JASON AND ELIZABETH	21
5	THE AWARENESS TECHNIQUES	27
6	EPILOGUE: BOREDOM IN HEAVEN	33
7	REFLECTIONS BY JAY	
	The Early Years	39
	Boyhood to Manhood	49
	Conscientious Objector	51
	Munich and Dachau	56
	Coming Home	63
	Issie's Graduation	65
	I Never Minded	66
8	REFLECTIONS BY AMY	
	Issie's "Friday Night Fix"	67
	Harmony Hill ~ Nottingham, NH	74
	Astrology Chart Consult and Boston School of Astrology	77
	A Classic: Astrology: A Cosmic Science	85
	Those Eyes … They Mesmerized!	87
	Her "Home-coming" Lift-off!	89
	"Your Cosmic Blueprint: A Seekers Guide"	93
	Sentiments Worth Saving & Prophecies Shared	95
	Lighting the Way	111
	Star Rovers and Astral Angels	131
	It Is All Right … and It Was	157
	Absent From The Appearance	162
	"Ode to Issie… Who IS!" and "Her Prayer"	164
9	MORE FROM ISSIE:	
	The Wounded Master	167
	The Voice Within	171
	Misc. Inspirations; Musings & Advice to Astrologers and Seekers	173
	As One Book Closes, Another Opens: This is Truth about the Self	205
10	INDEX OF ISSIE-ISMS	207
	ABOUT THE AUTHORS	208

Isabel Hickey, Jay Hickey and Amy Shapiro

PREFACE

For 30 years this book was a well-kept secret! Its message of hope has ripened with reflections and new insights into Isabel Hickey's wisdom and her life. We are glad that its time has come at last!

"I never let the title of my talk interfere with what I'm going to say!" Issie often told audiences with a hearty laugh and twinkling eyes. Unconfined by the limits of advertised topics, Issie– *true to her word* – gave listeners whatever her 'Higher Self' wanted to convey. No talks were ever the same and the fortunate souls who heard her were often changed for the better as a result. With a nod to Issie's wisdom and wit, this book is about *and by* a great Spirit who touched countless lives as an astrologer and spiritual way-shower: Isabel Hickey; *Issie,* as many of us affectionately called her, conveying the wonderful word play ... that she "*IS.*"

This journey has been a true metamorphosis. In its caterpillar phase, its working title was: *How Astrologers Touch Our Lives,* about how astrologers, *including Issie*, impact peoples' lives. It soon transformed in its chrysalis phase as a chorus of *many voices,* of people touched and healed by the compassion, love and good humor of Issie alone. To fly as a butterfly *or Astral Angel* took two wings! Thus, two souls whose lives were intimately intertwined with Issie's completed the journey in a tapestry of memories, observations and glimpses into history via letters, lectures, interviews and her precious last book: **NEVER MIND,** three decades after Issie's *graduation.*

You can dive right into **NEVER MIND** and let the rest of the threads carry you on an adventure as magical as Issie herself. May these many *meta-musings* bless and uplift you with grace. Issie taught: there is no *coincidence* or pure chance, so we gladly accept the grace-full enigma that the release of this book coincides with the launch of **Your Cosmic Blueprint: A Seeker's Guide** natal report at NewAgeSages.com and new edition of <u>Astrology: A Cosmic Science,</u> from which the report was adapted.

With Light, Love and Gratitude,
from Issie's eldest grandson and her once-young protégé,

Jay Hickey and Amy Shapiro, June 2012

NEVER MIND

Like so many souls born into a physical body in the early part of this century, I came into this[1] incarnation screaming. And why not? Before I was over the shock of leaving a warm, comfortable darkness for a cold, too brightly lighted world, I was held upside down by my ankles and had my derriere slapped. It would be 60 years before some doctors would realize how traumatic this is for the incoming soul. It would be longer than that before some would know the damage this reception did to the Kundalini center at the base of the spine. This is the creative center – the foundation of sexual energy. No wonder there is so much sexual aberration on this planet. But delivery techniques now used at birth are changing. There are entirely new approaches during the birth process by the more advanced practitioners in the medical profession. In the incoming Aquarian Age, the relationships between the soul and the body in which we live on earth will be better understood.

    Why did I come back to earth and start the whole process all over again? Like all of us, I chose to come back, and I chose my parents as well as the people with whom I would be involved in this lifetime. These choices have nothing to do with the personality part of us, or its desires. The personality part of us is only a one-lifetime deal. The wiser and forever part of us makes the decisions before we come into earth expression as to what we need to learn and to gain in this lifetime. We all have unfinished business and unresolved relationships to work out. There are those with whom we have strong love ties that we meet again, for Love that is real never loses its own.

> *Serene I fold my hands and wait*
> *Nor care for tide or foam or sea*
> *For what avails this hurried pace*
> *I stand amid the eternal ways*
> *And what is mine shall know my face.*

---

[1] Isabel meant the 20th century, as she had come into this incarnation in 1903.

There is a reason that is not reason. We meet someone and there is an instantaneous understanding and love between us. The heart remembers what reason does not know. There are those we meet to whom we have an unreasonable animosity. An ancient enemy is back again. In such a situation, there is a debt to pay for there has been injury, probably on both sides. We failed to love and appreciate each other in a past lifetime. We have been brought together again to learn to love and to serve each other. The two ties that bind us from life to life are love and hate. Love, and we never lose each other; hate, and we are bound together until we learn to be loving and forgiving. An illuminated teacher once told me that the n'th degree of hatred between two people was the direct cause of Siamese twins. If we take all emotion out of hate, we untie ourselves from being bound to another individual. How much better if the feelings be those of indifference rather than hate. The blessings we give to others come back to bless us. The hurts we inflict on others must come back to their source also. The easterners call this cosmic law, the law of karma – cause and effect. Space is curved. There is no such thing as a straight line in the universe. Everything sent forth must come back to its source.

When our soul patterns and the energies in the magnetic field of the earth synchronize, we are born again into a physical body. I was born August 19, 1903 in Brookline, Massachusetts. I was the second child. My brother John came into the family group two years earlier. There were two girls and two boys that followed us. Six of us – and every one of us different in soul structure and personality traits. Our energy fields and each one's relationships to our parents were entirely different. So it is with every family that is drawn together in a group. The same genes and heredity, for we have the same parents. But we have entirely different soul patterns. No one comes unbound into this livingness.

My to-be-father and mother met at a gospel meeting in a suburb of Boston while my mother was in training as a nurse at the New England Hospital for Women. She had emigrated from Canada. She was thirty years old when they met. My father was a good-looking bachelor, forty years old, who had come from Belfast, Ireland to live in Brookline. He had invested his income in real estate and was financially secure. He had a gentle charisma that was very attractive to females. Many of the women at the gospel meetings were "setting their caps" for him. That was the expression used in those days where "making a pitch" was concerned. The approach had to be made subtly and delicately. This was the era where women had to be ladies whether they liked it or not. In those days if a woman smoked in public, she was a fallen woman and was socially ostracized.

My father was born in May and my mother in June, yet both were born in the sign of Gemini. While both of my parents were born in the sign of Gemini, they were very different. My father had his Moon, (which represents the personality) in Cancer. My mother had her Moon in Sagittarius. In mythology, Sagittarius is represented by Diane, the huntress, to whom the thrill of the chase was far more important than the actual catch. Gemini and Sagittarius types, as a rule, are the most talkative of all the twelve signs of the zodiac. They never keep still, physically or verbally. The Moon (representative of the personality) in Cancer gives a quiet introverted personality that is home loving, sensitive and retiring.

Over the years many people have asked if two people born in the same sign are compatible. Sometimes the answer is "yes," and sometimes it is "no." There are ten energies in the birth chart and all influences must be understood and synthesized before a judgment can be made. My father was a heart person, and my mother, who had an excellent mind, was a head person. Never the twain did meet on a personality level. We cannot relate to one another on a head to head basis; only heart to heart. *Never Mind!* We say it all the time and never hear what it is saying.

On both sides of the family there was integrity, a disciplined approach to life and a religious background that gave the children strong moral values and refinement. Breeding is a quality that is too often happenchance in the human family. Strange! How careful we are to insure good livestock by breeding animals carefully. Yet, in the human kingdom there is no thought of such a course of action. Our emotions run our lives, not our intelligence. Culture is a soul quality. It has nothing to do with how much money or education is hanging on the family tree, though these things do give the opportunity to develop the culture that is within.

My father was a Fundamentalist. My mother had a Presbyterian background. While still in Canada, she was very much in love with a man who wanted to be a farmer. Having grown up on a farm and knowing how hard the life on a farm could be, she refused to marry him. She often stated that never, never, never would she marry a farmer. Shortly after she and my father married, he signed a large promissory note for a friend. The friend disappeared. My father was left holding the note for which he had to be financially responsible. To do so, he had to liquidate all his holdings in Brookline. With the money that was left, he bought a farm in Concord, Mass.

Over the years I have learned when we challenge life by saying very emphatically that we will never do a certain thing or act in a certain way, these seem to be the very things or actions we are forced to carry out. I have learned to be very careful. Every time I have said I would never take a particular action, it turned out to be the one thing I have had to do.

Growing up in the Victorian Age was not easy. Dogma, orthodoxy and creed were limiting and contributed more to self-righteousness than love. Sunday was a day that was completely the Lord's day in every sense of the word. No games, no books to read, except for the Bible. For growing up children, it was a very bleak day, especially in the wintertime. Like so many born ahead of their time, I could not accept the dogma and creed of that era. We went to Sunday School and I was the bane of my Sunday School teacher's existence. I realized later I was asking questions she could not answer. If I sinned, (and we were all sinners and were not yet "saved"), I would be thrown in the lake of fire and would burn in Hell forever! God was Love? Not so, in my mind! Why did I have a father who never took a drink in his life, and my dearest girlfriend's father was an alcoholic? God wasn't fair. If people died and their bodies went back to dust, how could Gabriel blow his horn and put them back together again? Why did they call Good Friday good, if there wasn't something good in it? Who would want to go to heaven and sit around all day playing a harp? It sounded very boring to me. None of it added up to my young brain and my much older mind.

As a little girl I loved Jesus with an intense devotion. Later, when He was often quoted and, in my observations, His precepts were not lived, I turned against Him. I did not realize I was "throwing the baby out with the bath water." Later I would bring the baby back. Later in life I would know that in the long ago, I had walked the shores of Galilee as one who had listened to His teachings and that I truly loved Him. Participating in Christian Endeavor (the youth group in our church) was one of the happiest parts of my growing up years. We had a teacher – Sarah Massie – who loved us and gave us principles that helped us all through life. I made a prayer that someday I could pay the debt I owed her by helping young people as she had helped us. How little did I know then how abundantly that prayer would be answered thirty years later.

In our growing up years, there was one Protestant Church (a united church) and one Roman Catholic Church in the town. We knew nothing of the various denominations of the Protestant faith. There was a great deal of bigotry and prejudice on both sides. The Republican Protestants felt they were of far higher caliber than the Irish Democrats who lived behind the railroad depot. The Republicans were the intellectuals ruled by their heads. The Irish Democrats represented the heart center. It was a devastating potato famine in the 1800's that brought about the immigration of Irish to this country. Reading the history of how Bostonians treated the Irish when they came to Boston is heartrending. They were treated abominably. Signs that said, *"Irish and Dogs stay off the grass"* were numerous. In some of the job advertisements in the newspaper, there was a qualification: *"Irish need not apply!"*

When we realize how far we have come in evolution since those days, we know we have progressed in brotherhood. We still have a long way to go, but there has been progress.

At home we had Bible reading and prayers before bedtime. Sometimes we had to memorize Bible verses. We would look for the shorter verses. I remember a day when my brother, John, spent three hours looking for the shortest verse in the Bible. With great glee he gave it out that night. "Jesus wept."

When I was eleven years old my appendix ruptured and peritonitis followed. In those days there were no antibiotics. When infection set in, if you were not strong enough to throw it off, you died. One day our gruff and crotchety, fast-talking doctor came – took one look at me and said, "I won't be back tomorrow, she'll be dead." My mother was very upset. I said, "Don't worry, I'm not going to die now. I'm going to live a long time like I did the last time. I went out at sunset then, for I wanted to see what was on the other side of the sunset. This time I'll die at sunset too, but it won't be for a long time." My mother said, "Nonsense child, we only live once." "Oh, no. We live many lifetimes," I replied. That was my first intimation of rebirth.

After purchasing the farm in 1913, we moved to Concord. Living on a farm was a terrible shock and disappointment to my mother. Her anger and resentment stayed with her all of her life. In those days, if a woman was unhappy in a marriage, she had to stay whether she wanted to or not. Women had no rights. There were no jobs a woman could get except housework. Her husband held the purse strings, and she had no rights of any kind. What a long way women have come since those days. It would be very difficult for the youth of today to realize what the first twenty-seven years of this century were like.

There were no washing machines, no vacuum cleaners, no supermarkets, nor gas or electric stoves. Everything had to be cooked on the big black stove that was in the kitchen. Wood or coal were used both summer and winter. In the summertime, the kitchen was a very hot uncomfortable place. There was no running water. We had a hand pump on the edge of the black sink and a well in the yard from which the water was drawn. Oil lamps had to be cleaned and filled every day. Except for barrels of sugar, flour and other staples, everything edible was grown on the farm. Vegetables were grown and preserved in jars for winter use. All pastry and bread were homemade. Chicken, beef and pork were raised and killed for food. There were no refrigerators. Ice was delivered by the iceman every day except in the wintertime. There was no such thing as a birth control pill and big families were needed to help with the work. We had hired men to work on the farm, and a hired girl who worked in the house who was paid $4.50 a week. They all worked hard and so did we. We had our chores to do and did them with little complaining. By the time I was nine years old, I was doing much of the cooking. I was fifteen years old before I saw my first movie. They were silent movies, and a piano played the background music to go with the movie.

The First World War in 1917 changed the world completely. It would never be the same again. There were no radios until 1921. Television was still a long way off. The first radio was a small crystal set. You had to put the plug to your ear to hear it. Only one person could listen at a time, and everyone had to take turns. Music in the home was either played on a piano or a gramophone. That title was to be changed to Victrola later. There was a huge horn on the gramophone from where the sound came. An ever-present trademark was a shepherd dog with his ears cocked and the inscription, "His Master's Voice" beside him.

World War I started in England in 1914. The United States went into the war in April of 1917. War was glamorized and so was patriotism. Bands were playing, flags were flying. The men going off as soldiers marched to the depot in Concord where many emotional goodbyes were said before they boarded the train for Camp Devens. From there they were shipped to France, while the bands played, *"There's a Long, Long Trail Awinding," "Over There," "Goodbye Broadway," "Hello France," "Pack Up Your Troubles"* and *"It's a Long Way to Tipperary."*

Troop trains full of young men were shunted from the tracks that led through our farm – coming from Framingham and changing tracks at Concord Junction to go to Devens, then on to France. Many of them would never get to France. In the influenza epidemic, hundreds and hundreds died. I have seen the station platform at Concord Junction (they call it West Concord now) piled so high with caskets that there was little place to walk.

The slogans were everywhere. There were a few wise people who knew that, "make the world safe for democracy" meant "make the ammunition makers multi-millionaires." They did not dare to express themselves for the knew they would be harassed and called traitors. If anyone of age refused to go to war, it was worse. Yellow feathers or yellow ribbons were put in their mailbox or given to them in public places. The song, "I didn't raise my boy to be a soldier, I didn't raise my boy to go to war," was played oftener than some people liked. They effigy of the Kaiser was burned in the village square of many towns and hamlets throughout the nation. Those of German descent, though American citizens for many years, were bombarded by hatred and prejudice and suffered name calling, stone throwing and property destruction. The warmongers and ammunition makers knew how to whip up mass emotions hiding the real reason for war. Today the people are not so easily fooled. The Vietnam War took all the glamour and the deceit out of war making.[2] We are evolving as souls, slowly but surely.

I was thirteen and my older brother John was fifteen years old when the war broke out. One evening he went into town to go to the dentist. When he came home, he told our parents he had joined the Army. He was very tall for his age and had told the Recruitment Officer that he was nineteen. Our parents wanted to have him released,

---

[2] Sadly, in 2003, misinformation and scare tactics under the presidency of George W. Bush led American armed forces to invade Iraq.

but he told them if they did, he would run away and they would never see him again. So they complied with his wishes and John celebrated his sixteenth birthday in the trenches of France.

John was the first wounded soldier in our town to return home from France. The man I married when I was sixteen years old was the second wounded soldier to come home. I was very unhappy at home, and I wanted to leave. My husband was a Roman Catholic – and a good one. My mother was very prejudiced against Catholics. I eloped and for some years I was an outcast. Always, if we need a lesson, our High Self brings us to an experience that will give us a chance to learn it. Later in life, after she got sufficiently over her prejudice and got to know him, she admitted my husband was the best son-in-law she had ever had. He was patient, kind, tolerant and bore no one any evil or bad luck.

That age had its values and charm. Morals were built in at an early age. Such a thing as talking back to our parents or our teachers was unheard of. We would be punished physically – and it hurt. It was a romantic age and we were innocents in a way that would appear very strange to the youth of today. If a boy had a date with a girl, he had to come to the door, ring the bell and get permission to take her out for the evening. If he kept her out too late, there was not another date. If he wanted to marry her, he had to ask her parents' permission. If it was refused, there were elopements and the couple was ostracized by the family. When a boy came to call on a girl, they might sit on the porch or go to a band concert at the village common. There was no crime as there is today, and we could walk the streets in safety.

I was very unhappy in my young years for I was an alien in the family group. I did not understand them, and they did not understand me. No blame, as the I Ching says.[3] So many families have a soul in the family different from all the rest. They are spiritual catalysts though they know it not. There was a dream in my younger years that I never forgot. In a group of Rhode Island Red hens in a barnyard, there was one grey hen. Because she was different, she was either picked on or ignored. So many times, what we do not understand, we fear.

---

[3] The I Ching is a divination method that Isabel introduced to Amy, who later co-authored with Jo Onvlee, *Questioning the Oracle* and *The Gift of the Tortoise*.

THE TWENTIES AND THIRTIES

THE TWENTIES

It was *1921*. The war was over. Our servicemen were coming home. The prohibition law that was railroaded through legislation while our boys were overseas was in effect. It brought the gangsters and Mafia into power. They have never loosed their grip on this country. People that wanted liquor either made it in their kitchens or bathtubs. There were speakeasies behind locked doors. You had to be identified before you would be admitted. Many people died from the effects of bad liquor. Can we legislate morality? Can we deny a person the freedom to put into his or her physical vehicle what he wants to? We were given free will by our Creator. Only when an action interferes or encroaches on someone else's free will is legislation acceptable.

We, as a nation, were in the throes of throwing off the pain and suffering of the First World War. We had been naïve and gullible. We sincerely believed that we had gone to war to make the world safe for democracy. We did not know that we were being manipulated by forces we could not comprehend. A few wiser people spoke and tried to tell us the truth, but they were condemned and considered unpatriotic, even traitors. We did not know that the war was all set up by the munitions makers. Read the Lanny Budd series of books written by Sinclair Lewis. He told the story but had to put it in fiction if he wanted to live. Taylor Caldwell has told the story in "The Eagles Gather". How many will believe? I don't know, but I think the world is getting wiser. Suffering helps us to grow up.

In the *"twenties"* Henry Ford was helping to usher in a new era. He made it possible for the average working man to have a "flivver" and to get out on the highways and byways and expand his horizons. The first Fords were touring cars. They had isinglass shields that could be put on the sides when the weather was inclement. The first engine starters were a tool that had to be put in a hole in the front of the car and then cranked. Tires were made from solid rubber. Driving thirty miles an hour was excessive speed. Mr. Ford was prophesying that we were going to have two hundred years of prosperity. People were buying everything that they wanted and could not have during the war years. The sky was the limit. The roaring Twenties were with us. Never had it been so good. Stocks were climbing higher and higher every day. Happy days were here again. Or were they? On October 29, 1929, the stock market crashed. We were thrown into a depression such as we had never known. It would be a while before realization would come to those of us who had been brought up before 1930. The world we had known was gone forever.

THE THIRTIES

The years from 1929 to 1936 took its toll on all of us who had families to feed and clothe. When the stock market crashed, everyone suffered except for a very few who had not trusted the stock market. Many millionaires became paupers overnight. Many of them committed suicide for they could not accept the idea of beginning over again. Many who lost everything built again on a better sense of values and found life much happier. A friend I was to meet later in life told me she had been a millionaire before 1929. She had had everything money could buy. Yet she was desperately unhappy and bored. She said that the loss of her money was the best thing that could have happened to her. She studied biochemistry and the use of cell salts for healing and helped people attain health through them. She never knew a boring moment from the time she lost her money until she died forty years later.

Up until Franklin Roosevelt was elected President, there was no social security and no employment benefits. Very few people today have any idea what we owe to President Roosevelt. There was little welfare. One reason was that welfare was only sought as the last resort. It was not easily attained. People had a strong moral code and an innate independence. They did not want to be takers without giving something in return. They wanted to work. Welfare was considered alms and no self-respecting person wanted to be the recipient of alms.

Today the welfare system in America is out of control. Generation follows generation on welfare and have no idea of giving it up. Too many people do not work and have no intention of working when they can get welfare. This is sad, for many of these individuals are young people and in what could be their most productive years. Many of the young girls are having babies and not marrying the fathers for they would have to give up welfare. The more babies, the more welfare payments they receive.

One would have to have lived through the thirties to have known what it was like. Jobs folded and there was no work anywhere. Beautiful houses on Beacon Street and Marlboro Street in Boston were sold for six and seven thousand dollars. Today[4] the same houses are selling for one hundred and fifty thousand dollars. Mortgages were foreclosed because people could not pay for their homes. Gasoline was ten cents a gallon. Food was cheap. The best hamburg was 25 cents a pound. Milk was 12 cents a quart. Butter was 15 cents a pound. Smoked shoulder was 8 cents a pound. Most of us ate smoked shoulder far oftener than we had steak. That was 50 cents a pound. Men were grateful if they received a salary of $12.00 a week. If they were paid $25 a week, they were considered very fortunate.

The people who had the hardest time were the blacks. Even when they worked and received a salary, it was one-half of what a white person was paid. Strangely enough, it was the people with money that took the most advantage of them. The Klu Klux Klan were in power and their idea of an evening of fun was to ride into the negro neighborhoods, grab anyone in a black body, tie him to a horse and drag him through the streets. They would rape young girls and women and God help anyone who went to the police and complained. These things took place in the South, but the prejudice in the North was more undercover. But it was there and to some degree still is. In the fifties when my daughter went to Louisiana as a physical therapist on a polio epidemic aid assignment, she addressed a black male patient as Mr. Adams. She was called down for using "Mister" and was told to call him Adams. She said he was one of God's children as she was, and she would give him the same respect. In the 30s, the only title a black male was given was *boy*. To this day, that title stirs up tremendous antagonisms among the black community. A friend of mine had a son, who, as a US Marine, served his country honorably and well. After he came home from overseas, he was driving through Virginia. On a very hot day, he went into a drugstore to get a cold drink at the fountain. Because of his skin color he was refused service. Today that brilliant

---

[4] Since Isabel wrote this in the 1970s, property values have since skyrocketed.

young man is a federal judge in a city near Atlanta, Georgia. Times *have* changed. Though it still has a long way to go, humanity is on the march to humanness.

The depression was at its height for seven years. Hundreds of young people left home because their families could not feed them, and they did not want to be a burden to their folks. They rode freight trains from state to state looking for jobs. Many of them found work on ranches and farms working for room and board. President Roosevelt was inaugurated in 1936. The first thing he did was to close the banks. We went off the gold standard. Was it by chance that the same day that the banks closed, and we went off the gold standard, that Uranus (energy that rules destiny and the utterly unexpected event) went into the sign of Taurus, which is considered the money sign of the zodiac? Gold has always been the symbol of spirit. Those who were awake spiritually knew we were taking a step downward. Material values were replacing spiritual values.

On the day of Franklin Roosevelt's inauguration, few listeners really heard his first sentence: *"I will lead my people on the path they themselves have chosen."* Roosevelt was a wealthy man, but he cared about people. The Republicans and the Conservatives who had not suffered from the depression hated him. He brought this country back together again. *"There is nothing to fear but fear itself."* He started the Works Program Administration (WPA). He not only gave people jobs, but he gave them back their self-respect. People did not earn a large salary, but it enabled them to come through the most difficult years this planet has ever known. Bridges were built, new roads made possible, old buildings in the cities were renovated and made livable. He created the Civilian Conservation Camps (C.C.C.). These camps were created for young men and scattered all over the country away from the cities. It took them out of the concrete jungles into the wide-open spaces where living was more natural. They were fed and clothed and were taught vocational skills that would enable them to get jobs when the depression was over.

Work projects helped the creative people as well as the laborer. There were writers' projects, drama and art projects. Talents in all areas were not allowed to go to seed. It was Roosevelt who created Social Security and unemployment insurance. He wanted never to see this country go through such a depression ever again. In every negative situation there is always a positive side. People were helping people. We were all in the same boat. As little as we had, we shared it with those who had less. If anyone knocked on the door (and people did) and said they were hungry, we shared what we had even if we did not know when or where anymore would be forthcoming. Unknown to ourselves, we were practicing a cosmic law that is forever true. GIVE and it shall be given unto you. We knew what hunger meant, so we gladly shared what we had. And more came. Somehow it was all right.

THE PERSONAL YEARS – 1921 TO 1933

The years between 1921 and 1933 were the most difficult years of my life. I did not know when I married that the head injury that my husband had sustained in France in World War I was going to affect his mind. He was hit on the left side of his head by shrapnel, which tore away three inches of his skull. At the site of the injury, the brain was unprotected, as it was only covered by skin. A blow of any kind at that spot would be fatal. One could see the brain pulsating there. The Veterans' Bureau doctors had spoken of putting a plate there, but there was a big chance it could mean his death or damage that would affect him mentally. They decided to leave the injury alone. One result of that injury was that he had a headache every morning of his life.

I was very unhappy at home, and so I left at the first opportunity. I married at sixteen and had a son and daughter before I was twenty years old. Ever has it been that if we run from tests, we meet them around the corner. Sometimes we meet much more difficult ones. My husband was older than I. He was a good man, hard-working and mentally stable, except for three or four days around the full moon. On those days, he would become irrational and difficult to handle. During that time, I could not turn my back on him for if I did, there could be a physical attack. At those times, I would have to sleep with the two children in the bed with me so they would be safe. He never intended to harm them in any way, but he would hold them to him so tightly they would be frightened and cry. That would make him hold them tighter. Many nights I would find him standing in the doorway with a demented glare in his eyes. I would say very quietly and gently, *"Kieran, go back to your bed. It is all right. Go and get your sleep so you can go to work in the morning."* He would leave and go back to bed.

I realize now that I must have been guided, but I did not know it then. I would get a very strong impression not to let him ever see that I had any fear, and to always treat him gently and lovingly. At these bad times he would always go to work. His fellow workers thought he acted strangely at times, but he was congenial and friendly at other times, and he was well liked. He could always relate to men better than women for he was basically shy.

A day came when I knew something had to be done. I was driving him to work one morning. It was the time of the full moon. Suddenly, without any warning, he jumped out of the car and tried to throw himself under the wheels. A big bus was coming toward me from the other direction. To this day, I do not know how I avoided hitting him or the bus. When he got up, he ran and hid behind a tree. When I called him, he came, climbed into the car, saying nothing, and I drove him to work. Before nightfall I went into the Veteran's Bureau and had a consultation with three doctors. They felt strongly that he should be committed to a mental hospital. They said that in his mental confusion, he might kill me and the two children. I refused to sign the papers that would commit him. At that point in my life I would have loved to be free; even free of earth-plane living. I had to think of my responsibility to my two children. It would have made life much easier for me if I agreed to the doctors' decision, but I could not do so. I asked myself how would I like to be locked in a mental hospital if I was all right twenty-six days a month and not right during the other three or four days? I could not bring myself to having him committed.

I decided that I would leave him for a while to see if that would help or change things. I took our children to my mother's home, and she agreed to take them for the summer. By that evening I had a job taking care of a bedridden elderly woman. During the day I took care of an eight-room house, cooked the meals and did the washing. At night I was up and down from bed answering her needs. My salary was fifteen dollars a week. Three months later my husband and I went back together again. Later, I was to know that my decision not to have him committed was the biggest test of my life up until that time. The only quality I had at that time was a blind faith that if I did what was right nothing bad would happen to us. As that old poem says: *"Dark as the night that covers me, I thank whatever Gods there be for my invincible soul."* That sums up the way I felt. If we do not go into the darkness, how will we know the light?

In those difficult years some of my women friends and I went to spiritualist meetings. They were held on a Sunday afternoon in a small hall in Waltham, Mass. After I went a few times, the conveners asked if I would play the piano to accompany their hymns for the afternoon and evening sessions. They scheduled a snack between the meetings which gave me an opportunity to meet the mediums when they were not on the platform. At the time, they had their snacks, they talked and gossiped about other mediums. They were extremely judgmental, and I found their behavior very distressing. I felt badly but I stayed at the meetings for I was paid a small amount of money, which I needed. I sensed that their meetings demonstrated an inner law there even though it was being misused. I somehow felt that our loved ones still lived. I knew intuitively (without knowing how I knew) that this appearance world was not all there was.

Invariably, when I received a message at a meeting, I was told my husband was going to die. Again and again, the same message came. I did not know the mediums were reading my subconscious wish. I would have been horrified if I did. That little untrained subconscious self knew that I consciously would not leave him. He had no family but us on earth. So my *"Subby"* fantasized: *"If God would take him, I would be happier. Also, my Subby would be free of tension without doing him any harm for he would be free of his difficulties."* The mediums reading for me could read the subconscious and its desires and would give it back to me on the conscious level. Mediums can read the unconscious as well as the conscious desires and thought forms in our magnetic field. What we want to hear, whether unconscious or not, will be given to us. If one goes to a psychic for a reading, it is best to cleanse the mind and the feelings of any desires. Let the prayer in the heart be: *"Let only that which is for my highest good be given me."*

It is very fortunate for us that when we are young souls, we lack the concentrated power to bring our thought forms into manifestation. The death wish, held for another and consciously dwelt on, can take the victim out of the body. That energy comes back to its source and takes out the one holding the thought. I have seen this happen in my counseling experiences. One woman that I counseled was married to a very wealthy man whom she had married because of his money. He was getting on in years, and she wanted him to be on his way. He had a very strong will and was determined he was not going to die. The battle took place on the mental plane. The first time she came to see me she gave me his birth data and wanted to know when he would die. I said, *"He will not die for quite a while."* (For those of you who are astrologically minded, he had Mars very close to his Sun in his

Birthchart. These are the people who have unbelievable ability to hang onto the body no matter how sick it is.) She was very angry with me. *"He is turning cyanotic and the doctor has given him less than a week,"* said she. I replied, *"Sorry, he is going to live some years more. If you continue to hold the death wish for him, you will not live to get his money."* She retorted, *"That is crazy."*

Though she did not like what I told her, she kept coming to see me occasionally for she always felt better after we had a session. Four years later he did die. The will was to be probated and she was to have the money in one year's time. Seven months after her husband died, she died. My *'little'* self would have loved to say, "I told you so!" That's the unredeemed part of me. There are no saints on earth, you know.

It was attending those spiritualist meetings that started my search for truth. I realized there was truth there, but it had to be sought. The Spiritualist Creed is a beautiful declaration of Principles. Two of them I have never forgotten. The first, *"The door to reformation is <u>never</u> closed against any soul here or hereafter."* How could it be? God is Love, always was and always will be. How could He stop loving part of Himself? The other one that sunk deep into me: *"We make our own Heaven or Hell by how we obey or disobey nature's laws."* Later I would learn the true meaning of that principle.

From the time I woke up spiritually there were no more prognostications that my husband was going to die. We were together only one month short of fifty years.

JASON AND ELIZABETH

It was Sunday morning at Harmony Hill in New Hampshire. Thirty of our group were coming from Boston to spend the day. I was busy in the kitchen making ten pies for dinner. In rushed a redheaded middle-aged man saying, *"Mrs. Hickey, you have to help me." "Who are you?" "I'm your neighbor Eric Worthington. I live in the grey house up the road."* The house that he was referring to is about five miles away. Our retreat house is on a dirt road that runs from Nottingham to Deerfield and the few houses on the road were far apart.

"What can I do for you?" "I want you to come up and de-haunt a house for me." I was amazed for very few people knew of my work with earthbounds.

"What is the matter?" "There is a ghost in the house. I've lived there two years and I've known about it, but it never bothered me and I let it be. I know it is there for I hear things being dragged across the floor in the attic. There are other kinds of noises too. Once I sent for the police and two of them came up. When the racket started, one ran up the front stairs – one ran up the back. Both of them had guns in their hands. Shortly, they came back down and said "Eric, we can shoot what we see, but we cannot shoot what we can't see. We're getting the h --- out of here." With that, they left.

I said, "Well, if you've lived with it this long and it hasn't harmed you why are you disturbed now?" "I have the house up for sale, and the racket has become worse. Last weekend, I had a couple come from Connecticut who are interested in buying the house. They stayed overnight and during the night the psychic noises were so bad they got up and went home. They were frightened. They never came back. I want to sell the house. I know you can help me." Later I found out he was somewhat psychic. He had been the redheaded kid in the original Our Gang movies.

I told him after I had finished the day and the crowd had gone, I would come up and bring a friend called Joe with me. Joe was born in the sign of Pisces and was very sensitive to unseen vibrations.

After the group had left Joe and I went into the Chapel Room and had a meditation. I was tired from all the busyness of the day and knew better than to work in the psychic field without protecting myself spiritually and having a rested physical vehicle. When we went to his house, it was about 10:30 p.m. He showed us the house. The moment we came to the upper landing at the top of the front stairs, we both stopped. We knew simultaneously that this was where the psychic disturbance was focused. Somehow, we knew that there had been a fight in the front bedroom, and it had ended at the top of the stairs when someone was pushed or had fallen down the front stairs. A neck had been broken and the person was dead when the body landed at the bottom of the stairs.

We each tuned into our Higher Selves and asked that the focused energy there be dispersed and that it be returned to its source and lifted into Light. We said a prayer of exorcism. Then, we went downstairs. Eric. He told us the racket started about eleven o'clock each night. He said when it started, we were on our own, for he took refuge in the kitchen behind a big chair. We were in the living room. Off the living room was a dining room. In it was a large round oak table. In the center of the table was a heavy brass candlestick.

Suddenly there was a large noise as though something from the next room had been thrown across the room. We ran in. The brass candlestick was lying in the far corner of the room. Eric had fled into the kitchen. We sat for a half hour and then returned home. Evidently, the exorcism worked long enough for him to sell his house and he left the neighborhood.

A middle-aged couple moved in and spent a year there. One day the woman dropped in to visit. I said nothing about my past visit to the house but asked very casually if she had ever had any experience with psychic phenomena. She said, "Not too much, but I am sure there is a psychic entity in our house, although it doesn't bother me much. I have a German musical stein on the mantel over the fireplace in the living room and sometimes in the middle of the night I hear it playing. It is the kind that only plays when it is lifted up. I went downstairs a few times and there was no one there. So now when I hear it, I let it be. One night my husband was sitting on the side of his bed and someone slapped him across the face. He was furious for he thought his son (who did not like him) had done it. I proved our son could not have done it for he was in a sound sleep in his own bedroom."

Time went by. They sold the house and moved closer to their work. The bank took the house back and it was empty for a long time. One summer afternoon three of us were sitting on my lawn, and I told them about the house. They were intuitives as are so many people on the spiritual path. They wanted to see the house, so we drove up. The minute we stepped on to the lawn, Rosalie froze. There was a huge tree on the lawn beside her. "I am not going a step farther. There is a body buried under this tree. It was buried in lime." She went back into the car. Sherry and I walked out behind the house. She said, "Someone pulled some trunks out of the attic of this house and burned them here in the back yard."

We were puzzled, but curious. What did it all mean? We came back to Harmony Hill and Sherry received an impression to take a pencil, and she would be told what the mystery was all about. An entity called Margaret wrote through Sherry that she would tell us the story, for the people concerned needed help.

In the late 1700's, the house and farm were owned by Jason Stevens, a sailor. Part of every year he went to sea, and the rest of the year he lived on the farm. It was lonesome living there alone, so he decided to marry. While he was traveling the seas, the ship stopped at a port in Nova Scotia and he met Elizabeth. Elizabeth was considered an old maid in the village where she lived. She was twenty-five years old and hadn't married. In those days, if you reached that age and had not married, chances were strong that you never would. You were considered a spinster. So when she met Jason, and he asked her to marry him, she agreed and came with him to Steven's Hill Road in Nottingham, New Hampshire. Jason, born in the sign of Scorpio, had the most negative qualities of that sign. Scorpio people are either very high in consciousness or very low. There do not seem to be any middle-of-the-road types. Jason was bad tempered, possessive, passionate, jealous and very difficult to get along with. He had no friends and was a loner in every sense of the word. Elizabeth was lonely, for it was deep in the country and there were no neighbors nearby.

One day she spoke to a young man going by on the road, leading a cow to pasture. Jason was furious and made her pay dearly with mental abuse for daring to talk to a man on the road. Elizabeth was very unhappy and wished she never had married him. Soon she found she was pregnant, which made her very happy. She would have someone to care for and love, and not be alone anymore. One night, when she was over seven months pregnant, Jason demanded his "rights" as a husband. Because he was rough in his sexual approaches, she was afraid he would injure the baby. She refused him and the fight started. She jumped out of the bed and ran out in the hall. Jason was in a vile temper; they wrestled at the top of the stairs, Elizabeth went hurtling down the stairs, and was dead when she reached the lower hallway. Her neck had been broken. He had not intended to kill her. He was very frightened, knowing he could be tried for murder.

He dug a grave out beside a tree and buried her in lime. He took her trunks with her clothes in them from the attic and burned them in the back yard. Then he told everyone she had gone back to Nova Scotia. He was full of fear that someone would find the body. So he stayed there alone on the farm for five years.

After those years passed, he decided to go back to sea. He did, and was killed in a bar brawl in a coastal town. As soon as he left the body, he came back to Nottingham and his house. Riddled with fear and guilt, he did not dare leave. Someone would find Elizabeth's body. He had no consciousness of time. He was caught by being locked up in his guilt and filled with fear that he would be found out. He had created his own hell and couldn't forgive himself. Elizabeth too was earthbound for she could not forgive him either.

When the story was given to us, I knew why. We were the channels to be used by the forces of Light to set them free. Sherry had the ability to see clairvoyantly. Rosalie would be used as a battery, and I was to do the talking. Into the Chapel room we went, and offered ourselves as instruments for Elizabeth and Jason's release.

Elizabeth came first. Because she was still living in the experience, she had no idea that it had all happened over one hundred and fifty years ago. She did not want to forgive Jason. She kept saying, "He killed my baby. He killed my baby." I had quite a job convincing her it was over 150 years since that had happened.

Finally, she agreed to forgive him and go forward into Light. I convinced her that she hadn't lost the soul she carried under her heart for seven months. Further, I reassured her that if she let go of her resentment and hatred for Jason, she would find that soul again when she went into Light.

Rosalie and Sherry were pleased and thought our session was over. They flinched when I said it wasn't over, for we also had to be the channels through which Jason would be set free. "Oh no." "Oh yes. Isn't he just as dear to the heart of God as Elizabeth?" They agreed and we made contact with Jason. He was sitting at the top of the stairs crying as though his heart would break. "I killed her. I killed her. I didn't mean to do it." The hardest part of dealing with earthbounds is to get them to hear you as well as to let them know you are there to serve them and that you really care about them and do not judge them. It was his fear someone would find the body that made him try to scare off anyone who came to live in that house.

I finally got through to him and convinced him it had all happened in the long ago, and he could go free if only he would forgive himself. He did not have to stay locked in that moment of time – the worst moment of his whole life. I asked him who he had loved the most in that life. "My mother." So, I asked the Invisible Helpers to bring an angel who would personify his mother to lead him into Light. (After all, in that length of time she may have incarnated again.)

We all heard him say, "Mother" in tones of pure joy. He had gone home – and so had Elizabeth.

Then we had an unexpected joy. We had our reward. We were projected, in consciousness, to a beautiful cathedral on an inner level. The presence of the Christ was there, and we were blessed. No words can describe that place, the Presence and the blessing. It was an experience none of us shall ever forget.

With movies like "The Exorcist" and "Rosemary's Baby" and many more horror pictures coming out, a great fear of the psychic worlds has been engendered. It is important to realize that not all entities functioning in the psychic realms are evil. Ninety percent are 'stuck' between this plane and the next one. There is an electrical belt between this plane and the next. It looks like flowing water, but it is not water. People have seen this belt clairvoyantly and have thought it was water. I have wondered if this is the reason for the myth of the River Styx and the old gospel songs like "Shall we gather at the River." Those who are closer to this side of that belt and who cling to the earth, no matter what the reason, need help from this side. We need to help direct them towards the other side where there are invisible helpers who will help them.

So many of them become earthbound, stuck because of guilt, fear or ignorance. Jason and Elizabeth were caught for different reasons. Jason was earthbound, for the minute he left the body, his consciousness had one thought: "I killed her. I must get back so the authorities won't find the body. I will be in bad trouble if they do." So he came back and harassed anyone who moved into the house, to frighten them into leaving. Elizabeth was bound to the circumstances of her death, for she resented and hated Jason for what he did to the baby. She didn't seem to care about his killing her. He had killed her baby. That was why she couldn't forgive him. When she came to the realization of what she was doing to herself, she forgave him and was freed.

An interesting impression came to me after the experience ended. Within three months, the porch would be painted white and I would know the house was clear of all intruding psychic forces of energy. It was. In the next house to Harmony Hill lived a man whose mother had been a Stevens. He was an ancestor worshipper, so I knew he would know the history of the Stevens family. Very casually, I inquired of him as to whether or not a Jason Stevens had ever lived on the road. "Yes, he lived in the house on the right about five miles up the road. It was in the 1700's. He had a farm there and followed the sea in the winter." "Was he married?" "For a short while. Then his wife went back to Nova Scotia where she had come from. He was a difficult person and he wasn't a friendly person, so he had no friends. He died away from here during one of the times he was at sea."

THE AWARENESS TECHNIQUES

During the years when I played the piano for a spiritualist group, two different mediums who did not know each other, gave me readings at different times that I thought were crazy. The readings said that when I was in my sixties (such a long time away to someone in their thirties), I would meet a man from another planet. Can you imagine anyone believing that in the 1930's. He would be bringing a knowledge and a technique to the planet that had never been here before. He would be tall with white hair. I was one who had been picked to help disseminate the knowledge he was bringing to the planet. These readings were so 'far out' I might not have remembered them if two mediums had not told me the same thing. At that time, I was a housewife and mother, and my world was bounded by the demands of those activities.

Years went by. As I have related earlier my spiritual livingness began when I was thirty years old. By the time I was in my sixties I had been working on my character and serving others to the best of my ability. I was deeply involved in group work in Boston and during the week I had astrological appointments. One afternoon I was expecting a young lady who had made an appointment with me. There was a knock at the door. When I opened it there was a young man standing there about thirty years of age. He said, *"I have come to take my cousin's place. She is unable to keep her appointment and I would like to take her place."*

I invited him in and when I had calculated his birth data, I saw that if he was not in religious life, he had missed his calling. He was dressed in sport clothes and looked like a man about town. But his chart showed that he had a very spiritual side to his nature, and he had come to earth to serve God. He revealed that he was a priest. When he relaxed a bit and decided I was not a fortune teller, he told me that he had come to prove to his cousin that astrology had no validity to it and was basically fortune telling and was not reliable. He told me later that two things *'threw'* him that day in my studio; the picture of Christ over my organ, and the vibration of God's power in that room. I explained that the studio was a place where there were many hours spent in meditation (personally and with a group). Any place dedicated to God's Love and healing carries a vibration that sensitive people can feel. That day was the beginning of a friendship that has lasted through many years and will always be. That friendship had started many lifetimes ago though neither of us knew it that day. Richard entered into many of our group activities and through our discussions, his ministry became much more meaningful to him.

One evening when Richard and Al, one of my group, were visiting, they said they would like to be hypnotized. I had never been an advocate of hypnosis and did not think it was a good idea. I told him that we had spent eons of time building up an inner center and learning appropriate use of will. Why give that will to someone else to manipulate? I did not want to become involved with hypnosis. A week later in meditation, I was impressed by my Higher Self that I was to do some experiments in hypnosis. I was shocked. I really did not want to do it. The same guidance came again. I have learned to be obedient but sometimes I question the guidance. So I responded, reluctantly: *"All right. I will do it, but I won't look for a hypnotist. If you want me to do this, you send me one."*

The next Monday night at my weekly astrology class, I talked with a young student who was new in the class. I asked him what other interests he had in addition to Astrology. *"I have studied hypnosis for five years."* (Then I knew my High Self was up to something, though I didn't know what it was.) *"Would you be willing to come to my house some Sunday evening and do some experiments?"* He responded enthusiastically, *"Of course."*

He came on a Sunday evening. Richard was the first one he hypnotized. He began by taking him back through his life, year by year. A pattern began to emerge. Richard's father was tyrannical and cruel and seemed to hate Richard. Beatings and abuse happened all too often. The man was cruel to his wife as well as his son and resented the love they had for each other.

When the hypnotist reached Richard's fifth birthday, he turned to me and said, *"I have never taken anyone farther back than five years old."* I suggested, *"Take him back to his birth."* On hearing my suggestion, Richard said, *"It is my birth day. I hear my mother screaming. I want to get out."*

With that statement, Richard, who was sitting in a big easy chair, curled up in the fetal position. Suddenly he relaxed and said, *"I am out. My mother is very beautiful, and I love her very very much. My father is standing at the end of the bed. I don't like him. He is a mean man."* He then went on to tell how, right after his birthing, he was taken from his mother. He did not like that because he was taken to a cold bed and the lights above were so bright, they hurt his eyes.

I then asked him to go back in time, before he was in his mother's womb. He replied that he had been a woman. I asked him to tell of his life as a woman. He described his life as a woman at the time of the Civil War. She was married to a man who was killed during that war. She had not loved him. It was an arranged marriage. After he was killed, she told of taking care of a wounded Yankee soldier. She fell in love with him. He did not love her. When he left, she followed him into the Midwest. She told how he left her there and of her death of the 'cough' in a shack, in a muddy town. She had deserted four children, the youngest only four years old and she died feeling great sorrow and guilt that she had left them.

Al, the other young man visiting that evening, went back to a life as a young man in the 1800's in Texas. He was shot to death by a jealous man who thought the woman he loved, cared for Al. Al and the woman were friends and that was all there was to their relationship. Al was surprised to see his body lying on the street with blood on it. He was feeling no pain. He spoke of how easy it was to get out of the body. One moment in it – the next moment out of it – with a great sense of freedom.

From that night on, Richard was clairvoyant. Many times, as he counseled people in his rectory, he could see their past life problems that were responsible for their difficulties in this one. One day a young man came to him with a problem. He said he could only talk to his spiritual advisor about the situation. He said the problem made no sense to him and he would be ashamed to talk to anyone else. He described an irrational fear that began immediately after his 22nd birthday. There was no basic reason for his fear. However, he had stopped working and refused to leave the house. His parents and girlfriend were upset. They thought he was heading for a mental breakdown. His fear was that he would regurgitate anything he tried to eat. He was sure he would vomit if he put any food in his mouth. He had never done so, but the strong fear was always there.

As the boy talked, the priest had a vision. He saw three men on an island in the pacific. It was the time of the Second World War. He had an impression that the men had been in a U.S. plane that had been shot down by a Japanese plane. Before the plane sank, they had released a raft, mounted it, and drifted to the shore of a deserted island. There was no vegetation of any kind on the island. Each day they hoped that either a plane or boat would find them, and they would be rescued.

Nothing happened. Finally, one of the men died of starvation. The other two, in order to live, decided they would eat his flesh. With sharp stones, they hacked some of the flesh apart. As the young man tried to swallow the flesh, he choked on it. He was unable to get it down or up. He died. Incidentally, he was the same age at the time as he was in this lifetime, when the fearful compulsion overcame him.

Richard was in a quandary when he saw this psychically. During his training in the seminary and his priesthood, he had not been exposed to the theory of reincarnation. Yet, he knew instinctively that he could not help the boy unless he told him what he had seen. If he did tell the boy, would he accept it, and would it be meaningful to him?

He remembered some teaching I had shared with him. The High Self in all of us has all the wisdom we need to guide us. All we need to do is to ask for it. Whenever we are in need, if we lift our consciousness to that Self, it will be given to us. He was so relieved when the boy said, *"That makes sense."* – the subconscious remembers. From then on, the boy was free of the irrational fear because he understood its source-experience.

This was the first *'seeing inwardly'* experience that Richard had after the Sunday night hypnotic session. Naturally, we all had become interested in what hypnosis might do as a tool to help people we counsel. Imagine my disappointment in my next meditation to get the impression, *"No more. This is it."* The message did not add up. What does in the world of appearance? When one turns the Will over to the Essential Self, frequently you are not told *'why'*. You have to trust and obey. Later you are shown the reason.

Some weeks later I went to a National Astrological Conference in Miami. I was asked to speak on *'Astrology and Reincarnation.'* In the talk, I told of Richard's experience with the young man who had choked to death in another life. After the lecture, a lady came up to me and said, *"It is not necessary to hypnotize anyone for them to go back in other lifetimes. I have a teacher here in Miami who has taught us a very simple way to go back and see for ourselves what we have done, what we have been, where we have been and what we have failed to learn or have learned in past lives."*

She said that if I cared to do so, she would take me to him that night. I went. He was the owner of a secondhand paperback bookstore. How little I knew when I walked into that store that night that a prophecy of thirty-five years ago was going to be fulfilled. The man's name was William Swygard. He told me that he had come from another planet and had brought a technique that had not been used before on this planet. He said that I was one of those that had chosen (before I had come to this planet), to disseminate the knowledge to the world. It is a simple technique that eight out of ten people can do with little effort. It is not hypnosis or trance. It is a *'do it yourself'* technique spelled out in very simple language.[5] It is a matter of creative imagination (can there be an image without it being a reflection of something?) It is a good idea to have someone help you in the beginning. Questions have to be asked. No one knows what will be experienced until the individual does the technique.

This technique proves many things. We have lived many times in many different races; in many different bodies, male as well as female. Prejudice of any kind is stupid. If we are anti-anything, we are setting ourselves up for a lifetime in that kind of condition. How else are we going to know the unity of all life and that we are part of each other, and part of the Creator that sent us forth to learn to love – to learn – to live – to learn to appreciate.

---

[5] A free download is available at www.scribd.com/doc/17054671/Multilevel-Awareness.

EPILOGUE: BOREDOM IN HEAVEN

It was a beautiful day in Heaven – but then – it always was beautiful in those halls. The angels were always good and never thought of not obeying the will of God. They always had; this made Heaven filled with peace and harmony, which was wonderful – but God <u>was</u> bored. Nothing ever happened; He always knew exactly what they were going to do and knew they would "*Yes"* Him all the lifelong years and days that were ever to be.

It was wonderful to be the Lord of such obedient beings, but He had to admit He **was** bored. So He pondered – and He pondered – and He thought – and He thought – after He had *'thunk'* for a long time, He had an idea. He, like all His creatures, had to give birth to an idea before anything could happen. The Idea, like all ideas, grew from a need.

God was bored with the *'as is'* and wanted to play a bit. So this idea began to simmer in the Universal Mind. Why not create a new world, one that would be different from all the rest. One where they didn't love Him because they didn't know anything but love, but one where they didn't have to love Him unless they wanted to. A world where they could learn how to create like Him. (They'd find out after a bit it could get very weary.) A world where they could have a choice between two opposite forces and decide for themselves of their own free will which end of the pairs of opposites they'd choose to take. He smiled for He knew for a long time they wouldn't guess that both were ends of the same pole.

This was going to be fun; a planet where they weren't automatons but gods in the making. If they learned of their own free will to run themselves and then the planet, He'd have bigger and better jobs for them for He had millions of universes that needed running. Each little god in the making would one day be big enough to be a God in his or her own right.

God knew that when He took a deep breath a world was born but this one <u>really</u> required some thinking for it was going to be different to all the rest. He had better do a great deal of thinking before He breathed out this one. (If only those children He was going to put on that world would remember to think before they breathed out their creations, all would be well with them.) This world was going to be on its own so He had to decide what were the laws that would go out with His breath for once He breathed it forth – like all creations – it had to be on its own.

The first and most important law of all would be free will. The right to chose or reject; the right to decide whether they wanted Him or ? ? ? Or What? There wasn't anything but Him really; how could there be anything outside Him!

At this moment seven angels came flying along past the throne room. They had just finished sweeping the Milky Way with golden brooms. *"Wait a minute. I want to talk to you."* They stopped and bowed low before Him.

They looked so beautiful – and so willing – it did seem a shame to give them such a job. Running a planet where nobody had to obey them or give them any of the glory. It was going to be rough for they wouldn't know how they were going to be used or abused from moment to moment. It was going to be their toughest assignment, for once they started on the job, they couldn't quit until the job was done – until every mortal He would put on this new planet would be like unto Him. Eons of time would pass before every child on this earth planet would stand in the halls of Heaven, Creator in his own right. But – after all – what was Time to an angel. A thousand years would be as a day to these shining ones. Time was a ball they'd bounce between them until Time was no more.

The most important thing for the moment was to pick someone that would represent that which seemed to be opposed to Him; the opposite to Life or Spirit or God – he would be maligned and misunderstood; he'd be blamed for everything that went wrong; he'd never be appreciated for tho' he would be the greatest of them all, he would be unhonored and unsung down there on the new planet.

Who of all these seven could be given such a job? Only one of the greatest of the Suns of the morning could handle this job successfully. His mind turned to the fairest and best and brightest of all those angels before Him awaiting His orders.

"Lucifer?"

"Yes, Lord."

"You are called the brightest and fairest of all the angels in my Kingdom. They call you the Light Bringer. Are you willing to hide your Light under a cloak of seeming darkness and play a game for me?"

"Yes, Lord."

"I'm going to breathe out a new world – and you are going to help your brother Michael, archangel of the Sun, run it. He'll represent Me outwardly; so will you, but inwardly. No one will know you are part of Me. You'll be called Saturn down there and some will call you Satan. You'll be blamed for everything that goes wrong for you'll represent the second principle; the law of limitation. It's your job to limit – to restrain – to check – when the earth children make the wrong choices you will be the angel they will meet – and for a long time they will not understand so they will curse you rather than bless you. Michael will represent Me as Will in its finest sense. Mars, standing there beside you will have the job of representing the energy that will drive that Will either toward you, Saturn, which will limit and restrict it – or toward Michael who will glorify it in My Service.

Mars, you will be Lord of Energy as well as the driving force of desire. You aren't going down into that dual world without a companion for everything on that planet must have its counterpart; and your companion will be one the whole world will love though they won't understand her until they have passed through your kingdom into hers. You will be the driving force that spurs them on, but she will be the power that will bring them Home again to me.

I give you Venus, daughter of the Mighty Ones, to be your spouse. She, who will be hidden deep in the heart of every earth child; take her with you, Mars, if you value your safety, for without her you'll be in dire distress on that planet. Without her love your power will be perverted and misused. Guard her well; you are her knight going forth to battle for your beloved lady, and only when you ride in her defense will your banners be held high and your honor unspoiled.

"What was that you said, Mars?"

"If you and Venus needs must travel yonder you will need the help of your brother Mercury. That rascal! Since heaven began you three – Venus, Mercury and you, Mars, have stuck so close together that even I – God – can't tear you apart. You think love and energy aren't any good without a mind or consciousness to use them? Perhaps you are right, but Heaven help the earth children when you, Mercury, get in there and star pitching. You can set things askew quicker than any other angel in my kingdom. Mercury, you and quietness just do not go together. If they will only accept you as the connecting road between heaven and earth, all will be well. But if they set you up as a god and start to worship you – forsooth you will lead them a merry chase.

"It's your job to reflect all the rest of you down there, but you are a mischief-maker and will take great delight in leading them down every path you choose to wander. You'll think up enough trouble to keep them from getting bored. And boredom is bad business. If I hadn't felt bored today, all of you wouldn't be on your way to a new experience – heading for a world on its own – one where they will have to run themselves and only when they ask My Help, will they get it.

"Now let's see. Saturn, Mars, Venus, Mercury – you have your work cut out for you. Come on Jupiter. By Jove, they will like you down there. Your enthusiasm, your genial and generous expansiveness will give them great joy. They'll call you the nicest names: old man luck, old moneybags, the greater fortune. Through you they will learn that through giving they will gain. You will be considered the most virtuous of the gods, but you will need your brother Saturn to balance your forces. Only a few down there will know that too much of even such a thing as a virtue can be a vice.

"Come here, Luna, daughter of an ancient past and ruler to-be of rhythm on this new world of mine." A very feminine angel came forward shyly. She was the soft and clinging type with an unearthly glow about her that appeared to flow in and through her constantly changing from light to dark.

"Your job is to be the mothering force of this new world. You will help to bring the earth children into it and take them off it when their exile is through. You will be loved by all young lovers for there will always be a mystery about you. If the feminines on this planet will take a leaf out of your book and keep a certain amount of mystery about them and use your quiet receptivity all will be well with them. They are all your daughters and, if they will understand, your power is no less than that of your Lord, Michael, but different in radiation and on an entirely different level. There will be some of you in every child born down there, and if they understand you, all will be well.

"Now you all have my orders. With my indrawn breath I draw my worlds back into myself and with my outgoing breath a new world is born. There it goes. Go with it at my command and when the last Light is lit on that world of mine you may come home again to your Father's House. But not before. Go forth as givers of my laws to the children of men – and REMEMBER …

Lo I am with you always unto the end of the world"

REFLECTIONS BY JAY

THE EARLY YEARS

At 7:29 am on June 11, 1947, I took my first breath in Waltham MA. My grandmother, Isabel Hickey, budding Astrologer, had stationed a nurse-friend in the delivery room for one purpose only: to record my first breath. For the next 33 years and several days, Issie and I were to share and enjoy the planet together. Her wisdom, faith, and guidance are the cornerstone of my inner peace in this lifetime.

My first conscious memory of Issie came at age four and a half at the Hancock Tower in Boston. She held my hand as we entered the building. A doorman opened the door and asked me if that was a brand new coat I had on, and would I like to get my picture taken. Inside the lobby was a model of the Hancock Tower 3 or 4 feet high with a camera in one of the windows, to take pictures of children. I had no idea what was happening when, with Issie's permission, he picked me up and held me in front of the model to take my picture. I kicked and tried to get away with enough force that he set me down. He said to me, "if I give you a dollar, will you let me take your picture?" and handed me a dollar. I had absolutely no clue what a dollar was but took it and let him take my picture. The photo taken that day remained for many years on the desk where Issie did her astrological counseling.

Before I was a teenager, Issie told me she had saved the dollar and put it in the back of the picture frame to give to me on my 21st birthday, but it was stolen. Issie told me she was very upset when she found it was gone. She also told me that she knows, in this life, she is not to elevate things of the physical world, but that of the spiritual world, and let it go.

We lived in a duplex in Watertown, Massachusetts. My grandparents, Issie and Sarge, lived on the first floor; my parents, John and Tia, and eventually five boys, lived on the second and third floors. Originally, the arrangement was reversed. One day, at about age 23 months, I had gone upstairs to visit Issie. She was working in her study on the second floor.

As described to me by Issie, it was a warm day; the window was open with a screen to let in the fresh spring air. She didn't pay attention for a moment, and then turned to see me sitting on the windowsill leaning on the screen. And then I was gone out the window, a two-story drop with a concrete abutment under part of the window. Issie said she screamed so loud that my mother came running from downstairs, and they met on the stairs.

Issie said to my mother, *"Jay fell out the window!"* and they both ran out to get me. I was gone. Issie said for a few seconds they were dumbfounded. They ran back to the front of the house and looked up and down the sidewalk. There I was, walking 75 or 80 feet up the sidewalk without so much as a scratch.

Issie told me in later years she thought she was going to have a heart attack when I disappeared out the window. She also said that my astrological chart showed that I was protected in this life. I have tested that premise many times over the years. In later years, when she told the story, even then, there were times she would become flushed thinking about it. I think that is the reason Issie and Sarge moved to the first floor.

Maple Street in Watertown was very typical of the 50s. There were two-family homes shared by two generations: my father's generation recently home from war, were starting families and careers; my grandparent's generation, having been through their own war, and a depression, wanting to do what they could to help their children. It was a wonderful place to grow up. I had four brothers, our grandparents lived downstairs, the neighborhood was full of children our ages, we had a yard we could play in, an overgrown vacant three or four acre lot that hid a lot of us kids in the overgrowth, and the Charles River was at the end of Maple St. It was a time when kids could be kids. The Trolley cars went from Watertown to Boston and stopped at the top of Maple Street for pickups and drop-offs. As we later found out, for a dime we could get to downtown Boston and back, and we did. If Tia and Dad ever found out, that we, at 8 or 9 years old, were traveling on the Trolley to Boston, we would have been in for it. Needless to say, it was a very good place for five boys to grow up.

In that context, Issie introduced me to a new world that would form my life and future. Issie had purchased a summer home in

Nottingham, New Hampshire, and asked Tia if she could take me with her for the weekend. I was a couple of weeks from my fifth birthday at the time. Tia said yes. Thinking back now, to my fall out of Issie's second story window, I'm amazed that Tia and my father let me go.

My first trip from Watertown to Nottingham, prior to the highway system being built, was two- and one-half hours; we had to travel through a number of town centers, which meant traffic. Another first for me was motion sickness, which would last for many years. In addition to the stops for motion sickness, Issie would always stop along the way for a break halfway through the trip. The break most times was at a roadside ice cream stand with homemade ice cream. After having been sick to my stomach, nothing was better than homemade ice cream.

Through the years, our time traveling back and forth was a time of discussion and knowledge transfer. Issie and I talked about everything during those trips. She told me how and where she grew up, the concepts of spirituality, how astrology worked, how to develop inner peace, and to trust God. She told me of people, like Gandhi, who strived to live the teachings of Jesus. Most importantly, no matter what age I was, she would ask what I thought and felt during our discussions.

Though the trip from Watertown to Nottingham took two-and one-half hours, in reality it was light years away. As we crossed into New Hampshire, the traffic disappeared, the homes and businesses thinned. We left Route 125, which ran north from Haverhill, Massachusetts, onto Route 152, which ran west, a country road with farms, fields, and forests. As we got closer to Issie's summer home, there were fewer and fewer homes. We passed the town center of Nottingham, basically a small store called Duds, with a gas pump, a Town Hall, and a Church.

We took a left onto a dirt road after the church. I had never seen a dirt road before. I could see the dust in the side mirror, rising up behind the car as we drove the road. I turned and kneeled on the seat and watched a large cloud of dust, rising like a sandstorm, in the road behind us. Issie was laughing at my curiosity of a dirt road.

Two right turns and a few minutes later, Issie announced, *"we are turning onto our road, Stevens Hill Road, only one more mile!"* That mile of pine and hardwood forest would be walked and driven thousands of times by my brothers and me. The last of the trip was up a hill that leveled and opened to a huge white Colonial with overgrown fields, an apple orchard, and stone walls made of granite.

The house seen from the road, front side yard (L), back yard (R).

She pulled into the yard, stopped, turned to me and asked, *"What do you think?"* I have no idea what I said, if anything. I remember clearly to this day, the smell and feel of the spring grass when I got out of the car, the openness, no other houses, no noise of children playing, no traffic and Trolley noise, just quiet, absolute quiet. In the movie *The Wizard of Oz*, is a scene where the movie turns from black and white to color; that's how I felt standing in the yard of Issie's summer house for the first time. I was overwhelmed. It didn't seem real. But it was.

Issie was excited to show me the house. We went in for the grand tour. I remember the fireplace was higher than I was tall; I could walk right into it if I wanted. It was wider than both my arms stretched wide. The water came from a well house in the front yard. A metal bucket attached by rope wound round a wooden rolling pin type thing (only much bigger) with an iron handle, was lowered and raised to get water. In a room off the kitchen was a pantry that included a hand pump that, once it was primed with water from the bucket, would bring water to the house. As an almost 5-year-old, the rooms were endless. Although this was my first time at *"Harmony Hill"* (Issie's name for it), I felt at home.

My impression of the house revolved around fire and water. Issie lit a small fire the first night for my benefit. I was totally impressed.

The colonial was built in 1806, with an addition added at a later date. The addition was almost as large as the original structure. There were 21 rooms, including a summer kitchen, pantries, numerous bedrooms, closets, and a large living room (the original kitchen). The fireplace that served the original kitchen had a place to hang a pot for cooking. The hook and pot were still there, as was a beehive oven on the left side of the fireplace, originally used to bake bread. As was typical in a colonial of that era, the chimney served the kitchen fireplace cook area, as well as the four bedrooms on either side of the main chimney. Two bedrooms on the first floor and two on the second floor all had fireplaces.

The bathroom was off the original kitchen, through a washroom with a large washbowl and a pitcher of water from the well, for washing our hands. Past the wash area was a door that opened to a three-hole wooden toilet. There were wooden covers over the holes, a bucket of ashes and scoop to put ashes down the hole of your choice after you, as Issie said, did your business. I don't know how long it was before the birthing room off the living room was made into a "modern bathroom." I would guess four to six years. Even so, my brothers and I continued to use, as Issie called it, *the 1806.*

This was a great place for my brothers and me to explore. For many years, we discovered many hidden treasures, such as many places to hide from each other, old newspapers from the early thirties, and an old Victrola record player with 78-rpm records; turn the crank, the records would play. There was no electricity; the refrigerator ran off propane, as did the globe wall lights in the kitchen and living rooms.

The barn was gone when Issie bought the house and property, but the stone foundation remained. The property consisted of forty acres of fields, pine, and hardwood forest, the house, and a cemetery, where a number of the previous residents resided.

The overgrown apple orchard still produced apples; there were also pear and peach trees and high-bush blueberries. All of these, which Issie, a very good cook, would turn into most excellent Pies and Muffins. If we picked them, she would cook them.

My first day at Harmony Hill, Issie and I arrived early after-noon. After the tour of the house, Issie told me she was going to make us lunch, and if I wanted to go through the house and pick a bedroom to sleep in, it would be my bedroom for as long as I wanted, or I could go outside and explore.

The bedroom decision was my first choice. Issie told me, *"the smaller room off the living room to the left of the fireplace is going to be a chapel; all others are available."* I chose a first-floor bedroom to the right of the fireplace. No way was I going upstairs by myself. The room was large 16 x 18 feet, with twin beds, bureaus, a fireplace, and four windows with multiple small panes of glass.

At home, I shared a smaller room with my brothers. I had not thought of the actual sleeping in my own room alone until this moment; I was immediately frightened. I went to the kitchen and expressed my concern. Issie stopped working on lunch and went with me to my room. She said, *"You will never be afraid in this room, because it is special."* She then went from one window to the next and closed the Indian shutters, which covered all the windows. The room was dark with the exception of light coming in through the open door. She said nothing could get me with the shutters closed. I was convinced that I was safe.

Issie would play the piano in the living room until I fell asleep. She played hymns and songs she grew up with from the First World War era through the 1950s. To this day my favorite hymn is *"I walk Through the Garden with Him."* The nightly piano playing became a tradition until I was in my teens and went to bed after Issie.

From my first weekend at Harmony Hill I felt at home. It was as if I had always lived there and had come home. What I didn't comprehend was that I was about to meet the first members of my extended family. Issie and I had arrived Friday afternoon. We did the tour of the house, I picked my bedroom, and we carried in groceries, ate lunch and settled in. During the evening, Issie lit a fire in the fireplace and we talked. Issie told me a few people were coming for the weekend to help us work on the house.

At that time Issie had a studio in Boston where she did Astrological Counseling, taught Astrology Classes and held Meditation groups weekly. From these groups, volunteers came forward to help

Issie at Harmony Hill with cleaning, painting, yard work, anything that needed doing. Saturday morning, 10 to 12 people arrived prepared with supplies, work clothes and willing hearts. The Saturday work sessions lasted for years with hundreds of people from every walk of life involved. It was my first experience of people working, laughing, and having fun. There was a core group that came consistently over the years. The ebb and flow of life always seemed to change the dynamics of the group with new additions and subtractions. For Issie, they were one of God's Blessings. As I grew, they became my friends, counselors and confidants.

Issie set the project priorities; the Chapel was first on her list to be completed. During my first summer, the Chapel room was cleaned, painted, wallpapered, and a new rug put down. The Chapel included a pump organ with pedals that had to be pumped with your feet in order to play, an antique couch from her mother's home in Concord Mass., several high back chairs, an existing fireplace, and depending on the season, flowers. Lilies of the Valley and Lilacs were my favorites. The Chapel could seat nine or ten people, and more people often sat on the floor. After the chapel was completed a dedication service was held; thus began many years of meditation, prayer and respite from the world for the many people who came to Harmony Hill.

Issie spent time with me alone me in the chapel, teaching me to pray and meditate. I remember asking her, "What is the difference between prayer and meditation?" She said, *"prayer is when you talk to God; meditation is when you listen to God."* Issie and I arrived Friday afternoons before others arrived and would almost always spend time first in the Chapel.

Sundays were a day of rest with minor things being done. Typically, the group slept in Sunday mornings after having worked all day Saturday, followed by Saturday nights in discussions ranging from Astrology to karma, reincarnation, politics, teachings from the great masters, and anything that came up. Issie and I had an agreement: I could stay up as long as I wanted and listen to the discussions, as long as I had a nap on Sunday afternoons. Many times, I woke up Sunday mornings having been carried to my bed after falling asleep listening to the Saturday night discussions; I would always ask Issie how long I made it before I fell asleep. As agreed, I would take a nap on Sunday afternoon, falling asleep to Issie playing the Piano.

Photo of Issie at Harmony Hill in summer.

    A routine developed for me. I spent my weekdays in Watertown and weekends in Nottingham at Harmony Hill. The summers there were the best. Issie and I could leave Watertown on Fridays, and even on an occasional Thursday, and return on Monday mornings. Our season at Harmony Hill ran from late April or early May to mid-to-late October, depending on the weather.

    Issie and I, and later my brothers, would come to Harmony Hill during February School vacation, to check the house. It always amazed us how much snow was there, most times two feet with high drifts from the wind. The road was plowed by the town, leaving mounds on both sides of the road.

    Issie parked in the middle of the road, which was now a single lane due to the snow. We would wade into the house for the shovels we needed to clear enough room to turn the car around in the yard, and not block the road if someone needed to get by. Issie always picked a storm-free day to make the trip; most were bright sunny days with the bluest skies. Issie carried a dustpan and brush, sweeping hundreds of hibernating flies from the floor and windowsills as we went through the entire house, checking to make sure everything was

OK. It was usually colder in the house than outside, so we ate our lunch outside on the porch. After lunch, we spent a short time in the cold chapel, and then it was time to head back to Watertown. I loved that trip; it meant we were not far from spring and being at Harmony Hill for real.

During the winter, Issie was busy with Astrology Classes and counseling. She had a meditation group she called the *Astral Angels* that met at her studio Wednesday evenings on St. Botolph Street in Boston. Many of the people that came to Harmony Hill in the summer attended the Wednesday Meditation group. It was always nice to see them again.

As I grew older, a late school night became less of an issue, which allowed me to attend the meditation group on a more regular basis. On New Year's Eve, the group celebrated with a meditation and a nonalcoholic party and shared their wishes for the next year. I attended the New Year's celebrations well into my teens.

The early summers at Harmony Hill with Issie were years of accomplishments on both spiritual and physical levels. We finished most of the major projects related to the upgrade of the house. The last major project was having electric lines run to the house from more than a mile away. Issie had mixed feelings, as did I, about how that would change Harmony Hill and the peacefulness of this place.

My understanding and growth related to the spiritual world mirrored the changes of Harmony Hill itself. With Issie's help I was able to understand the concept and how it felt to reach inner peace in meditation and bring forth that peace to deal with the tornados of everyday life. During the many years since Issie taught me the gift of inner peace, I have had people comment on how calm or peaceful I am in stressful situations. I would tell them how my grandmother had her own chapel in which we learned of the spiritual world, and no question went unanswered. The response usually was one of two things: *"You and your brothers were so lucky!"* or *"You had a What?!"*

Issie would say life is no different than going to school. There are always going to be tests; your choice is how many times do you want to repeat the same life test before you move on. She taught me about what she called my three selves: the subconscious she called my *Subby*, the conscious (my waking) self, and the super conscious (my higher) self – the God connection. She would say, *"Trust and use these connections as you grow older. They will guide you in the direction you have chosen to go. If you get stuck, let go and let God."*

My time with Issie during my school vacations included going to a retreat, seminar, or conference ranging from three or four days to a week. My first memory of traveling together was to the Vedanta Center south of Boston. I was six years old. I remember some of the men wore turbans and robes and it was peaceful like Harmony Hill. While Issie met with the Swami, one of the brothers took me to the garden. He asked me if I knew how to be still and quiet; I said yes. We sat on a bench. He placed seeds in my hand and told me to extend my hand and be still. Within seconds, a Chickadee landed on my hand and took one of the seeds and flew away. To this day I can remember the lightness of it on my hand.

We attended a retreat on Star Island off the New Hampshire coast when I was seven years old. I was free to roam the island, attend the lectures and meditations as I wished. My directions from Issie were to be careful climbing the rocks near the ocean; mealtimes are scheduled, be back for meals or I may go hungry. I did not miss a meal. I liked the Meditation time, lots of people, music, and singing.

Two days before the end of the retreat, Issie told me a Hurricane was coming and we were going to leave a day early. The following afternoon we boarded the boat to head back to Portsmouth and home. The boat could accommodate twenty or so people. There was an enclosed area with lots of windows on the deck for us to sit out of the wind. As people were boarding, a boy my age, that I had met at the retreat, and I went outside on the front of the boat and sat on the deck with our feet hanging over the side.

There were ropes, one low and one higher, to keep people from falling overboard. The lower rope was in just the right place for us to rest our arms. As the boat pulled away from the dock, the water was so calm we could see the crabs scurrying beneath our feet. We headed out of the harbor counting the crabs. As soon as we left the harbor, the front of the boat lifted out of the water, so that I slid against the boy next to me, and it came down into the sea with a splash. We both were hanging over the side of the boat with the rope under our armpits and dripping wet.

The boat was rising up again as I felt a hand pulling me back onto the deck. The captain's teenage helper had pulled my friend and I back onto the deck together. He took us into the enclosed area with the adults and got something to dry us off. Issie and the other adults were very concerned and all talking at the same time. It had happened so quickly and was over in an instant. I had no concept of how close my friend and I had come to exiting the planet.

The rest of the trip from Star Island to the mainland was very rough. Many of the people on the boat, including me, suffered from motion sickness. I was wet and cold and sick; the short trip to the mainland seemed to last forever. Issie told me years later, the Captain of the boat told her it was the worst trip to the mainland he had experienced in almost thirty years. If he had it to do over, he would have not left the Island that day.

Issie would remind me when I was older, more than once, of my two close calls, going out the window and the trip from Star Island and would tell me *"I know you are protected according to your Astrological chart, but please don't test it while we are together; I'm going to have a heart attack,"* then would always laugh. I did test my protection several more times but not in Issie's presence.

BOYHOOD TO MANHOOD

For many years Issie and I continued our summer getaways attending conferences, retreats and all manner of astrological get-togethers. We traveled to the Finger Lakes in NY, the Edgar Cayce foundation at Virginia Beach. My brother and I went with Issie cross-country by automobile to Santiago, CA for an astrological conference. I had turned sixteen and was able to help with the driving. At sixteen I would have driven the whole way if she let me. We zigzagged our way across the country, stopping to see the sites, and for Issie to touch base with friends and speak about Spiritual Astrology and do charts.

After our return from California I was, for a couple of years, Issie's chauffer to her speaking engagements throughout New England. We had a great time traveling to her lectures. We had time to talk and catch up. Our trips to Harmony Hill together were less frequent due to my schedule. I now had a job at a supermarket, had my own car and was finishing High School.

I had decided to attend a technical school to study carpentry. I had loved working on the house at Harmony Hill and wanted to continue in that direction. Working outside was a bonus. I spoke to my father about going to a school to learn carpentry. He was adamant that I would not attend a trade school. His impression from his high school days was that Trade Schools were where they sent juvenile delinquents.

Issie and I discussed the issue during one of our drives to a speaking engagement. She asked if I would like her to speak with him. I said yes. When we got home that evening, she asked me to wait downstairs while she spoke with my dad. A short while later she came downstairs and said he would let me attend the tech school if I wanted to. I had expected my Dad not to change his mind. I asked what she said. Issie said she prayed on her way up the stairs for the right words to say to him. Issie listened to why he thought it was not a good choice, and then said, *"John, Jesus was a carpenter."* What did he say, I asked Issie. *"He said yes, its your choice."*

I graduated high school in May of 1965 at the age of seventeen with a background in carpentry. Three days later, with Issie's blessing, I moved to Harmony Hill for the summer. Thanks to my High School carpentry teacher, I had a job helping a friend of his build a house not far from Harmony Hill.

Issie was pleased that I was staying at Harmony Hill although, on occasion, she said she wished she could do the same thing. After my first week, Issie asked if I minded being there alone. I asked her if she remembered the first time I came to Harmony Hill and how nervous I was about sleeping in a room by myself. *"Yes,"* she said, *"I showed you the Indian Shutters, and you were comfortable. I'm such a wise person!"* she said laughing. I told her I haven't been nervous here since that day, and we both laughed.

The summers were great for Issie and me. As we had when I was young, driving from Watertown to Harmony Hill, we had time to spend to together catching up. On the weekends, there were people coming to spend time, working, visiting and partaking in the Saturday night discussions. On Sunday evenings, they would head home leaving Issie and me to spend more time together. We would sit out on the porch talking while the evening changed to night. The air would change with the slightest breeze, and the whippoorwill that had been singing in the apple orchard across the street, would be done for the night.

Issie told me her family had a farm in Concord. Massachusetts where she had grown up. She said it was hard work and long days. At the end of the day, she and her older brother John would sometimes sit out, like we were, and talk while the evening passed to night. Issie said she and John were very close and she loved and admired him and they both wanted to leave the farm for a new life as soon as they could.

John left the farm at sixteen to become a soldier and fight in World War One. John lied about his age and was in the trenches in France for his seventeenth birthday. He was wounded by poison gas and sent home. He died at twenty-one from the damage to his lungs by the gas. The loss was sadness for Issie that lasted her whole life. She told me, *"I still miss him but know it's only temporary; I will be with him again."*

Issie left the farm at sixteen and married my grandfather Joseph Hickey, who had also been wounded in the war. She said he was her way off the farm. They had two children; Helen, and a son John named after her brother John. Her son John was father to me and my four brothers.

Issie told me her marriage to Joseph was difficult. He had a head wound from the war that caused horrendous headaches, resulting in outbursts focused at her and the children. She said they decreased in intensity and duration as time went by and it became more bearable.

She said the circumstances of her marriage in a very roundabout way led to her study of prayer, meditation and astrology. She would tell me, *"the road to your destination can sometimes be more important than we realize, pay attention."*

CONSCIENTIOUS OBJECTOR

During the summer after my graduation from high school, I turned eighteen and received a letter from the Selective Service asking me to register. I hadn't thought about the possibility of getting drafted and going to Vietnam until this time. It was 1965 and protests against the war were scaling up as was the war itself.

Issie and I were sitting on the porch at Harmony Hill when we talked about it. She asked me how I felt. I said, *"everything I have learned and understand says life is precious. I won't take a life. I don't want to go to prison or Canada. I will serve my country but not take a life as part of that service. I don't want to go to Vietnam to kill* people." She said, *"I will get your astrological chart and be right back."*

She came back, sat down and said, *"I know your chart inside and out you will not go to Vietnam,"* then started looking at the chart and said: *"nothing will happen for several years. At that time, you have something important to do that will not be what you are expecting."*

I asked if she knew what it would be. She said, *"something you are equipped to do, are you hungry?"* That meant that's all you are ready for or that's all I can give you at this time. We ate lunch.

During the next eighteen months I was married and living in New Hampshire fulltime. I had applied for Conscientious Objector status with the Selective Service office in my hometown of Watertown, Massachusetts and given a date to appear. Issie told me not to be nervous; she had asked her groups to pray for me the day of the hearing.

I remember entering the hearing room and seeing 12 or 13 people sitting around a large conference table with one empty seat for me at the end of the table. They asked me to sit down. I did and was not nervous. I felt at peace, like I was in the chapel at Harmony Hill. The people at the table were passing around a letter taking turns reading it. When they were done, the Chairman said to me, *"this is a wonderful letter written on your behalf,"* and the others around the table nodded in agreement. They asked me few obligatory questions. I explained my belief system to them and that I am willing to serve but not kill.

The Chairman said, *"you will receive a notice of the decision in a few weeks; your request will be approved."* I asked who had written the letter and was told his name. It was one of Issie's friends that had been coming to Harmony Hill from the beginning and had watched me grow up. I was so excited when I left the hearing, I called Issie to tell her the story.

At this time Issie, was spending more time during the summer months at Harmony Hill working on her book and other projects. I lived close by and, during the week, I would stop in. Issie and I would have dinner, then spend time visiting on the porch, catching up. It was a nice time to visit and quickly became something we looked forward to. The weekends were still busy with lots of company and not conducive to spending one-on-one time together.

The weekend dynamic at Harmony Hill started to change when an infusion of younger people started coming. Issie had started a meditation group in at her studio in Boston for younger people which she called *"the Friday Night Fix."* Issie said the Friday Night Fix was made up of kids, she called them *her kids*, others called them *Hippies*, from teens to twenties, in search of truth, understanding and inner peace. She was teaching through discussions, astrology, meditation and her wisdom, the things my brothers and I had learned and mostly took for granted that everybody knew these things. Many weekends during the summer included people from the Friday Night Fix. That meant meditation time in the chapel or on the front lawn, lots of music, interesting discussions and trips to the local pond led by my brothers and me. It was a special time with people the same age as my brothers I were, and a validation that Issie's teaching was being passed to a new generation.

During the summer of 1968, I received a letter from the Selective Service saying to report on August 22nd for induction into the army. At Harmony Hill during one of our weeknight visits, I told Issie about the letter and date. We sat out on the porch while Issie reviewed my astrological chart. She was smiling, a good sign, as she reviewed the chart and said, *"this date confirms you will not be going to Vietnam."* She said, *"the August 22nd date is also confirmation of something important needing to be done in this life. The timing of this date is going to set off all kinds of events of importance in your life. This is a good thing."* she said. I was not so convinced sitting on the porch that summer evening. However, the timing was unbelievably important as I came to see.

I was inducted into the Army and sent to Fort Sam Houston in San Antonio, Texas to be trained as a medic. I was assigned to a company of forty or so men that were all conscientious objectors. About half of the group was Seventh Day Adventists, the remaining were people like me and had requested and received Conscientious Objector status. We did our basic training together. When we moved to the Medic Training Center on the other side of the base, we were integrated into barracks with other army soldiers who were not Conscientious Objectors.

At the training center, we were in groups of sixty men and in a class of six hundred. Every couple of weeks a class would graduate and be assigned. Of the six hundred, approximately half were National Guard and went home after the training to serve with their local units. The remaining were getting orders for duty stations, mostly Vietnam.

We were trained as combat medics and told repeatedly that we would end up in Vietnam. That was my expectation, in spite of what Issie had told me about not going to Vietnam. The medical training finished on the twenty-first of December and I was to receive my orders for assignment on the twenty-second of December, exactly five months to the day from when I was inducted into the army.

On the twenty-second, our Sargent told my group that, because it was Christmas, most of us would not get orders until after we returned from leave. The Sargent said the Army didn't want to upset our families at the Holidays; we would get our orders after we returned. Then he said, *"If I call your name, you are to go to the Captain's office for your orders now."* He called three names out of my group of sixty men, including mine. In total, 32 of us out of the class of 600 were to report to the Captain's office and receive our orders before Christmas.

Once there, we were told to line up in front of a desk and be quiet. The first person in the line was asked if his shots were up to date and does he wear glasses; after the response, the Sargent said *"Vietnam"* while handing the orders to him. This process continued; then he got to me. After I answered the questions, he handed me my orders and I turned around to go to the barracks.

He asked me where I was going. I said back to the barracks. *"No!"* he said, *"Where do you think you are going to be stationed?"* I said, "Vietnam." The Sargent said, *"You are going to Germany. The first 16 are going to Vietnam the second 16 are going to Germany. If any of you men want to switch orders with each other, you can, it's up to you."*

I was in shock, but I did hear one of the guys behind me say, *"Holy shit! Unbelievable! I'm going to Germany!"* I don't know if any orders were exchanged. I was out the door heading to a phone booth to call my family, and thinking of Issie being so absolutely sure I would not have to go to Vietnam. I went home on leave for the holidays with orders to fly out of New York to Germany in early January.

I arrived in Frankfurt, Germany in mid-January of 1969 with a group of eight or so medics. We were replacements for those going back to the States to be discharged from the military. My group of replacement Medics was told by a Captain that they didn't need medics here, *"I don't know why you are here; we are going to send you south to see if you are needed."* "South" meant a number of US military bases between Frankfurt and Munich. After two weeks of stopping at every military base between Frankfurt and Munich, the three of us not chosen at other bases along the way ended up at a small ambulance company close to downtown Munich. The first thing we were told was we were not needed and will be sent back to Frankfurt in the morning, to start the process all over again. I had a flash of spending my entire time in the military, living out of a duffle bag, traveling back and forth between Frankfurt and Munich, being rejected on a daily basis.

A Sargent who had been reading our personnel files asked the Lieutenant if they could *"keep this one,"* and pointed at me. I later found out the Sargent had confused my Conscientious Objector status code with that of someone who had been trained as a Us Army Ranger. I was not about to explain that he was making a mistake. That was not done. I didn't know it at the time, but Munich was prominent in what Issie had told me, about doing *"something important and unexpected."*

The medical company I was assigned to was attached to a military hospital located in a military housing development, also close to Munich. We also provided ambulance service to several dispensaries south of Munich. The dispensaries served the military and their families when they vacationed in the lake and mountain regions of Southern Germany.

There were around sixty to eighty in our medical company including support staff. We were located in a compound that included a military intelligence group, the University of Maryland Munich campus, library, gymnasium, cafeteria, and the motor pool. It was unlike any military base I had ever seen: no gates or guards. If you were single, you had a room in a building designated for the single soldiers; if married and not career military, you were assigned an apartment in a German housing complex a mile from the base.

I was assigned to the emergency room at the hospital as an ambulance driver. The majority of my time in the military was spent helping people. I was able to put to use what I learned from Issie, in being able to communicate inner peace in stressful situations, and to share with those whose life was near the end, that there is more to come.

Five months after I arrived in Munich, I was joined by my wife, and we moved into a 3-bedroom apartment provided by the military.

Having three bedrooms meant we had room for friends, family and travelers. At that time, the late '60's, early '70s, many people were traveling around Europe with backpacks and rail passes. There were no issues with picking up hitchhikers, and we did, with discretion. We met people from all over the continent and British Isles. Some stayed with us for a night or two, others for a week or two. One couple stayed every time they came through Munich. We made many new friends along with a core group of friends that lived in Munich. Most of my friends were civilians and were only reminded that I was in the military when they saw me in my whites heading to the hospital.

MUNICH AND DACHAU

Issie and I had been exchanging letters from the time I left the States. Most of the time, it took two or three weeks to get a reply. It's hard to believe how communication was so different then. My son Jon is in the Navy now and he can email or call me from the middle of the ocean.

Issie sent me a letter saying that my Parents and Aunt Helen would soon be going to our ancestral home in Ireland and would like to visit with me in Munich. Issie said she and Tom Jackson would like to come sometime during the summer for a visit. I told them that will be great, to let me know the time the plane will arrive, and I will pick them all up at the airport.

It was great to see them. I gave my parents and aunt the tour of Munich, including great food, during the several days they were with me. By this time, I knew Munich like the back of my hand. Munich and Boston were very much alike, narrow streets, old buildings, universities, streetcars, parks, great food, rock concerts and friendly people. My parents and aunt loved Munich. They felt like I did, that it was very much like Boston, minus Fenway Park.

They were amazed that my military service was more like a civilian job. I told them it was because I live in the married quarters; they have us check in every two weeks to make sure we remember that we are still in the Army, and our haircut is regulation. We got our duty schedule once a month, that's it. Both my father and aunt served during World War II. They said, *"Boy, times have changed!"* I told them I was lucky, very lucky, and I knew it. The visit was over so quickly, I was sad to see them go. Tia reminded me that in a couple of months Issie and Tom will be here.

Issie and Tom arrived during the summer for their visit. I picked them up at the airport in the evening and could see they were exhausted from the trip and time change. We went to our apartment for something to eat and they rested. Issie's idea of rest was to take a nap for an hour or two. We spent until 2 or 3 AM catching up on all I had missed since I left for Germany. I told Issie about using what I had learned from her teachings, how I was able to use her teachings at the hospital, and how effective they were in comforting some of the people, even those with terminal cancer. She was very pleased.

I told Issie we had a group of a dozen or so friends we hung out with here, and that they would like to meet her. I told them what a great astrologer and teacher she was and some of the things she and I have done. They had very little understanding of what Astrology or meditation is all about. Issie said, *"If they can come over Saturday evening, I will explain the basics, and we can teach them about meditation. Have them give you their birth dates and times of birth if they know them, and don't include their names."* I knew our friends were about to have an unexpected experience and receive a new understanding of their existence and purpose.

I didn't expect that she had a surprise for me.

We spent the week sightseeing, eating at several great restaurants and visiting. Issie and Tom both said they liked Munich, *"It's very much like Boston!"* I laughed and told them that my mother and father said the same thing when they were here.

Saturday evening, about a dozen of our friends scattered around our living room, with the overflow sitting on the floor. Issie was sitting on the couch looking at the birth dates of our friends. Before she reviewed the birth dates, she had explained how Astrology works, and how it can be used for good or misused. She explained how important being in contact with your Higher Self is, and that meditation is a tool that can help that happen. She told them if they have questions, to ask them, don't be shy.

They asked lots of questions! Most of them were getting this information for the first time. Issie started reading the charts from the birth dates and times she was given. As she would point out different personality traits of the person's chart and provide a profile, the spellbound friends would pick out who it was that Issie was discussing. There were lots of questions asked and answered.

Issie explained that this is only the surface of what the chart can disclose at an in-depth reading. *"I want you to know this is not hocus pocus. It's a tool that can help you gain knowledge of who we really are, and what we bring into and need to work on in this lifetime. It's time for a break; I have one more thing to show you afterward."*

After the break, Issie told us the story of meeting a person from Florida several months ago. She was teaching astrology in a group setting with many people in which she also discussed reincarnation in relation to the astrological chart. After her presentation, she was invited to meet to a man named Bill, who owned a bookstore, and had developed a simple, effective technique by which people could view past lifetimes. Issie said that the people she was with asked her, *"What are you doing? You don't even know this person! He could be crazy!"* Issie said, *"Where's your sense of adventure? We'll go as a group and check this out."* Issie went with some friends to Bill's bookstore to meet him to learn his technique. After explaining the process, Bill guided them to see some past life experiences, after which Bill told Issie and her friends to pass this along to others.

Issie said to us, *"His technique works. I was able to remember things I had done and who I had been in other lifetimes. When we got back to Boston, we tried Bill's technique with our group, and it worked with almost everyone. A few people had to try several times before they went back. That's the story about Bill; would any of you like to try it?"*

There were a lot of volunteers to be the first to try it. Issie had us lie on the floor and went through a relaxation process that started with concentrating on our breathing and getting to a state of whole-body relaxation. She walked us through the technique she was taught by Bill.

Issie led everyone that wanted to try the technique back in time to other lives; with the exception of one person who had not been able to relax, everyone that wanted to try it was successful. When we were done, she said we can try it with each other; that we will be able see more detail, the more we practice. It was well after midnight when we ended the evening. Typical with Issie when she was teaching, she was the most invigorated of the group. Then, as was her custom at the end of a class, Issie led the group in meditation.

When I was young, Issie told me that after teaching a class or lecturing in the evening, she had a difficult time getting to sleep. Many times, she would read until dawn, before she could sleep. The stacks of books in her bedroom that I wondered about as a child then made sense.

Issie and Tom left Munich a few days later for home. Not only did I miss them, so did most of our group of friends that had met her. I was told by my friends she was the coolest grandmother and I was so lucky.

The next time Issie and I were together, I had finished my military service. I had flown home from Germany to Fort Dix in New Jersey to be discharged from the military. I had a plane ticket for my trip back to Munich in thirty days; I now considered Munich my home.

I enjoyed catching up with my family and friends. I loved being back at Harmony Hill, sitting on the porch with Issie and talking. I told her I felt out of place here in the States and not sure why. We discussed my going back to Munich and what I was going to do. I told her we were going to travel south for the winter to Greece or Spain, we weren't sure, then come back to Munich to work and live.

She said, *"when I read your chart before you left for the military and said you had something important that needed to be done in several years, that time frame is coming up. When you are in Munich, at that time you are meant to be there."* Issie asked if I was still meditating and praying. I said not as consistently as I should. She said, *"get back on track and pray for protection; we will pray for you at the meditation group."* Issie wasn't asking me, she was telling me, and that was a first. It made me nervous for an instant; I didn't ask any questions because I didn't want to know.

The month home was over quickly. I was on a plane heading for Munich thinking about what Issie said and praying for protection. I let the curiosity go but did follow through with the meditation and prayer.

The next several months were spent prepping for our trip. We headed south from Munich to the Mediterranean in the fall. We followed the coast to Spain and Portugal where we spent most of our time. It was wonderful there. The weather was warm and not many tourists that time of year. With the expectation of working during the winter and continuing our traveling in the spring, we decided to go back to Munich and be with our friends for the Christmas Holidays.

If I worked in a support position for our military stationed in the Munich area, part of our benefits would be an apartment. I went to the personnel office the first thing on Monday and was told there was a position managing a gym opening on Thursday. The gym was located at the Army base we had in Dachau, about ten miles from Munich, a thirty-minute drive if there was traffic. I was told the job included an apartment.

He then asked if I had any experience. I said yes. I thought how hard could it be to run a gym. He told me, *"you're hired,"* then said, *"I can't believe you walked in today, we have been trying to fill this job with no luck for weeks. The fellow that was doing your job has stayed for weeks waiting for a replacement. He has to leave the end of this week for the States."*

I filled out the paperwork for the job, was given directions to the base at Dachau, and was asked to go out to the base and meet with James at the gym. James will go over my job duties. If I can do that, I will be paid starting today and will have an apartment in a couple of days. I walked out of the personnel office with the directions to the Army base in Dachau in hand.

During the trip to Dachau, I was thinking about the timing of getting this job. *Right-place-right-time* had happened before in my life, usually for reasons I hadn't foreseen. My thoughts quickly went to why, after having been stationed in Munich for eighteen months, I did not know anything about an American Army base so close by.

I arrived at Dachau. The base was guarded by Military police. I pulled up to the gate, showed them my identification and employee identification card, given to me by the personnel office. The MPs said I was all set, I asked for directions to the gym, and was off.

The buildings on the way to the gym appeared to be old office type buildings made of brick. Most of the buildings appeared to be vacant. I noticed a few soldiers out walking. It was January, cold and foggy, with a few inches of dirty snow on the ground, and basically dank. My first impression was, *"This place is depressing; I'm glad I wasn't stationed in a place like this."*

I arrived at the gym which looked like all the other buildings, except a little larger. I stepped out of my VW bus and felt something not quite right. I got back in the VW and sat, deciding whether to even take this job. I really didn't like this place. After a few minutes of wondering about my negative feelings, I decided that if this wasn't meant to be, I wouldn't have fallen into this job. The job also meant, I will have an income and an apartment.

I went inside the building to meet James. The gym was empty. I looked around, not much there, a full-size basketball court, weights and some equipment for working out, a shower and bathroom, and a small office-equipment room.

It was old, but clean; I liked it and felt more comfortable about being here.

James came in thirty minutes later and introduced himself. He had been at the base office, letting them know he finally had a replacement and was leaving. James was retired military and liked it here. He told me his parents were getting along in years and had some medical problems. That's why he was going home to Georgia, to care for them. James went over my responsibilities, handed me the key, and said, *"Good luck, I'm out of here. There is a schedule of your hours, and the hours you are to be open is on the wall in your office, the Sargent will be by to meet with you in the next couple of days."* He stopped in to meet me about six weeks later.

I was able to tell my wife and friends that evening, that I found a job, had already worked my first day and would have an apartment shortly. When I told them the job is in Dachau, my friend who was Jewish said, *"that's where one of Hitler's concentration camps was located."*

Other than knowing that millions of people were killed during World War II, the age group I grew up in didn't know about what had happened in Germany. It wasn't taught in our schools. My family never discussed the war. By the time I was in school, our county had been in the Korean War and perceived the Russians as our main threat. World War II was in the past.

After visiting the memorial museum on the other side of the base, and talking to the soldiers that used the gym, I came to know the horror of the Dachau concentration camp by learning what had happened there. I was told the American Base at Dachau was part of the original concentration camp; we used some of the buildings at the end of the war for our base, and still did. I realized, why, when I entered the Dachau base the first day, I was so uncomfortable that I wanted to leave. I also remembered what Issie had said about praying for protection, and I had been.

The first weeks I was there, I met most of the soldiers and support staff. Most of them offered up stories of seeing or hearing ghosts; some waited to see my reaction, others to see if I had seen anything unusual. I told them, *"I haven't seen anything, but I feel them. I could feel them when they were close; like when you know someone is behind you even though you hadn't heard them approach."* One of the soldiers said, *"That's weird."* He had just finished telling me a story about seeing an old woman with a shawl walking on base and how she disappeared in front of him.

One of the people I met those first weeks at the Dachau Army Base was a girl from California named Leeann. She was working at the base, teaching photography to the soldiers. The military had equipped a small building with all the photographic equipment needed for someone to teach photography. I met with Leeann a few times after I was done working at the Gym. She taught me how to develop my own film and more about using my camera. We were talking about where we lived in the States, and I mentioned Issie. She said, *"I have heard of her and her teachings. You are her grandson!"*

We talked for hours and came to realize that we shared much of the same knowledge I had received from Issie about prayer and meditation. Leanne told me, *"we are not here at Dachau at the same time by accident."* She said she lives in a room here at the photo shop, and wanted to show me something. She led me to the basement, a large room with white tile from floor to ceiling with a drain in the middle of the room.

She said, *"this is where they did experiments on people, a lot of people."* It was so real I couldn't say anything. She said, *"I know."*

She told me, sometimes at night she's awakened by screams down here, *"I come down, sit on the tile floor, and pray for the spirits to move on."* I said, *"I couldn't do that."* She said, *"You don't need to; you're here and understand about earth bound spirits."*

To this day, I'm not sure what she meant about "being here." I did know that she was one of the most fearless people I ever met.

I told Leeann that I had written Issie, telling her the stories I was told by the soldiers and civilians about the history of Dachau Army Base. Issie sent a letter telling me that all of her groups were praying for release of these souls. Issie said by the time I get this letter, hundreds of people would be praying. In my second letter to Issie about Dachau, I told her about Leanne. Issie replied, *"Leanne being there was confirmation that something on higher levels was going on and being resolved. We are praying for resolution, and for you and Leanne."*

COMING HOME

Two months after starting the job at Dachau, I was awakened from sleep by a voice telling me that I needed *"to go home within two weeks."* I then heard the same voice talking to my sleeping wife. While sleeping, she responded to the voice, and a short conversation followed. She did not wake up during the conversation. The following morning, I said to her, *"We need to go home to the states within two weeks."* She said ok, and started planning the trip home.

That was not what I expected. We had saved money for traveling that summer. We had friends, a place to live, and nothing waiting for us at home. We were on a plane headed home before the two-week deadline. What I didn't know was that another right-place-right-time event was going to happen in my life, and the timing was critical.

It was strange being home. It was like being in two places at the same time. Many times, I would think, *"let's go here for dinner or to a show,"* only to realize that those places were in Munich, not here. I was also questioning coming home. Being home also meant spending time with my parents, four brothers, Issie and at Harmony Hill, all of which I now appreciated much more. I had missed New Hampshire more that I realized.

Not too long after we returned home, we went back-roading. Back-roading is defined as getting off the main roads and finding places (historic homes, farms, etc.) and things you had not seen before. This particular day, I noticed a road, close to where we were staying, that I had not noticed before. We turned onto the road to see where it went. We passed some very old homes as we were climbing two very steep hills. It was May, and there was still snow in the shaded areas on the side of the road. I thought this road must be a challenge in the winter.

We got to the top of the hill to find an empty 1779 colonial with two-story Lilacs and so many Lilies of the Valley around the house you could smell them from the car. The farm fields were overgrown but we could see Mount Kearsarge some forty miles away. The following week, I researched who the owner was, a man named Richard, who, with his mother, used it as a summer residence.

I called Richard and explained who I was and, with a little boldness, asked if they would they consider us as buyers if they ever sold the home and property. He was gruff and said they had no intention of selling the property, and if they did, they had a list of ten or eleven names of people who also wanted to buy it. I asked Richard if they could put us on the list. He was noncommittal and said goodbye. I let it go.

We settled into being home; we rented a house, got jobs, even went back to visit our friends in Munich for Christmas that year. I was spending time with my family and visiting with Issie at Harmony Hill on the weekends and during the week when she was there.

One Saturday morning in July, I was awakened by the same voice that told me to leave Munich, telling me to call Richard about the house on the hill we had seen fourteen months earlier. After I hesitated, I gave in and called around 11:00 AM. My expectation was of an unpleasant experience.

Instead, Richard said, *"I was going to call you this week, to see if you are still interested in the house. The last person on my list of people interested in the property, called this morning around nine to say they decided they were going to build a new home instead of fixing an old one."* I was amazed that he had even put us on the list, and now was asking if we are still interested. I said, *"we will buy it,"* without having ever seen the inside of the house, knowing the asking price, or how much land went with the house.

Richard asked us if we wanted to meet with him tomorrow to see the inside of the home and walk the property? We met with Richard the next day and toured the home and property. During the time Richard and I were walking the property, he told me that the person ahead of me on the list to purchase the home had called him back Saturday afternoon and said they had changed their minds again. They wanted to buy the house. Richard told them he was sorry, that it was sold.

That evening at Harmony Hill, I told Issie the story of looking at the house and that the only four or five hours it was available in fourteen months was the time I had called.

She said, *"The date of your induction into the Army set you on a chain of events that needed to be accepted by you. If you had broken* the chain along the way, you wouldn't be sitting here telling me this story. Your chart indicated this, and your choices have confirmed what your chart indicated to me. We all have free will to accept or not accept the choices put before us. You know if you just listened to me all the time you would be better off!" and laughed, followed by, "Would you like some pie?" I had missed her humor when I was gone. She had a very good sense of humor and timing.

Two months later, in September of 1972, we moved into the home surrounded by eighty acres.

ISSIE'S GRADUATION

I was in my mid-twenties when I took my last summer trip with Issie. We went to an astrological conference at Carleton University in Ottawa, Canada. Issie had friends, also astrologers, who lived in Ottawa. They had traveled to Boston attending Astrology classes and stayed several weekends at Harmony Hill. They had become friends of Issie's.

They invited Issie to speak at a conference they had helped create at Carlton University. Issie spoke several times, with large crowds attending. She taught Astrology classes followed by a meditation after the day and evening classes. Issie and I stayed with her friends at their home near Ottawa. Issie and I liked staying in a home setting. It gave Issie a better chance of resting, and not having people stop by to visit, like at a hotel.

That wasn't to say we didn't stay up late talking with our hosts. They loved the stories of Issie and me driving to groups all over New England to speak to a dozen or so people about Spiritual Astrology. Now she was speaking to hundreds. They were amazed when Issie told them of the early years at Harmony Hill and all people involved.

When we returned from Ottawa, I noticed Issie was tired. I asked if she was all right, and she said she was good, just needed more rest than she was getting. We had one of our weeknight dinners at Harmony Hill a few weeks later. I asked her again how she felt. She said, *"My heart is not keeping up with my mind, that's all. I'm alright."* Nothing was said again about her health; that's how she was.

Over the following years Issie continued to teach astrology and meditation in Boston during the winter months. The warm weather months were generally spent at Harmony Hill working on her books and enjoying her friends and her favorite place. We had maintained our midweek get-togethers at Harmony Hill. We had time to catch up and watch the evenings settle in, from the porch, as we had done for many years. As always, before I left, we would spend time in the chapel together.

Shortly before Issie *graduated* (that's how she described death to me when I was a child), she said, *"We come from spirit to earth, to learn and grow, just like you do in school. Eventually, we graduate this school, leave our body here, and go back to spirit."*

We spent our last evening together on the porch at Harmony Hill catching up. As I was leaving that evening to go home, she said, *"I have something for you,"* and handed me a small travel case saying, *"This is for you. Hold onto this."*

When I arrived home, I looked inside the travel case and saw the birth chart of my two-year-old son on top of a written explanation from Issie. It was late, so I put the case away to review later.

Issie graduated the next week at Harmony Hill, her favorite place on the planet. She was buried in the cemetery at Harmony Hill on a sunny June day, with many of her family and friends to see her off.

The void she left in many lives was substantial yet mitigated by her teachings and of continuity of spirit.

Issie told me on one of our many road trips, *"The veil that separates us from spirit and earth is very thin; we are still connected even when we can't see each other."*

I NEVER MINDED

For more than thirty years, Issie's last completed book, <u>Never Mind</u>, sat in an attic, stored under my son's astrological chart, the chart Issie gave me the last evening we spent together.

As Issie would say, *"Timing is not coincidental."*

REFLECTIONS BY AMY

ISSIE'S 'FRIDAY NIGHT FIX'

I first met Issie at age 14, in May of 1966, then again that summer at her Harmony Hill retreat in Nottingham, NH, near my 15th birthday, two life-altering encounters that led me to study with her that September, during my sophomore year at Brookline High School. Looking back, 46 years later, it feels like lifetimes ago, yet the memories still resonate clearly. Astrologers will not be surprised to learn that transiting Uranus was conjunct my Mercury at the time. During the hundreds of astrology classes I took in the next five years, I learned how that transit awakens one to their calling.

Some personal background: As a teen, difficult family circumstances had caused me to lose my childhood faith in God; how could a loving God let humans suffer such injustice and hurt? Life felt meaningless amidst all the angst in the world as well. My generation was adrift, drafted into or protesting the Vietnam War of the *establishment*. As the civil rights movement took root and the assassinations of President Kennedy, Martin Luther King, Jr. and Bobby Kennedy sent shockwaves through America, Feminism was emerging, as women in our culture were done tolerating institutionalized inequities. With new birth control access, Baby Boomers had causes and ways to *"tune in, turn on and drop out."* The oft-told joke, *"if you remember the '60s, you didn't live them"* failed to account for the thousands of my generation who were lost to war and drugs. The slogans *"Make love, not war"* and *"flower power"* were pleas for *humanity* and for a return to nature's simpler values.

This was the backdrop against which Isabel came into my life, through my mother, Dorothy Amdur, with whom my sister and I were living in Brookline. Mom was an accountant at a law firm in Boston, and had become friends with her co-worker Mary Hickey, Isabel's sister. During one of their lunch hours, Mary brought Mom to visit

Isabel for an astrological consult. Mom came home from work that night excited to tell me that an astrologer had told her, based on my birthday, not to worry about me, because one day I would make her very proud. She also told Mom that she wanted to meet me, and to bring me to her Friday night class! The idea that I may one day do something to earn parental approval seemed a sellout to my then-hippie psyche, and I wasn't keen to be seen in public with my mother to meet a lady whose prediction I didn't relish. But curiosity got the best of me, so I agreed to attend, as long as I could bring a friend.

Mom agreed, so I invited my most hippie-looking friend who was up for an adventure. Like me, she had long dark hair, dark clothes and no make-up. I wanted her opinion of this odd older woman who wanted to meet me, true to another '60's motto: *"trust no one over 30!"*

Issie's 2nd floor office on St. Botolph Street in Boston's Back Bay area was near the Public Library, Public Garden, Hancock Tower, Museum of Fine Arts, Fenway Park, colleges and universities. Tucked into a clean, quiet room with a sturdy wooden desk, cushioned rocker, and padded metal folding chairs in rows on an intricate oriental rug, was this intriguing lady. Little did I know that she was about to become my first spiritual teacher. No adult had ever greeted me so warmly.

My friend and I had never met anyone like Isabel. Full-figured in her 60s, she had an impressive nose, thin lips, a blonde braid crowning her head, brilliant blue eyes and a playful, welcoming smile. She reminded me of my Grandma Rae, whom I adored.

Issie's braid crowned her head.

Once we were all comfortably seated, Issie began to talk in a soothing, pleasant voice. Her words flowed easily and unrehearsed, filled with insights about life, love and other important themes. It soon became clear, this was not an astrology class; it was her Friday night discussion and meditation group. My Jewish upbringing had included experience with prayer, but not the kind of prayer Issie taught. This was my first exposure to meditation, eastern mysticism and the laws of karma, grace and prayer in English!

I learned that night that the ages of the body and soul are not the same and *"if we knew better, we'd do better,"* so we may as well forgive others who – like each of us – *"do the best we can with what we know at the time."* True enough.

Absorbing it all, I was eager for more, until Issie said: *"You know, there's no such thing as an accident!"* I'd been a queen of accidents in my family, so this did not square with my scars or memories of plaster casts, broken bones, stitches and surgeries. Nope, if anyone knew, I did: accidents are real! Aren't they?

Issie went on, *"We are vibratorily connected to everything that happens to us,"* and that through our *auras* we radiate and attract that which reflects our consciousness. Accident-prone folks, she suggested, are like balls of tension growing inside an egg until the repressed anger, needing to be expressed, breaks the outer shell (body) in an *accident* to release the pent-up energy.

Indeed, through the years, I had repressed anger toward injustices that were beyond my control. Issie spoke the truth again.

My mind reeled with revelations, insights and a fragile new hope for a more meaningful and purpose-driven life. Mom had found someone really special! This was a lot to digest in one evening, and we weren't half done! And then came *KARMA*!

Issie explained that *"we are vibratorily connected to everything and everyone, and from more than one life;* that karma is the cosmic law of cause and effect in motion, and that if we believe our souls exist *after death,* logic dictates that *infinity could not stop at birth – it must run before birth* too!

Each lifetime is like a grade in the *school* of life to help us learn lessons, develop talents and skills. *"We do not come unbound into this livingness"* she taught that night, and often in the following years. *"We do not start here, and we do not stop here; infinity goes in both directions."* With that message, Issie cracked a huge psychic nut for me, one that takes a lifetime to fully digest.

Issie's wisdom was a healing balm for my soul. Reincarnation and karma made sense of otherwise senseless situations and renewed my faith in a compassionate Creator. If we must account in this life for past life deeds, then we can't know by appearances what unseen forces drive circumstances, to teach us essential life lessons. As she added *grace* and *dharma* into the mix, my anger at God dissolved, and my sense of gratitude returned. We can choose not to perpetuate those karmic wheels! Very cool!

Issie dimmed the lights and began guiding the meditation; I was open to whatever the universe offered. We took deep cleansing breaths to release tension and relax further, inhaling healing energy and exhaling tension, and *thanked* our bodies for all the wonderful things it does for us … *"you don't have to tell your lungs to breath, or your heart to beat …"* It felt good to thank our bodies! Don't they deserve our thanks, after all?

We joined voices in a series of *Om's* and drifted in silence. At one point, Issie suggested: *"imagine your Spirit standing behind you; she is beautiful, and her hands are on your shoulders, pouring warm healing energy through your entire being."* With that suggestion, I saw and felt a beautiful spirit behind me, a soft firm pressure of hands on my shoulders, pouring healing energy through me.

After the meditation, as the lights came on, Issie observed, *"physical light is so much harsher than spiritual light."* True again!

Before leaving that evening, I told Issie of my experiences in the meditation. This seemed to delight her. I assumed that others must have experienced their angelic presences too, so I was surprised at her surprise! Of course, I now realize what a special gift were those first visualizations and visitation.

Thus my transformational journey began with my biological mother leading me to my spiritual mother. I would be remiss not to add, how much I love my biological mother too, and how glad I am to have been born to her. She was an early Feminist pioneer who thought outside of the box and broke through many 'glass ceilings' as a champion of women's rights, and helped me to find my way. And thanks to my spiritual training with Issie, I was able to give real comfort to Mom in her last days on this Earth in April 2012, while completing this manuscript, by helping her to picture Issie among the loving souls on the other side, who would welcome her home.

That first evening with Issie in 1966 was so powerful that I needed no one to validate my experience, and in the following five years, I brought many friends to Issie's meditations. Some were curious, others were deeply troubled; all felt touched by her love, light and grace. The healing that Issie channeled uplifted countless lives, and I have often said, being in her presence and learning by her side was such a blessing, that if Issie had been a cobbler I would have become a cobbler, too. That she happened to be an astrologer was always secondary; her primary calling was as a healer.

Issie's weekly meditations became lovingly called the *Friday Night Fix* because they uplifted and energized dozens of youth who found so much peace, healing and revelation in them that they no longer sought those sensations with drugs. As its popularity grew, Issie had to keep finding larger spaces. Thanks to her daughter Helen, who was Dean of BU's Sargent College of Physical Therapy, the Friday group's biggest and last home was Boston University's beautiful Marsh Chapel.

The evening included a discussion of topics of spiritual significance, guided relaxation and meditation, with a focus on breathing, visualizations, chants, song, prayer and group healing wherein we said names of people in need of healing. We might sing *"Kum Ba Ya"* or *"I am an acorn; make me a tree ... I am a bubble, make me the sea,"* say the Lord's Prayer and The Great Invocation, about which Issie often discussed their meanings in depth.

The Great Invocation, recited by many seekers, has over time, been made more inclusive by substituting *humankind* for *men* and substituting *compassionate grace* for *Christ*. The Invocation helps us to open our minds to light, our hearts to love, and invite grace and purpose to guide us, regardless of one's religious affiliation.

Said mindfully, these words can be tremendously uplifting and empowering for good:

From the point of Light within the Mind of God, Let light stream forth into the minds of men; Let Light descend on Earth.

From the point of Love within the Heart of God, Let love stream forth into the hearts of men; May Christ return to Earth.

From the centre where the Will of God is known, Let purpose guide the little wills of men; The purpose which the Masters know and serve.

From the centre, which we call the race of man, Let the Plan of Love and Light work out, And may it seal the door where evil dwells.

Let Light and Love and Power restore the Plan on Earth. So let it be and help us to do our parts.

Many synchronicities with Issie's group meditations were later verified when a friend or relative whose name (unbeknownst to them) I had spoken aloud in our healing circle, would call me later to share a revelation or healing they received that evening. Our thoughts *do* generate far more energy than we realize, so training our thought patterns to generate positive and constructive ripples into the universe helps us to better serve others – and ourselves.

This was strikingly illustrated one Friday when a good friend shared in Issie's group what had transpired at work, at the Boston Public Library. As she returned books to the shelf, she noticed across the room a nun who looked a bit forlorn. Issie had encouraged us to inwardly direct healing to anyone whom we felt was troubled, by mentally projecting *'God bless you'* to that person.

My friend had sent a silent *'God bless you'* to the nun, and was stunned to hear the nun say aloud, *"Thank you, dear!"*

"Thank me for what?" the girl asked, to which the nun replied, *"You just blessed me!"* I would never doubt the power of positive prayer after that!

On the other hand, negative prayers and thoughtforms can do a lot of damage. Issie taught that in prayer, it's essential to visualize the outcome you want, not what you fear. This was brought home most clearly when I visited Issie in the hospital after she'd had knee surgery. She was glad to see me and gave me this message for the Friday group: *"Quit praying for me – you're killing me!"* She felt everyone's prayers that pictured her suffering in pain, and they were making her feel worse, and slowing her recovery!

I have since had many validating more experiences of these principles, and know that the power of visualization is real. We are what we think, and what we think often enough begins *thinking us*. Part of the challenge of *'never mind'* is to discipline our minds as much as our deeds, so that our minds are not our masters, with us as a slave to our thoughts; a tall order that takes a lifetime to achieve.

Two great souls often co-led Issie's Friday night discussions, Tom Jackson and Mitch Blake. Both radiated joy and were loved by all. Tom often accompanied Issie at lectures across the country.

This photo from Jay's collection shows Tom at Harmony Hill.

It was an unusual sight in those days, for a tall, slim graceful dark-skinned man to be with a pale, grandmotherly-looking woman. As Issie often said, *"absent from the appearance is present with the power."* Tom's deep voice and sparkling eyes conveyed his joy in carrying the spiritual torch, and his faith in me as a fellow light-bearer.

The following quote from a letter to Issie, by a grateful attendee, conveys a similar feeling.

"What a joy to share a Friday night with you and Mitch again. The receptivity of all these souls, often just starting on the path, draws through each of us the most amazing amount of His Light and Love. I had never felt such a high vibration or been used as quite a channel before. God Bless you and Mitch for this Service. So many are helped and fed."

As those who attended Issie's meditations know, words can not fully convey the experience. Even my beloved father, Myer (Mike) Shapiro, who worried about losing his teen daughter to a *cult,* learned by attending Issie's *'Friday Night Fix'* that she would cause me no harm and her insights were sound. Thereafter, my development through Issie's influence had great ripple effects on us, inspiring wonderful heart-to-heart conversations. To Dad's credit, cult figures in those days *did* lure young people into fatal situations in the '60s and '70s so he was right to find out who his impressionable teenager was spending time with and why.

One of Issie's suggestions regarding frustrating, upsetting or highly problematic situations was: *"put it on the inner altar and ask for guidance."* I have followed that advice countless times over the years, and always found it to be helpful. If *"altar"* stirs mixed emotions as a negative trigger for you, come up with an image that helps you to, as Issie also said, *"let go, and let God."*

Eighteen years after meeting Issie, I had a family of my own, and we joined a Unitarian Universalist congregation near our home. Being accepted by the members was great, and they were glad to accept my offer to run a Friday night meditation group. From 1984 to 1988, it was open to the public on a drop-in basis, very much like Issie's group. Our meditations left us feeling at peace, spiritually nurtured and ready for the coming week.

HARMONY HILL ~ NOTTINGHAM, NH

My first meditation evening at Issie's St. Botolph Street studio turned out to be her last Friday group before leaving for her summer retreat in Nottingham, New Hampshire. Her astrology classes were also done for the season. Sensing my disappointment that her meetings had ended, before we left her suite, Issie told my mother to bring me to *Harmony Hill* in New Hampshire for her summer picnic with her students. 'Harmony Hill' sounded both a little hokey and magical; I hoped it was more of the latter. It was, and it became the highlight of that summer!

We arrived late morning and were directed to park on her spacious, well-manicured lawn. Our spirits were not dampened by overcast skies and threat of rain. Mother and I, and her friend Bernie, who had driven us, were warmly welcomed. Much of the day is hazy in my memory but two conversations still resonate vividly.

Issie sat at a small table in her enclosed porch, paring, slicing and setting apples into crust-filled pie plates. I was mesmerized by her calm joy in this simple mouth-watering task and didn't want to break her concentration. I had never seen anyone prepare an apple pie without a recipe!

She asked me, while forming the pie, *"Do you know much about astrology?"* Eager to impress her, I replied, *"I know I'm a Leo!"* having no idea what that meant, and added a hint, hoping Issie would explain, *"I'd like to learn more!"* I did not expect her reply: *"Then you'll have to study with me in the fall!"* she said with a smile. I instinctively said, *"Ok!"* All the while, my skeptical teenage mind thought: she's just being polite; she couldn't possibly want me to study with her! She would soon prove me wrong again.

The day passed in pleasant conversation, ending with a group meditation in Issie's *chapel room* where I was lifted again to new planes of consciousness, as healing energy filled the room. When it was time to go, my mother and her friend and I said our good-byes and walked to our car. After so a wonderful day, I felt sad to leave.

Then, to my great surprise, Issie walked a long length of lawn to our car, gave me the biggest hug, put her hands on my shoulders, gazed into my eyes, smiled and gave me the date and time of her first class in September of her Boston School of Astrology, adding, *"Will I see you there?"* I was stunned; she was serious about me studying with her! I clumsily managed to say, *"Okay!"* mystified that this wise lady who I had met only twice was so genuine and made me feel so special. That was another first.

In the summers ahead, I enjoyed a dozen or so picnics and retreats at Harmony Hill. The name beautifully reflected the surroundings and experience. Even the 1806-wood outhouse put us in harmony with nature!

The 'Healing Tree' in the stone wall across the road.

My favorite spot on the property was *the healing tree* as Issie named it. It was in the middle of a stone wall on either side, with the trunk curved perfectly for sitting on the wall with your back hugged by the tree. I sat there every chance I got, with a sketchpad and found something to inspire a drawing.

I recall Issie's grandsons Jay, Donny and Tommy, doing chores, splitting firewood, and mowing the lawn. As we chatted, took walks and played checkers, their respect and affection for Issie was evident. I marveled at their luck in having her as a grandmother and relished feeling a part of their extended family. Similarly, whenever I meet an astrologer who learns of my time with Issie in my youth, they remark on how lucky I was, and I agree!

Guests who stayed the night or weekend at Harmony Hill were expected to pitch in too with chores, to help clean, cook, do dishes or yard work. *Discipline means disciple-in,* Issie taught! One sunny day, Issie asked me to help "the boys" weed and of course I was glad to join them at the flowerbed. The job was bigger than I expected, and I began to lose interest and daydream of wondering off with my sketchpad to find new inspiration to draw, and letting the boys finish weeding. As I sat on the ground by the flowers, my weeding slacked. Seconds later, the soft pressure of a hand on my shoulder startled me. Issie whispered in my ear words to this effect: *"You have to show the Invisibles you can be trusted to finish a small job before they'll trust you with a big job ... if you want to be a Light Worker!"*

Whoa! The ground below me seemed to dissolve with my sense of reality. My cheeks must have blushed as I lowered my head and resumed weeding, speechless. Conflicting feelings erupted as I fought tears of guilt for having wanted to abandon the boys to indulge myself; tears of joy that Issie cared about my spiritual development enough to share her wisdom; tears of awe that if I proved worthy, I could be a *Light Worker* like Issie, and lastly tears of laughter; how psychic was she, anyway? I was no longer just weeding; I was awash in major revelations and realized that *my ego needed weeding* at least as much as the flowerbed!

The fireplace at Harmony Hill crackled in the evenings as we learned how to release earthbound souls who we sensed hovering over the adjacent cemetery and shared ghost stories, past life visions, inner plane explorations, laughter and fellowship. Before turning in for the night, we gathered in the Chapel Room for a guided meditation to close the day and empty our minds so that we might open ourselves during sleep to a different kind of wakefulness. Sleep at Harmony Hill often brought prophetic visions, intriguing dreams or out-of-body experiences.

In the deep silence of one of our late evening meditations, I began hearing a low, steady thump; the longer I listened, the louder it grew. After the meditation, I mentioned to Issie that I'd heard a loud rhythmic pounding in the stillness and wondered what it was. She lit up, laughed and said without a hint of hesitation, *"That's the heartbeat of the house! I hear it all the time!"* Issie taught that each house has an overseeing Spirit that will help us if we call upon it, in buying or selling it, or to better understand your ties to it. Tune in, and see for yourself!

ASTROLOGY CHART CONSULT AND ISSIE'S BOSTON SCHOOL OF ASTROLOGY

The first time Issie discussed my chart with me, I was still fairly new to astrology and very curious, to say the least. The experience went far beyond a *reading* of symbols. As Issie shared what my chart revealed to her, I could feel her shining a warm light into my soul. Eventually I would come to understand as I learned astrology, why she told me the things that she did, but in that first consultation, her ability to turn what looked like flat symbols into profound insights about me was amazing, and still amazes me, looking back.

Much of what Issie told me was not news to me but were things that no one else knew about me. Some of her predictions were eerily mysterious and took years for me to fathom. One was that I would *"live two lifetimes in this life,"* based on my separated Jupiter-Saturn opposition. As a past life therapist, I have relived dozens of past lives, integrating their lessons into this life, so you might say that that prediction turned out to be an understatement! She made several more predictions that day that are still unfolding.

I had to know; how did she do that? Issie somehow knew that I was meant to study with her even before we met, when my mother first gave her my birthday (8/13/51, 11:14 PM EDT, Boston, MA).[6]

---

[6] When we published this book in 2012, I thought my birth time was 11:12 PM. I have since learned that my birth certificate shows that it was 11:14 PM instead.

It was a true blessing to have found Issie at such a young age, and her teachings have guided me ever since.

In my years of study with Issie, she interpreted my chart many times privately and in class, helping me mature in understanding of my personal challenges. Her insights blended principles with heart-centered intuition, turning the mundane into the extraordinary. Issie often shared her secret of success with her students; that before seeing a client, she would always *tune in,* ask for guidance and visualize her Higher Self connecting with the other person's Higher Self, and showing her what that person needed to hear for his or her highest good. This faith gave her confidence to broach sensitive or difficult topics. When Higher Powers guide the session, the experience serves both the client and astrologer well. Using this tuning-in method, I more often than not receive guidance for someone else that is also just what I need to hear for myself. This works for any interpersonal situation.

Issie embodied the meaning of *to consider – to be with the stars (con-sider),* ever-moving cosmic energies letting us glimpse our spiritual heritage in an infinite universe. With this positive a foundation, it was natural for me to call my astrology practice *"Good Heavens!"* which grew to include radio and TV shows, articles, columns, a newsletter and website in the 1980s and 1990s. I would close my weekly radio show with this sign-off: *"May Good Heavens shine as our lives intertwine, that together – through love – we may know the Divine!"*

I began attending Issie's Boston School of Astrology in 1966, while a sophomore at Brookline High School. Before long, I was attending beginners and advanced classes, taking public transportation into Boston, notebook in hand, hungry for knowledge. I was her youngest student, but as Issie taught, the body's age is not the age of the soul. This explained why I loved befriending many of the older women in her classes, and in other parts of my life (also shown by my Moon in Capricorn in the 9th house). Besides intellectual learning, Issie's lessons and demonstrations were full of compassion and laughter. Peeling layers of karmic implications, we uncovered paths to grace, healing and enlightenment in individual natal charts.

Issie's style of teaching reflected her natal Mercury in Virgo's orientation to detail, balancing technique with intuition to bring a chart alive, connecting with the person on a soul level. Issie's Moon-

Neptune conjunction in Cancer in her 8th house, trine Mars in Scorpio in her 12th house, gave her the gift of *seeing* others' souls; which I personally experienced on many occasions. With so strong a Mercury, Issie always found astrological correlations – sometimes several – to what her intuition told her. Her spiritual core attuned her to profound meanings of Pluto, asteroids, esoteric rulers and more. Her Pluto in Gemini in a Mutable cross with Uranus, Jupiter and Mercury shows her true thirst for knowledge as a Light Worker.

Pluto in Gemini being also Issie's Ascendant ruler shows her clairvoyance and intuition to *see in herself* the dual nature of Pluto as a force for transmutation – its *Minerva* side – and degeneration. As she would teach in her second book, the path we take is our choice.[7]

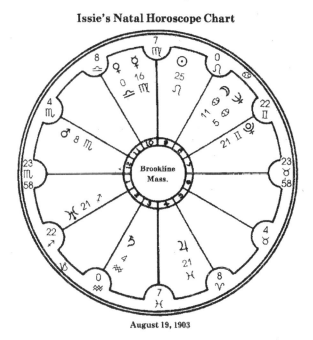

Issie's Natal Horoscope Chart

August 19, 1903

A tremendous reader, Issie spoke eloquently on a wide range of topics, and how they related to astrology. She taught many predictive techniques; horary astrology, transits, progressions, solar and lunar returns. My cup overflowed with information, hope, possibilities and inspiration in her class.

---

[7] Additional natal energies: N. Node 7 Libra, Juno 24 Scorpio, Chiron 17 Capricorn, Eris 23 Pisces, Vesta 3 Gemini, Pallas 15 Virgo and Ceres 27 Virgo.

I managed to keep up with most of my regular high school work, and while history and science were my weaker subjects, my interest in astrology led me to care more about them, as I wondered how transits reflected historical events, and how science follows other cosmic laws. I would race through my regular homework so that I could study my astrology notes between Issie's classes.

Being new to Brookline during high school, and very shy, I neither expected nor sought attention at school. But my extracurricular interests piqued the curiosity of peers, teachers and staff as my astrology focus deepened. I would weave it into my academics as I learned about mundane astrology and how certain planetary influences resonated with historic events and epochs. I read a book in French on astrology for a French paper, carved planetary symbols into linoleum blocks in art class, and wrote about cosmic law for English assignments.

In my second year of studying with Issie, I began to interpret charts for relatives and a few close friends. A buzz began about this at school and more of my chums asked me to do their charts. I wanted the practice, so I was always glad to oblige. One day in my junior year while I was in art class, a student messenger came to tell me to go to the House Master's office – immediately!

Yikes! Was I in trouble? I was polite, never sassed adults, never even bickered with students. My journey to my House Master's office was full of trepidation about what awaited. When I arrived, he was waiting for me.

I gulped and asked, *"Mr. ___, I'm Amy Shapiro; you wanted to see me?"* He said excitedly, *"You're the Astrologist?"* I gulped again and said, carefully avoiding the appearance of publicly correcting him on the incorrect term *'astrologist'*, *"Well, I've been studying astrology, yes."*

He quickly shooed everyone out of the outer office, beckoned me to his inner office, shut the door and directed me to sit opposite him at his desk. I braced for bad news, and thought, here goes, I'm being expelled. I was completely unprepared for what happened next. My House Master wanted me to do his chart!

He gave me his birth data along with a note to excuse me from a study hall that Friday. I was to return to his office in three days for a demonstration! I was both petrified about how it would turn out and curious to see if my skills might impress him. With only his chart and my ephemeris in hand, I stunned us both by nailing many sensitive personal facts. He thanked me for an enlightening experience. I left wondering if I'd overstepped any boundaries but in hindsight, the opposite was clearly more the case.

The upshot came in my senior year, when some student friends lobbied that same House Master, to grant them permission to earn Independent Study credits by taking an after-school astrology class with me at my home. He approved the request, and one girl only managed to graduate due to my 1-credit course! The satisfaction of that teaching experience, and my House Master's recognition of astrology's value, inspired me to pursue astrology as a career.

Two years after graduating from BHS, the phone at my Cambridge apartment rang. It was my old House Master, wanting an appointment for a second consult. He added: *"this time I'm going to pay you!"* During that *professional* consult, I was saddened to hear of his woes, which I had hoped he would avoid – about which I had advised him years earlier. He had been amazed that the harsh potentials I had seen in his chart occurred exactly when I had said they might, relative to his personal life.

It was not how I had hoped to be right. I would have preferred hearing that he had avoided some of his suffering by heeding my good advice! My hope was to soften others' hard destinies, so I took little comfort in astrology's reliability as a predictive tool. Seeing clients dismiss my preventive advice led to a deep soul searching. What use was it to see how people could avoid hardship, if my advice was ignored?

I came to realize that we are each responsible for acting in our own best interests, and that my role as an astrologer was not to shield people from their karma, but to shed compassionate light on possible ways to navigate their lives with a cosmic compass or beacon. I could urge people not to sail into lightening storms, but I couldn't keep them on shore or steer fate for them!

Many wondrous results also came from my consults. I'll never forget a female client calling to say that because I had urged her to be vigilant of unusual growths during harsh Jupiter transits, at her last internal exam, when her doctor found nothing, she asked him to reexam her, to be sure. He turned pale upon finding a large growth he had missed on the first exam, and which required urgent life-saving surgery. Outcomes like that renewed my faith in astrology's potential as a source of hope, courage and wisdom.

My interest in the mysteries of the human psyche, and people's struggle to act in their best interests led me to earn a Master's Degree in Psychology at Boston College. I wanted to be confident that, along with my ability to discern the meaning of cosmic forces in the natal chart, I could wisely counsel clients. To my happy surprise, my professors often echoed Issie's teachings, as did later instructors at Harvard Medical School's Mind-Body Institute, New England Society of Clinical Hypnosis and other stress-management courses.

The field of Education was not ready to embrace astrological insights by a Guidance Counselor, in support of youngsters and their families. I did use my academic credentials as a Head Start Advisor for many years and taught early childhood education courses at Endicott College and for Wheelock College. I also founded the Cape Ann School of Astrology, through which I taught astrology in my home and at Endicott College's adult education program, sharing Dr. Oskar Adler's esoteric course, *The Testament of Astrology,* years after completing my studies at Issie's Boston School of Astrology.[8]

Knowing astrology gave parenting a transcendent dimension in raising my sons, especially in times of doubt, when knowing their transits helped me steer the best course in their development. I have also loved counseling parents on their children's charts and their family astro-chemistry, as a tool for insight into family dynamics. Astrology had even helped me as a teenager, in understanding why my own parents' marriage failed; their astrological chemistry echoed their personalities and their charts showed why they were better apart than together. To understand what forces were at work was tremendously uplifting psychologically and spiritually. Imagine if every child of divorced parents had the benefit of this understanding!

No textbook could replicate the joy of Issie's live classes, with their spontaneous insights and her many eager students. I loved analyzing charts and speculating on how planetary configurations might manifest. Issie often called upon me in class to offer my thoughts on a chart. This was an incredible gift to me, a shy teen who had never before spoken in front of a group! Issie helped me to

---

[8] My adventures of teaching this work are described in *Dr. Oskar Adler: A Complete Man*, and his course is also available at NewAgeSages.com.

overcome my shyness with a powerful visualization. She taught that if we want to continue to expand our understanding, we *must* share our knowledge with others, and empty our *cups* in order to receive more knowledge, until eventually, the bottom of our cups would open fully, allowing our Higher Selves to pour light, love and healing energies through us uninterrupted, and we would become *channels*.

We learned that, just as *consciousness is reality*, two people with the same chart could have vastly different fates, based on their circumstances and their karma. *"We do not come unbound into this livingness"* Issie reminded as we looked to a 12th house ruler, it's aspects, the *dignities*, mode dominance, and outer planet connections to inner personal planets, for clues of what the soul carried into this life. Like creating a new recipe each week, basic combinations of meanings formed a cohesive picture of each soul's evolution, blended with a good dose of intuition.

Natal aspects, transits, progressions, horary charts, solar returns and esoteric rulers were all fodder for Issie's lessons. We felt renewed by learning to speak this universal language, punctuated by insights that could tickle a funny bone or lead to a tender tear. Every human condition was in the chart, plus medical and mundane correlations. Love, compassion and the recognition that we each *"do the best we can with what we know"* were central to each evaluation.

The Precession of the Equinoxes, *Ages* and speculation of when the Piscean Age would finally yield to the Aquarian Age were intriguing! Issie's prophecies on that seemed both too fantastic and fatalistic yet have come to pass or are unfolding at this moment, regarding many global shifts and accelerations.

Issie taught that *how* we convey what we see in a chart is as important as our knowledge of the planets, signs, houses, aspects, etc. She taught us not to dodge awkward subjects that may be revealed in a chart, and not to dwell on the negative, but to see the strengths and challenges in a chart and find the inherent balance and life purpose, and to encourage people to build on their strengths and work on their deficits. This therapeutic approach encompassed karma, grace and reincarnation. Issie taught how to find clues in the birth chart as to what lesson or karma was burdening the soul, the soul's purpose and how they might transmute their karma with grace and forgiveness. She taught that when we see something harsh in a chart, we can best address it by tuning in and asking our Higher Self what was in that person's highest good and have faith that the right words will come. With a true desire to serve our clients best interest, Issie taught, we can discuss any issue without fearing a negative response. If we want to serve others' spiritual needs, which is why most people seek astrological guidance, we must reach beyond our own ego insecurities and trust Spirit to show us the way.

I tested that theory! Once, while doing charts at the Sphinx Bookstore in Cambridge, MA, a young man in his 20's came for a session. Seeing a heavily loaded 8th house was a concern, so I prayed for the right words to broach the subject, of what role death played in his life. Just as I inwardly heard the words, he blurted, *"When am I going to die?"* Having myself a Sun-Pluto conjunction, I was fine with death as a topic, and grateful that my Higher Self had braced me for his question. He was suicidal and desperately seeking spiritual guidance. After that, I understood the real importance of letting my intuition guide the session, trusting it to show me what needed to be addressed. It has been like that for me ever since.

Issie taught that our Cardinal, Fixed and Mutable aspects show the nature of our karma. Cardinal karma (Aries, Cancer, Libra, Capricorn) reflects *deeds* from a past life, requiring *correct action* in this life. Fixed karma (Taurus, Leo, Scorpio, Aquarius) implies *misuse of will* in many lives, requiring a *willingness to relinquish control* in favor of being of service. Lastly, Mutable karma (Gemini, Virgo, Sagittarius, Pisces) calls for *attitude adjustment* to replace negative mental chatter by visualizing positive outcomes. Countless life cases have validated this.

Empowering as this perspective was, I also learned by trial and error that not everyone cares to explore such deep levels. Just as we may sometimes want just a snack or a treat, and other times a full meal, our individual developmental stage will determine our desire and capacity for self-reflection. Each person who seeks an astrologer for counsel brings with them a range of needs, some recognized and others sub-conscious or repressed. Most presenting problems have deeper roots that show in the chart. To also be a healer, an astrologer must cultivate a doctor's *bedside manner,* as well as many technical proficiencies. Issie understood and modeled this quality.

A CLASSIC: ASTROLOGY: A COSMIC SCIENCE

Issie's reputation and influence grew far beyond Boston, with a demand for her to write a textbook of her views on astrology. I recall seeing her writing *Astrology: A Cosmic Science* at Harmony Hill and later *Pluto/Minerva: The Choice is Yours*, both labors of love and tools for transmutation. Her style was simple and brief; she made a point and went on, methodically covering the basics. A few well-meaning advice-givers disliked her substance-over-style approach and pressured Issie to adopt a more stream-of-consciousness style. She stuck to her guns despite this criticism and huge sales resulted. Both books became classics, still in demand today. The binding of the first paperbound edition tore too easily with use, so hardcover editions and then translations followed, uplifting thousands of souls by her wisdom.

When I graduated high school in 1969, I'd been interpreting charts for three years. Astrology: A Cosmic Science, was published in 1970 with the help of her student, Bruce Altieri. I'll never forget Bruce telling me that he had a revelation after hearing Issie say, *"act as if and it will be so."* He decided that he had had enough of the emotional storms of being a Cancerian male, and so he consciously adopted a more Capricorn persona – his opposite sign! This gave him new perspective on his Cancer Sun sign and its *imaginative* power to enlist the subconscious in changing his persona. Issie inspired this kind of creativity, to apply astrological principles for spiritual development, and to have some fun with it in the process. I have applied this *act-as-if* principle with wonderful results in many situations. Another huge lesson Issie taught is that as astrologers we carry karmic responsibility for our words, which will burden or bless us. We are accountable for our insights and predictions, especially in sensitive topics. That is also why I went on to earn an M. Ed. in Counseling Psychology, to better use astrology as a therapeutic tool.

Issie inscribed my first copy of Astrology: A Cosmic Science: *"To Amy – my spiritual daughter, may she always keep the Inner Sun shining and stars in her eyes, God bless, Issie."* My love for Issie and gratitude for how she touched my life still move me. From 1965 to 1970, I spent hundreds of blissful hours studying with Issie, who truly was my *"spiritual mother."*

Rave reviews of ACS praised her contribution to astrology such as this one by Ellen Lamb, of the Selection Department of King County Library System in Washington, who wrote:

"It is indeed a pleasure to recommend this classic title. If you read only one book on astrology in your life, let this be the one ... a great, comprehensive treatment of the subject. In addition to offering authoritative, well-written information for all signs, house placements, nodes, etc., Hickey speaks with deeper wisdom and compasssion than any author I know. She is fearless in confronting the flawed personality and equally courageous in her absolute conviction that human beings have the inherent ability to overcome all."

Issie did not rest on her laurels. Her guidance told her to publish her intuitions on the newest-discovered member of our Solar system: Pluto, received in decades of meditation and studying natal charts. Her unique view was vital to astrologers, especially me, with a natal Sun-Pluto conjunction. In 1973, Issie published *Pluto/ Minerva: The Choice is Yours,* dedicating it: *"To Thomas A. Jackson whom we love and respect for his support and encouragement and friendship through all the years we have known him."* I was then age 22 and fully *blossomed* (as Issie would say), attending college, living on my own and seeing astrology clients. Issie's inscription to me in my copy meant the world to me; her beautiful script shown below:

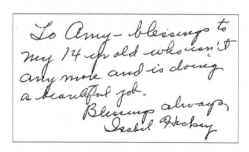

Pluto/Minerva struck a powerful chord with astrologers and was an instant success and classic. After Issie's passing, her daughter Helen continued offering Issie's books via her *"New Pathways."*

The Dec/Jan 1990 "Mountain Astrologer," gave ASC, and Issie this glowing review: "<u>Astrology: A Cosmic Science</u> is a comprehensive text-book ... especially to those of you who are interested in karmic, spiritual and evolutionary astrology. ... The author, who died (or, as she would have said, 'graduated') in 1980, was a much-loved and respected teacher whose work directly or indirectly shaped many of today's lecturers, counselors, and teachers ..."

If you Google-search *Astrology: A Cosmic Science* you'll see a wealth of sites with reviews of it, book sellers or writers who cite it as a source of inspiration, including this reviewer's excerpts:

"The strength of this book is the deep, rich context surrounding each topic... [It] reveals vistas of astrological truths ... assembles random bits of the universe in which you live into a pattern that makes sense."[9]

Issie continued to expand her understanding of astrology and all of the myriad of subtleties involved in chart interpretation, long after she published her classic ACS book. I know this because Helen Hickey had given me *the* copy of ACS that was Issie's in which Issie had made addition notations in the margins on a dozen or so pages, adding new insights and intuitions to her text, as they came to her.[10]

More voices of individuals touched by ACS to come later.

THOSE EYES ... THEY MESMERIZED!

If you ever met Issie, you would be struck by her eyes. Sunk deep, bright blue, she was more than merely present as she looked at you. Issie looked through your outer personality shell and ego façade, right to your soul. The eyes *are windows to the soul,* and Issie's translucently clear *windows* made her a true "Seer." This was driven home to me on many occasions.

The first time was at Harmony Hill. As I was leaving from my first visit, Issie put her hands on my shoulders to make sure we were seeing each other's eyes and asked if she'd see me in September for her astrology class; that *eye-to-eye* moment sealed our soul connection.

---

[9] The site, "Extra Torrent," did not indicate the name of the person posting.
[10] These extra insights and thoughts are in *Your Cosmic Blueprint: A Seeker's Guide* based on her textbook, available at NewAgeSages.com.

Once, at one of Issie's astrology classes, I asked her privately before the class started if she would consider using my chart for a class demonstration. I knew that she liked letting students discuss a person's chart and hear feedback about how accurate they were, and I needed help with a decision. Gazing into my eyes, Issie knew immediately what was troubling me, and told me exactly what I needed to hear. After that, she did not use my chart in class that evening, knowing that a group discussion was not in my best interest. Her protective maternal instinct, shown in her own chart by her Moon-Neptune conjunction in Cancer in the 8th house, (exactly conjunct my natal Uranus) was one of her best qualities.

I stayed for the class that evening but wasn't focused on the discussion. Processing what Issie had said about a Neptune transit I was having, I suddenly understood the link between two seemingly conflicting ideas Issie had often taught about Neptune. She used to call Neptune a *Cosmic Santa Claus* and that its lesson was *humility*. As I pondered that irony, a loud *"HO-HO-HO!"* echoed in my brain and made me see that his jolly laugh was really to help us stop taking ourselves too seriously!

A third example that comes to mind of Issie's mesmerizing gaze was at a Star Rovers evening. I was sitting next to her in the lobby of the hotel where our group held lectures; a distraught woman came over, knelt in front of Issie and poured out her woes. I don't recall her grievance, but I recall seeing her expression transform from gruff to peaceful before Issie had even said a word, as she felt Issie's light and love radiating to her. Issie's remarks then helped the woman to rethink her entire role in the matter, instead of blaming others. The woman was only open to Issie's message because of the healing energy that Issie had silently radiated to her. By the end of this exchange, the woman was smiling, happy and thanked Issie with a hug. Although I was sitting right next to Issie, I was invisible to the woman, her eyes fully occupied by absorbing the healing Issie was sending to her, a very powerful thing to witness.

A last example: We were at a holiday party at the home of one of her students. Issie had invited me to join her, and I was glad to attend. As I was underage, so I didn't partake in the spiked punch or alcoholic drinks. The room was crowded and too noisy for much conversation. Sitting together, sipping our sodas, Issie and I were content to just be and take in the scene.

Suddenly, a drunken man with bad breath pressed his face close to Issie's and spouted, *"So, you're the astrologer?"* in a provocative tone. She looked him in the eyes, smiled and said in a gentle yet firm tone, *"No, you must have me confused with someone else."* He started to argue, then must have forgotten why and stumbled off to another room and didn't return.

I was stunned, and asked Issie why she had told such a lie. She explained that because alcohol had led the man to be possessed by dark forces and incapable of rational conversation, she had to shield herself from attack with a protective *robe of light* and a *white lie*.

His leaving without a scene had confirmed her clairvoyance; *"absent from the appearance is present with the power."* Whenever he sobered up and reclaimed his body, he would have no memory of the encounter. Issie was unharmed by the attempted psychic assault, nor was the sad soul who would have humiliated himself and ruined the party, if Issie had taken the bait and fed his negativity. One look into his eyes told Issie that he was possessed. She passed the test with flying colors, while giving an unforgettable spiritual lesson to me, which I have had many occasions through the years to apply.

ISSIE'S "HOME-COMING" LIFT-OFF!

Issie taught, in meditation, to visualize your ideal place and fill it with your own favorite colors, paintings, plants, architectural and landscape details in your *imag-in-ation*. That beautiful place will await you on the other side when you leave the body, to welcome you home. It was at Harmony Hill, Issie's favorite place, where she had created a piece of heaven on earth, that she left the body in 1980.

While I was in college in the mid-1970s, we kept in touch and I looked forward to Issie's hug whenever I returned, as she whispered, *"Welcome home!"* In 1979, I came to hear Issie on a panel and shared the following quotes from it in *The Astrologer's Newsletter:*

> "Q: *What would you want to do, in terms of your life and goals as an astrologer?*
> **Issie:** "To have everyone live his Real Self, so he no longer needs his chart!"

Q: *What qualities should an astrologer have to be a good counselor?*
Issie: "Warmth, caring. It is my belief that every astrologer should be a healer, a channel for healing. And if you really care, it will show through."

Q: *What do you expect of the 1980-81 conjunction of Jupiter and Saturn in Libra?*
Issie: "This is the first time that Jupiter and Saturn have been conjunct in air signs for hundreds of years. This is terribly important. Libra is the turning point. If you're doing a race and you come to a place where you have to turn back, then you are doing that in Libra. Aries to Libra is involving yourself in matter; Libra to Pisces is the soul's journey back, evolving beyond matter. If you look at the planets from Jupiter on out for the next three years, you'll be very surprised at what you'll see.

Everything has come together between Libra and Pisces, and there are going to be many people who are sound asleep who are going to be taken off the planet because the speed is going to be so great, and the new energy coming in is going to be so strong, that if they can't go on with it, in mercy they will be given another planet to which to go.

This is one of the reasons every spiritual astrologer and teacher is working so hard to wake people up, because if they don't wake up by that time, they're going to miss the opportunity not only of this lifetime, but of many lifetimes. I don't want to sound negative, but if you're not awake, wake up, because you can be part of what's coming in. It's going to be fantastically challenging and wonderful. Jupiter and Saturn are both sacred planets, and they're bringing in something that's never been on this planet before, and it concerns social relations.

All of the crises, divorces, and break-ups that are happening are preparing the way for the right kind of people to get together and be together. The souls coming in on that Libra conjunction are going to be running the 2000-year period. There are some very high souls who are already coming into the babies being born right now. So, it's a tremendous challenge and if we'll only use it this planet can be the Paradise God intended it to be!"

Issie was clairvoyant about her death. When she told me that she knew she'd be leaving the body in the next few years and that she was *"passing the torch"* to me. I said softly, *"I understand,"* all the while hoping she may have misread a sign. She had foreseen going peacefully in sleep, just as she did. I believe Issie meant my work as an astrologer and healer, which continued. Her *torch* also came to include *this book,* which her grandson Jay faithfully safeguarded for 30 years – a mere blink of the Creator's eye!

At her memorial at Harmony Hill, her students, family and friends gathered to bless her on her way. As we joined hands in a healing circle on the lawn, I shared with the group a vision of Issie's Spirit being ready to rise with the help of a huge multi-colored hot-air balloon. Issie wanted us to release any fear that may weigh her down, and as we each released our fears, another psychic '*sandbag*' would drop from the metaphoric balloon to lift her higher, fueled by her Spirit's huge torch, as she *"let go, and let God."*

It was a sad and glorious day of good-byes and gratitude for our blessings. Issie said often with a giggle, *"the spiritual life is never dull!"* and that her gravestone could read, *"She was never bored!"* This poem, read at her memorial, had been found on Issie's desk:

> *Do not stand at my grave and weep*
> *I am not there – I do not sleep.*
> *I'm part of the thousand winds that blow,*
> *I'm part of the diamond glints of snow,*
> *I'm part of the sunlight on ripening grain,*
> *I'm part of the gentle autumn rain.*
> *When you awake in the morning's hush*
> *I am the swift uplifting rush*
> *Of quiet birds in circled flight.*
> *I am part of the stars that shine at night.*
> *Do not stand at my grave and cry,*
> *I am not there, I did not die.*[11]

Many gave tributes and messages besides me; astrologer David Lewis, Helen Hickey, Issie's sister Mary, Dr. Frank Jackson, Virginia Fleming, Patricia Allard, Ayesha and Wayne Grice, Sheagh Kendal,

---

[11] Mary Frye wrote the poem in 1932, while living in Baltimore.

Chuck Azzwelo, Lucile Bennis, Louise Walls, from across the USA and from Canada. Close long-time friend, Tom Jackson, shared these prophetic words:

"Issie's name should be written in the history books of astrology. Unborn generations should know about Issie. The philosophy that she had and taught is what the world needs. We will never have any peace in this world unless her philosophy is applied. Her name should never be forgotten."

My last pilgrimage to Harmony Hill was a warm day in 1983, with my then-2-year old son, Jeremy, who was born during that Saturn-Jupiter conjunction in Libra. I was pregnant with our second son Clifton and felt called to visit Issie's grave in the small cemetery not far from the house, and to see the old summer retreat.

The Light of "Harmony Hill" had waned with Issie gone but whispers of magic remained. Sitting with Jeremy on the lawn, my grief welled into tears, and my old-soul toddler put his arms around me to comfort me. In that moment, I knew that I was as blessed by raising a family as much by any esoteric pursuit. As Issie taught, *love never dies; it only changes form.* Magic was in everyone whose lives Issie touched, wherever our paths led.

The cemetery next to Isabel's summer retreat.

"YOUR COSMIC BLUEPRINT: A SEEKER'S GUIDE"

Years after Issie's passing, the publisher CRCS proposed to Helen Hickey the combining of Issie's *Astrology a Cosmic Science* with her second text, *Pluto/Minerva, the Choice is Yours* in a revised edition. Helen agreed, only if I would oversee the editing, to ensure that any changes were true to Issie's teachings. I was glad to lend a hand, and this led to another project with Helen, to spread Issie's message further. Helen loved the new cover that CRCS designed for the revised book, convinced that the time was right to join these two volumes with a fresh look.

Below are Issie's original (left) navy and yellow cover for ACS, and her black and white Pluto/Minerva cover design. Under them is the new cover, of the combined CRCS edition.

CRCS promoted the new edition with this press release:

"A perennial best-seller in hardcover, this classic work is finally available in paperback! This classic of spiritual astrology (over 100,000 sold in hardcover) is one of two defining works on the interplay of karma, reincarnation and astrology ... a comprehensive textbook of spiritual astrology, and it has had a large following for the last twenty years since original publication. ... Isabel Hickey was one of the most popular and influential astrologers of recent years. She lectured throughout the US and was one of the most important teachers of astrology for the baby boom group of practitioners. She can truly be called the most important pioneer and popularizer of spiritual astrology in the modern era."

Overseeing the revision reignited my love of Issie's teachings and sparked a vision of more people benefiting by her wisdom, if we were to adapt the text to be a computer-generated natal report. Helen agreed and in 2001, we signed on with Astrolabe to partner with us. As Helen and I adapted the text, we drew from our respective skills and background as therapists and writers, emailing our edits back and forth, often sensing Issie's *inner* support. Delays caused years to pass before the program launched in 2015. Helen had *graduated* in 2005, leaving me to see it through, along with another puzzle that took years to piece together, resulting in this book's publication in 2012.

Helen Hickey (1923 - 2005)

As Issie taught, *absent from the appearance is present with the power.* I know, in hindsight, that this principle drove our years of delays, giving us time to add valuable new interpretations of Pluto's transits.[12] The report, *Your Cosmic Blueprint: A Seeker's Guide,* now allows countless *m*ore souls to reflect on the indicators of their astrological charts.

The long delay also led me to find Issie's grandson Jay Hickey, who I'd last seen in 1980, to pass along precious family documents that Helen had given to me. Jay's delight in learning about these ancestral papers was far surpassed by my shock at his news for me,

---

[12] For more information on this report, visit NewAgeSages.com.

which led to us collaborate on this book. Helen passed along much more to me, returning us again to what *'never mind'* means, as none of this could have happened if I listened only to my rational mind, and not also trusted in my intuition!

SENTIMENTS WORTH SAVING & PROPHECIES SHARED

Issie often said, *"One thing that saddens me most as I travel the country and meet people is that so few people realize how beautiful and worthy of love they really are – if they only knew how beautiful they are on the inner level – their Higher Self – and that they ARE all-love, they would feel worthy and at peace inside and become happier in their relationships."*

An excellent way to enhance self-esteem, Issie taught was to keep the good things that people write about you in cards or letters. In times of self-doubt, they will help you remember that you are loved and valued. Even in today's electronic culture, the idea still holds true. One can also benefit from writing down positive things that people say about why they like or admire you. Issie herself had saved many letters that expressed gratitude, hope and love for *her* as a spiritual teacher.

In the winter of 2005, a package arrived from Helen, who was cleaning her home in anticipation of major surgery. Sensing that she would not return to her beloved apartment overlooking Boston Harbor, she mailed to me a package of papers. When I called Helen to ask why she had sent them to me, she said that they were papers of Issie's that she had saved, and always intended to do something with them, but could never figure out what that should be, and her intuition had told her: *Amy will know what to do with them one day.*

The conversation was brief, as I was more concerned about her well being and upcoming surgery. Since she said there was no urgency about the package, I put it on a shelf, where it stayed for the months while I kept in touch with Helen, visiting her in the hospital and at rehab, where she made a valiant but fruitless effort to recover. In the years after Issie's passing, Helen had sometimes asked me to interpret her chart, which led to intimate exchanges about her destiny. When she asked me about surgery, it showed brighter days ahead. We both sensed that Issie was getting ready to welcome her on the other side in the not too distant future.

After her surgery, I visited Helen in rehab and was amazed by how she urged her physical therapists to improve their professional standards; their attitudes always changed when they heard that their patient was BU's former Dean Hickey of Sargent College of Physical Therapy! Even at her frailest, Helen served, guided and enlightened others. Hundreds who knew her as a graceful soul and spiritual sister mourned her passing that March.

Months later, I opened the package from Helen and studied its contents. I'd written a biography of Astrologer, Dr. Oskar Adler, a huge project. Did I have the fortitude for a similar undertaking? To my delight, the package had this profile and photo of Isabel as a younger woman than during the years when I knew her.

ISABEL M. HICKEY
Astrologer

YOUR DESTINY AND THE STARS

This lecture by Isabel Hickey overturns all the popular misconceptions regarding Astrology. "The wise man rules his stars," says Mrs. Hickey; "the fool obeys them. Astrology is not fortune-telling. It deals with energies in man as well as in the cosmos." From Isabel Hickey's Astrology you learn that character is destiny; and you will learn how to improve your character, your ability, and your destiny.

ISABEL HICKEY brings to the lecture platform a wealth of practical knowledge in varied fields of human relationships. Lecturer, writer and teacher, she has had many years' experience in group instruction and in personality integration, as well as being a Personal Counselor. As personal consultant, she has worked with doctors and psychiatrists. She has been an executive secretary in the field of religious education and an editor of church publications.

Mrs. Hickey has a positive dynamic understanding of people's problems that gives them a clearer sense of values, as well as full co-ordination of body, mind and spirit. Her attitude is one of complete openmindedness. It consists of an unshakeable faith in the laws of nature, combined with perfect humility toward those laws, and a patient determination to learn them at whatever cost.

Seeing this photo brought to that mind something Issie had often said, that when the soul leaves the body, if someone could see you, they would see a much younger, more vital version of yourself, with no signs of degenerative disease or aging.

The package also contained dozens of letters and tributes to Issie by recipients of her compassion and wisdom. Letters by students, clients, astrologers and booksellers spanned Issie's last decade, many sent to *Fellowship House Bookshop* in Waltham. They expressed gratitude for her guidance and spiritual views in her books, lectures and meditations. Often a writer would ask for Issie's guidance about a personal matter.

To preserve confidentiality, no names are disclosed. If you are among the students, clients and others whose expressions of gratitude are among this collection, thank you for letting Issie know how much she meant to you; know that you meant as much to her.

The first excerpts are by fans of <u>Astrology: A Cosmic Science</u> (ASC); students, teachers and booksellers in the US and beyond, including Canada and Trinidad. All admired and respected Issie, who, as she traveled, met people who wanted to stay in touch, due to her generosity of spirit. Their anonymous words are supplemented with my reflections:

"Your book is an electric charge jolting me into a higher orbit – one of those exciting events that come along and puts us on the edge of our seats! It is no accident that "Astrology – A Cosmic Science" fell into my hands as I've been seeking this type of instruction since starting the study of astrology. With a grand cross and five retrograde planets, the negative interpretations don't fit! Yours do! I recognize a fine spiritual teacher when I read one. I have responded to no other astrology book as yours, which struck a true note. Richest blessings."

To find a fine spiritual teacher, as the above soul did in Issie's book, is indeed a rich blessing. The description of *'an electric charge jolting me into a higher orbit'* reflected Issie's natal Uranus in Sagittarius in her 1st house! She *was* electrically charged, radiating cosmic law. I once asked Issie why some of her students didn't seem to fully grasp the implications of karma and grace. Smiling, she said, *"Most are still asleep in matter and come to class just to soak in the love; only a few are awake."* Soakers, as she lovingly called them, were not ready to forgo their egos in order to step into the Light of Spirit, and onto a brighter path. Similarly, she reminded: *no chicken ever hatched with a sledgehammer; it takes warmth and love.* Issie's warmth radiated far, accelerating the development of those who were open to jolting themselves out of *'sleep'* and into a new orbit!

Issie also loved thought-provoking word plays. She once sent me a holiday card that remains above my desk still today. I'd just graduated high school and was renting my first apartment with a friend and occasional other friends who needed a place to *'crash'*. To make ends meet, besides giving astrology consults, I worked an early breakfast shift at a nearby hospital, scooping various kinds of oatmeal into bowls as my roommates slept. I was too tired in the evenings to attend Issie's classes and had been missing her and feeling self-pity at being stuck at a menial labor job, with no prospects for advancement. The front of her card shows a swath of black, and in bright pink script, this quote by Paul Goodman: *"to understand is to stand under which is to look up to which is a good way to understand it ain't easy,"* This enigmatic message was just what I needed.

Her note inside: *"God bless you, Amy. Have lovely holidays. Love always, Issie"* told me that Issie was missing me too and cared about me as a person more than just as a student. It also made me stop feeling sorry for myself in the hospital basement breakfast-line crew. I had my health and independence while others were ill, in pain and dependent on others. Each tray that I touched went to a patient who needed healing, even if I never met or saw the person. I *understood*: God had given me that job for me to be a *Light Worker* by blessing each tray that I touched on its way to a soul who was suffering. That revelation transformed my attitude about the job, and I began looking forward to that early morning shift for the rest of the time that the job lasted.

At a turbulent time in my young adulthood and in my family, Issie was my spiritual anchor, a rare and precious role in our secular culture. Many Astrologers spoke of a *Grand Cross* and *Retrograde* planets in depressive terms, but Issie taught that for each hardship in a chart, a way to grace can be found if we inwardly ask our Higher Self to show us where to find it in the chart. With a Grand Cross in Cardinal signs with natal Uranus, Neptune, Moon and Jupiter, I am so glad that Issie saw my potential in my chart, and not merely a soul weighed down by karmic burdens.

"We each" Issie taught, *"do the best we can, with what we know; if we knew better, we'd do better."* She understood, as I did years later, that my seven natal trines showed gifts to help me transmute the karmic challenges that my chart also expressed.

Speaking of Karma, and the astrological significator for it, which is Saturn, this next note by another astrologer refers to a poem on the back of Issie's original ACS, which came to Issie as a vision in her sleep as a profound message about Saturn; the poem follows.

"I find your book so enjoyable, we've become good companions. Thank you for the beautiful poem *"Saturn – Angel of Discipline."* Oh! How I understand that. I teach a small class in Astrology and could ask for no better text; unless they understand the inspirational side of Astrology, much is lacking. It's a wonderful pleasure to meet you through your book, now a most treasured item needed on every Astrologer's bookshelf."

SATURN – ANGEL OF DISCIPLINE

In the deep darkness of grief and pain,
I found the angel of Light again.
She wore no lovely garment of white
But was garbed in robes as deep as night.
I saw in her arms no flower fair,
Instead, a crucifix nestled there.

> She didn't walk with joyous tread
> Or offer me relief from dread.
> But I felt her peace and her quiet power
> And knew in that night of awe filled hour
> She was the angel of Eternal Dawn.
> Lifting her hood I saw her face
> And knew the glory that hid her grace.
> From earth blinded eyes too dim to see
> That only through her, could we ever go free!

At the present time (2012), with transiting Pluto in Capricorn (Saturn's sign) through 2025, this poem has enormous import for *the inspirational side of Astrology* and life in general as a vision to fortify seekers on their journey.

Issie's natal Saturn in Aquarius in her 3rd house reflected her thirst for knowledge that *she* could test. Issie urged us to do the same, saying *"don't take my word for it – test it yourself; if it works, use it, if not, throw it out."* She knew what she knew, and wanted us to know *inside* as well, and not to accept her ideas on blind faith. That she urged us to do *reality checks* when most of my generation distrusted anyone over age thirty, was a very wise and effective way to instruct. Issie also recognized that a new crop of individuals were positioning themselves as "New Age Gurus" and she warned us to beware of people who call themselves *Guru,* because enlightened souls are humble about themselves, not arrogant. Although many of us knew Issie as an amazing *Guru,* she never asked to be called that.

The next excerpts of Issie's book-fans are a chorus of praise and must have meant a lot to her because of all that she had suffered. Although her students embraced her spiritual views of astrology, many other astrologers of her time disapproved of her. Issie endured public insults and tasteless jokes at her expense in her lifetime and even beyond. Some astrologers perhaps resented her success. Other astrologers were courting favor within scientific circles, wanting astrology to be perceived as more of a science than as an art. Naming her book "Astrology: A Cosmic *Science"* had irritated some of those astrologers! Yet, if science relies on observations based on mathematics, logical inference, generalization and system-theory that is supported by evidence, then Issie's approach to astrology was both scientifically valid and spiritually fortified.

Not all of Issie's relatives accepted astrology or her becoming an astrologer. She had lamented that some of her family considered it *'hocus pocus'* and that they feared for her immortal soul. Issie did not *choose* astrology as her path; her inner guidance put her on this path, and she obeyed the call to the benefit of many thousands of souls. As a channel of Light and healing, Issie lifted astrology up, despite countless obstacles and naysayers. Issie prayed for those who belittled her, like *'pearls in her oyster,'* as she taught us to do regarding anyone we dislike. *Liking*, she taught, must be earned, but *love* is each person's divine right: *"even if you think the person's a stinker!"* she would laugh, *"surround him or her with God's love and light in your prayers, and watch how they'll change!"*

Just as many *sleeping souls* judged or misunderstood Issie, other more awakened souls defended her, as in the next letters show. For brevity's sake, Astrology: A Cosmic Science is shown as 'ACS.'

"Your Astrology masterpiece is a wonderful addition to our astrology library. I have practically worn it out! I love it; the vibrations are fantastic and I really relate to it. Thank you."

"What a happy day to find ACS. Of all the astrology books I've read, it is dearest to my heart. It was like meeting a long lost friend. It encompasses a way of life and a perspective I'd hunted for in other books. It helps me guide my clients and is a constant inspiration to me."

"Warmest appreciation and gratitude for your wonderful "ACS" and "Minerva /Pluto The Choice is Yours" – they help me understand myself and my destiny, to serve others and help them to understand their lives. In Love and Light."

"Your book is invaluable in teaching Astrology. I recommend it to friends and students for its spiritual approach. Have recently obtained "Pluto/Minerva" and really appreciate it."

"Thank you for ACS. I enjoy it and use it when delineating charts. I send you a thousand blessings. You give a true picture of this divine science and fed my hunger for true astrological knowledge."

"Your book is one of the greatest discoveries in Astrology. I am gradually digesting it, one idea at a time, and recommending it to my students."

"Thank you so much for your beautiful Astrology book. The clarity and truth of what you say is appreciated by all, especially people first starting their study of the heavens."

"Reading the Preface of "ACS" I was struck by the beautiful way you introduced the subject. It's a most lovingly written book, and will help me in my search for understanding."

"Thank you for writing <u>Astrology</u>. Your clear style enabled me to learn a great deal about myself. It also cleared up some of my inner conflicts and restlessness. Thank you."

"Your Astrology book is one of the best. I like your positive, constructive suggestions to difficult aspects and signs. I find your work rather therapeutic."

"ASC is wonderfully presented, very reachable and readable. We need much more work of this type in America."

"I can't begin to express my thanks for your marvelous ACS. The spiritual and Karmic side of Astrology, all-important for complete understanding, is ignored in other books. I have almost burst with excitement since being introduced to your book."

"I enjoy ASC and Minerva/Pluto, extremely fascinating, informative and enlightening."

"A friend who is into astrology considers your book the bible of astrology. I am excited and delighted – your insights have awakened my ambition and love for Astrology, confirming many things I have felt, in my chart and others. Thank you for sharing your knowledge."

"Through ASC, I learned that my responsibility is *"to flow with the rhythm of life."* I feel relief, hope and gratitude for such a wonderful, penetrating book. It seems a horoscope with many negative aspects may be the result of a person who lived previously but did poorly, or a more advanced soul who must develop his *'spiritual muscles,'* so negative aspects cannot tell if previous existences were successes or failures."

"I keep returning to your beautiful book. You have the most positive and useful attitude of any astrological author I have read. Your insight is gentle yet deep, as is your advice."

"Many thanks and compliments for the inspiring ACS. I learned of it thru an astrologer who described it as the best she ever read on the subject. She was right! It is a true friend for an Aquarian."

"You truly feel like a friend; ACS is an invaluable companion in my astrology studies. An intuitive drive for enlightenment and desire to find help for my health problems led me to astrology. Your approach and philosophy are the kind of astrology I want to learn so I can tread the path of enlightenment and help others."

"ACS is the first book I refer to when I look something up. I like what you say about being humble, a lesson we must all learn. When I opened your book. I couldn't put it down. It was one book I really relate to and recommend to anyone interested in astrology. Astrology helps me see the other's point of view and give me a better understanding of myself. Thank you."

"Once again I have taken a chart through your book for insight. Each time I finish, I want to thank you. I cannot put my physical arms around you to tell you with a hug how much I love you, for this book and Minerva & Pluto. Everything is coming to me now with such beauty and excitement step by step and each time I went through your book, when finished a little voice said "Let her know how you feel." So here are my thanks, a far away friend, yet so close."

"Your wonderful "ACS" is just what I've been looking for. You make our link with astrology as souls so clear. Thank you for writing the book."

"After reading ACS I have come to love you even though I don't know you. The keys to our spiritual mission are in your guidance. Thank you for an astrology text with real depth."

"ACS" is clear in defining traditional astrology, giving ample coverage to the beginning student. References to the spiritual, esoteric side of astrology interest many now that there is a trend toward expanding human consciousness."

These next four excerpts are from people who attended Issie's group meditations. Reading their letters brought me back to my first time experiencing one of Issie's Friday gatherings and to the countless positive ripple effects that they had:

"I want to express my gratitude and love for your being a positive spiritual influence in my life, through chart readings, meditations, astrology classes and your house in NH. The first time you told me to *'get my feet on the ground'* and *'serve or suffer'* I had no idea what you meant but slowly your wisdom seeped into my consciousness and I put my toe onto the path. You were the first person to care enough to tell me I was headed in the wrong direction. I am finding true freedom of surrender in service. As I travel this wondrous path to God and my true Divine nature, thoughts of you and your words pop up in my consciousness like a luminescent ray from the Divine Center of Light. I thank God every day that there are beings like you who are so selfless to stand and hold the lantern for other souls to see and feel the Light and Love of God. You once told me to read *Initiation* by Elizabeth H. [Haich] It was one of the best books I have ever read. God Bless You, Thank you and Love,"

"Thank you for turning my eyes inward to find myself and God. When I look at my life today, you were the threshold to me finding my way back home. What you said is unfolding."

"Meeting you was a reinstatement of my spiritual faith. I thank you and pray that you continue your work in the way that you have been."

"Your book is my favorite because it rings true. You left me a beautiful message when you signed it, about my head and heart working together –excellent advice."

* * * * * * * * * * * *

From seven seasoned astrologers and booksellers:

"You brought a torch of truth, and all of us lit our own Torch from yours. We grow brighter and richer from our experience with you. I say this not to feed your ego but to let you know what a beautiful channel you are for God to work through. Since your visit, many have been inspired to learn meditation and others are practicing regularly. My bookshop has become a center for everyday seekers to talk and discuss astrology and spiritual things. Your book and lectures are often the topic. God bless you."

"Bless you and thank you for opening the doors of spiritual understanding through "ACS." You must be a very old soul filled with great love and beauty to share so beautifully your deep understanding of the higher meanings of Astrology. I feel loving and comforting vibrations from you through your book, and situations with which I would have been unable to cope have been easier to bear because of your insights. In my search for a more Spiritual approach to my life, I was many times moved to tears as your explanations allowed me to glimpse the beauty of the different planetary vibrations, and cause and effect of being in the here and now. For years I've been searching for deeper meanings, for the reasons I am here. The Karmic interpretation of Astrology evokes in me all the awe and reverence of God (life) that one feels upon entering a great cathedral. I deeply feel that I must 'server or suffer' and 'let go and let God' and serve humanity. Again, thank you for starting me on the path to spiritual discovery, and bless you."

"ACS is the best book on Astrology – I find it exceptional. Why? Because of you – one can tell you're a good soul, evolved in scope and spiritual depth."

"ACS is wonderful! I have a considerable astrological library but it would be hard to choose one I like better, or have found more useful than yours. Thanks to your marvelous book, the pieces are beginning to fall into place."

"I was very impressed by "ACS" and compliment you on the excellent workmanship that went into it. It is straightforward, concise and intelligible. The attitudes expressed are highly positive, enjoyable and a fantastic basic text for classes. Keep up the fine work, as you enhance the field toward respect in scientific circles."

"ACS is by far the best on the market. I thank you for many who have gained so much from your inspired work and added prestige in the field of astrology."

"Interesting delineations, sensible approaches, satisfactory answers, well written, friendly style. Could you possibly outline your further views concerning the Avatar of the Aquarian Age – already functioning – in a black body?"

* * * * * * * * * * * *

Issie had made stunning predictions in the 1960's and 1970s; that the Avatar of the Aquarian Age would come in a black body. The Civil Rights movement was still in an early phase. One might wonder if the great civil rights leader and Nobel Peace Prize recipient, Rev. Martin Luther King, Jr. (born Jan. 15, 1929) fulfilled her prophecy before his assassination in 1968. King was so advanced, he skipped grades 9 and 12, began college at age 15, graduated at 19 and earned his PhD at Boston University in 1955. His pivotal *"I have a dream"* speech became a global vision. Nelson Mandela, another awakened soul in a black body (born July 18, 1918), could also be viewed as an Avatar. A prophetic anti-apartheid activist, Mandela's convictions earned him 27 years in prison, the Nobel Peace Prize and the Presidency of South Africa in the late 1990's after ushering in multi-racial democracy in 1994 by putting reconciliation above revenge. At the time of Issie's prophecy, no one foresaw America electing an African American as our 44th President. Barack Obama was a boy when Issie made that prophecy. Born August 4th, 1961, Obama, as a community organizer aided fellow Chicagoans in a time of economic distress and became USA President with a mandate for change in true Aquarian style, receiving a Nobel Peace Prize early in his presidency. As Aquarius rules groups and consciousness, the Aquarian Age calls each of us to strive to be Avatar-like. As Issie taught, *consciousness is reality.*

Issie made many other stunning prophecies. Decades before Pluto was discovered to be binary planet, Issie had spoken of its dual nature, calling us to choose darkness or light. That is why she named her second book: *Pluto/Minerva: The Choice is Yours.*

Decades before globalization, cell phone, the internet, online social networking or global warming, Issie spoke of an all-inclusive *interconnected web* of invisible energy of which we each part, and that Earth's *vibration would speed up* so much at the turn of the century that *souls who are unable to keep pace will, in mercy, be taken off the planet in large numbers.* Our 21st Century ultra-fast culture, and a stream of wars and natural disasters have provided evidence of her vision more times than I like to admit.

Other similar sentiments can be easily found with an online search. Lastly, among the papers from Helen, were some poems and a special letter by Harry Kemp, known as *the Poet of P'Town!* Most of Issie's saved letters dated in the 1970's, but Harry Kemp's letter of December 2, 1948 stands out from the rest. He was 65 at the time, and his *"Tramping on Life"* was a bestseller. William Brevda (*"The Last Bohemian"*) wrote that Kemp *"survived through the kindness of friends, by selling an occasional poem to a magazine, and by staging self-promotional events that he called "the art of spectacularisms. ... He had learned early in life that by calling attention to himself through some stunt or wild costume he could attract an audience for his message."*

To better understand Harry's letter to Issie, it will help to know that Issie believed and taught that benign celestial visitors, which she called *White Brothers,* were here to advance humanity. Many of her students experienced White Brother visitations in meditations or dreams. It was a tremendous validation that, 60 years after Kemp wrote of extraterrestrials to Issie, the Papal Vatican announced in 2008, that belief in alien and intelligent extraterrestrial life does not contradict faith in God! Here is Harry Kemp's letter:

The Provincetown Publishers
Box 507
Provincetown Cape Cod, Mass.

Dec. 2nd 1948

Dear Isabel Hickey:

To you that article on astrology must be just amateur stuff. And I know that it is not in my poetry you are interested. You are rightly interested most in what is the more important to you, to me, and to an increasing number of other people who realize that the hope of the world lies now, as always, in voices from other worlds – in Religion; in the Relation of The Divine Fact to the Soul of Man.

Arian has had the celestial visitors come to him for a long time; as veritable presences, not imaginary beings. And for those who accept this, it is true enough. Let all others believe it to be imagination; as not being ready for the revelations. His Psycharchs came to Arian with authentic potence many summers out here in the dunes.

At first it gave him a sense of imminent destruction; but soon he saw that there would be no harm to him, if he only kept honest and un-boastful about the visitations.

The ordinary world seemed soon what it really is, – one most extraordinary. Arian never left the "ordinary" world, but was merely given access to what ought to be open to many gifted souls. My reading public's reaction has been various: one or two have hailed the book as authentic and wait for further matter; several, on the other hand, have written me denunciatory letters; several advertisers have told me they do not approve, and wish to "withdraw their support." ..

But all I can do, of course, is to go on and on and on; like Columbus in Juaquin Miller's poem.

I have a sense of golden fulfillment within myself that nothing can tarnish...

Only last night I got a balling-out from a man who really meant to be friendly. I just sat and listened.

You are doing good work, and I thank you for encouraging me.

Here are a few lines that just came to me; to me out here in my small shack; that would, to most, be an impossible dwelling-place. But THEY came here – and still come – and that is an incalculable reward.

While cowards of possession, slaves to ownership,
Cringe underneath the lash of property,
The soldier, lying in his scanted tent,
Puts fear into walled cities and guarded palaces.
        In the Name of the Psycharchs,
        Harry Kemp

Others were also inspired to poetry. Among Issie's papers were three undated poems by her daughter Helen, and two students.

HAPPY, BLESSED, JOYFUL, ABUNDANT, SUPER, ENJOYABLE SPLENDIFEROUS, ALL-ENCOMPASING MOTHER'S DAY

As the "kids" say,
Who's the coolest of the cool?
That's Issie ......

As the teacher's say,
Who conducts the greatest school …
That's Issie
As her colleagues say,
Who personifies the Golden Rule? …
That's Issie
As her family would say,
Who's our most precious jewel…
That's Issie
As the Father would say,
Who's my most useful, Number one, Super-Duper,
Always-Available TOOL**… That's Issie
And who's my mother, my friend, my pal, my supporter, my
confidant, my dear heart
Who thank goodness, fits no earthly, but all the heavenly rules
THAT's (you guessed it) ISSIE!!!
From your Pisces, Your Fish, Your "Pigeon"
** 'cuz she's always "on-the-alert", ready-and-willing and
constantly doing my work to enlighten others, to lighten loads, and
to bring the WORD GOD IS LOVE,
GOD IS GOOD, GOD IS IN ME,
THUS I AM LOVE, I AM GOOD, I AM GOD

This next poem conveys the warmth and whimsy of Issie's classes:

The Astrology Students Lament *By Lewis G. Holladay*
I analyzed and synthesized
The planets and the signs,
I even considered the aspects –
The sextiles and the trines.
I then went to the angles bold,
And hidden houses too –
I puzzled through the night
Until I thought I knew.
Ah! But then I went to class
And heard my teacher do it –
And I came crashing to the Earth,
Because dear friend, I blew it.

This last poem is by a spiritual seeker in Issie's circle.

THE ASTRAL TRIP by Adina Walker

While in quiet meditation
A shaft of light upon me shone
Illuminating Emanation
Shining down on me alone.
It pulled me slowly from my body
Like a silver cord above my eyes
And set my psyche free to wander
Thru the vastness of the skies.
Out of body soaring ... soaring
Nothing to restrain my flight
As galaxies like grains of sand
Stretched out across the night.
Light years passed and still I flew
... still my spirit traveled
Upward thru the realms of light
... as mysteries unraveled.
I heard the music of the spheres
Round about my head ...
Ringing ... Ringing in my ears
(I thought that I was dead).
In awe I watched the cosmic vast
Unfolding silently about ...
A veil was lifted from my sight
And I perceived without a doubt ...
That all of illimitable space
Evolved according to a plan
Beyond the power to comprehend
Of utterly insignificant Man.

LIGHTING THE WAY

Most precious to me among Issie's papers were her notes for an astrology lecture that she had given at a convention in Miami in 1968. I was with her when she gave it and thrilled to see her notes forty years later. I was just 16, and Issie felt that it was time to expose me to the larger astrology world. I had been studying intensively with her for two years and had a good grasp of the basics. I loved participating in class whenever Issie called upon me to share my observations on the natal charts being analyzed, as she often did.

For the Miami convention, Issie and I roomed together. I rarely had a chance to travel far, and never without one of my parents, so it was a big adventure for me. It was my first American Federation of Astrologers (AFA) convention and a life-altering event for us both in many ways. When we arrived at the hotel in Miami, it was a very hot afternoon. After we settled into our room, before her talk, Issie encouraged me to enjoy cooling off with a swim at the pool, and to strike up a conversation with other astrologers, to begin to mingle.

Astrologers were everywhere! I was excited to hear others talking the language that I had grown to love. Because Issie had encouraged me to meet other astrologers at the conference, I worked up the courage to say hello to a few astrologers by the pool, eager to make new astrology friends.

When they learned that I was there for the astrology convention, one said loudly to the others in a rude tone, *"how ridiculous to bring someone so young."* Humiliated, I said nothing and quickly swam to the other side of the pool, vowing to keep to myself for the rest of the conference.

When I returned to our hotel room to change for dinner and the evening program, Issie sensed that something was wrong and asked me what had happened. I couldn't hold back tears of shame as I shared the story about my brief encounter with the astrologers at the pool, and my deflated feelings. Issie enfolded me in a reassuring hug, then looked straight into my eyes and said that I had as much right to be there as anyone, and that I had handled the situation well by swimming away and not getting huffy or rude myself in the face of criticism. Her warm embrace dissolved my shame as I realized that the experience had taught me that not all astrologers could *see the age of the soul, as Issie did*, but were still as asleep in matter, as were so many others.

Issie *did* see through to one's soul. I have countless memories of her gazing deep into my soul, and witnessing how, when someone asked her for guidance, their ego and layers of pretense would dissolve in the loving warmth and light of her gaze.

Imagine my further shock when, at the start of her talk that evening, Issie made a point of prefacing her lecture by mentioning me by name to everyone in the hall, saying how proud she was of her gifted teenager who was an old soul far wiser than my years, and who had started studying astrology with her at age 14, and who at age 16 showed great promise as an astrologer! Issie's public praise of me set the record straight for everyone else and put me on cloud nine the rest of the conference, which brought wonderful memories. As Issie taught, the *age of the soul matters most*, and that only when the heart is engaged with the mind can astrology bring joy, wisdom and healing to oneself and to others.

These vivid memories might not have resurfaced decades later as I stared at these notes, had it not been for Issie herself jogging my memory! At the top of the first typed page, in Issie's handwriting, was my name and the names of others of her Boston group who'd come to that conference! That incident at the pool caused Issie to change her opening remarks, to awaken some *sleeping souls* in the audience! I had never experienced anyone coming to my defense, never mind in such a public way. Issie herself never asked others to come to *her* defense, but others did, when the situation called for it.

While editing this manuscript, I happened to enjoy a phone visit with a fine astrologer who expressed chagrin that few young people seem to be learning astrology; she wondered what might attract more young people to want to consider astrology as a career. Looking back, now at age 60, I know that what attracted *me* as a teenager to astrology was Issie's teachings that astrology can help us find deeper meaning in life. I believe this need is as strong for today's youth as it ever was. Below is how Issie expressed this in her own words, from her saved notes, from that Miami Convention lecture ...

"Astrologers of ancient times were Initiates who understood the Cosmic laws and lived by them; therefore they were healers as well as astrologers. In the age we are living in we have the priceless privilege of bringing astrology into its place as a sacred science once again. In the past it fell into disrepute when it fell into the hands of the uninitiated and was used as a fortune telling advice and used to enhance the individual's ego and to swell his pocketbook.

Thirty years ago, when I was told from within that I was to study astrology (having been trained in it in a time my new brain does not remember) I was told that Astrology was once again to be raised to its rightful estate as a Cosmic Science and many of us had chosen to incarnate at this time for just that purpose. This means self-discipline and the willingness to get beyond the pull of the Unlit Self; the personality.

That is really what Astrology is all about; to teach us how to overcome the duality in ourselves; to reach a state of consciousness where we, having found our inner Center can help our clients to find their own True Self.

The blueprint we call the horoscope shows where we stand on the path of evolution. We do not come unbound into this livingness but we can go unbound out of it if we overcome the pull of matter and clear up what needs clearing. Our debits and our credits are clearly shown in our charts.

Newton's law of motions is true of the dual plane. To every action there is always an equal and contrary reaction; the mutual actions of any two bodies are always equally and oppositely directed.

KARMA: Action and reaction are exactly equal. The personality or world of appearance is under this law and when we function as personalities, we must take this law into consideration. The law of the Real Self – spirit – comes under the law of the trinity.

Physical science cannot formulate laws outside of the dual world. The manifestations of gravitation and electricity have become known but none of the scientists can tell you what gravitation and electricity are.

The LAW FRAMER and the OPERATOR they do not detect. What you or I call God – or whatever you want to call it – must be experienced. It can never be defined. To surmount the law of duality and to find the reality behind the world of appearance it is the sole purpose of our birth in matter.

IT CANNOT BE DONE IN ONE SEMESTER IN THE SCHOOL OF LIFE. Consider this planet as a school of learning. There are grades from kindergarten through grammar school, high school and college. There are Master's degrees that we will eventually attain. On the earth plane, while we are learning, we go to school; then in June we have a vacation and we have a respite from our labors. Then comes the reaping time in September, and back we go to school. The knowledge we have already acquired we still retain and we go on from there.

The blueprint we call the horoscope shows the place and grade we are in at this particular moment; where we go or if we go further is entirely up to us. If we fail we stay in the same grade until we do learn the lessons our Inner Self has set. The end is sure. How long it takes is up to us.

Let me discuss with you some of the clues that show where we stand as shown by the horoscope. The first thing an astrologer does having set up the chart is count the planets in Cardinal, Fixed and Mutable signs. Aries is where we start. The ***indepth*** astrologer knows that the afflictions in these elements will show where there are problems that must be resolved.

Afflictions in cardinal signs – whether square or opposition – shows the wrong use of our energies in the past life. They are the result of wrong action and can only be corrected by right action this time. They can be handled by constructive action in this lifetime. Otherwise they will manifest in fixed signs in the next lifetime and be so deeply ingrained as patterns of behavior they will give much pain and suffering.

Adverse aspects in fixed signs represent the harmful effects of self-will. They are the hardest to handle for they are lessons we have failed to learn through many lifetimes and are deeply ingrained patterns. They are tied with our emotional response to life and deal with egoic tendencies. To overcome the fixed squares and oppositions the giving up of the self-will and being willing to let go and let God is the only solution.

Mutable afflictions are the easiest to handle for they are faults just beginning to manifest. They are tied with the thinking.

Every aspect has a threefold affect: physical, emotional and mental. These habit patterns of ours start with our thinking, then affect our emotions for good or ill and if they are destructive eventuate in the physical body as disease. Our respiratory diseases are tied with mutable afflictions; our cardinal afflictions with tumors, growths and impurities that effect our kidneys and blood stream. Fixed afflictions, being chronic and crystallized in nature have to do with paralysis, and crystallization; for instance, arthritis (they have got stuck) and chronic back difficulties and heart trouble.

Each planet has a story to tell about the past that the brain (being new in each lifetime) does not remember. The most important planet is Saturn for she rules the personality and the world of matter. She is the ring-pass-not, the planet that stands at the portal to inner freedom and tests you to see if you have redeemed the ego and are fit to enter the inner Portals. Her place in your chart shows where your greatest weakness lies – and the place where you can have the greatest strength. The weak link in the chain when welded becomes the strongest part. Adverse aspects to Saturn show the failures of the past and the good aspects show our virtues that have been attained through work and persistence.

The Moon (especially in relation to Saturn) holds the secret of our past for it is the key to the past and the unconscious side of our nature. Study the position of the Moon, by sign, house and aspects and you will know the reason for the present conflicts in the person's life. Put the Moon on the Ascendant, using the degrees of the Moon on each house, and you will learn much about the dark side of yourself.

Neptune is of great importance for it has so much to do with debts owed; your obligations that you must meet in this lifetime either because you understand Neptune sacrifices gladly and joyously because it represents Divine Compassion or because you have copped out on your responsibilities in the past and you must make amends.

Mars, ruling the animal self, has a story to tell. Badly aspected, it represents the misuse of force in the past. Temper and accidents are tied together. Even insurance firms are recognizing this factor.

Uranus configured with Mars can give great violence but the same aspect, when redeemed, makes a person a powerful healer. Tremendous energy; its how it is used that decides the issues. An inner teacher once said to me: 'You can take the path of friction if you want to, but there is a better way. No matter which way you take the end is sure. You can walk, you can run, you can be shoved, you will be pushed, you can ride, you can be dragged; but up to the mountaintop you are going. You can go around the road or you can strike out and go up the mountain steps, a harder way but a quicker one. The choice is yours but the end is certain.

Illustrations: the brutal king – the triangle – the boy whose pal was shot. What we have found out in hypnotic sessions. The man and the judge he saw at 14 – you cannot run out on a problem for you will meet it around the corner. Hypnosis – back in consciousness.

You are vibratorily connected to everything that happens to you. The only way you can change what happens to you is to change what you are. Your keynote attracts situations into your life; change your keynote by changing your consciousness and you will change what happens to you. This is the Cosmic Law and it's up to us to help our clients understand this law. Prediction should not be the primary concern of the astrologer for anyone has it in their power, by changing their attitude, to change what happens to them.

Students and the changes in them in one season.

And now let me share with you something that gives you the reason for coming to earth."

* * * * * * * * * * *

The first illustration mentioned above, was of a boy who nursed anger at the murder of his friend, until in hypnotic regression, he saw that his lost friend was a brutal dictator in a past life, and his murder was karma from his cruel past. The last lines in Issie's notes referred to messages of hope and compassion. Issie often told beginner students to expect their first year of studying astrology to be *"as clear as mud"* while they learned the many details of interpretation. As the pieces fell into place, the student would learn to synthesize, and when intuition kicked in, it would all make sense. This was wise and compassionate counsel.

Her last line referred to an allegory about why souls incarnate, with which she closed her talk and her book: *"Why: An Allegory."* Credited to "Anonymous," it profoundly reflects Issie's philosophy and approach to chart interpretation.

"WHY" ~ AN ALLEGORY
~ Anonymous ~

"I leaned from the low-hung crescent moon and grasping the west pointing horn of it, looked down. Against the other horn reclined, motionless, a Shining One and looked at me, but I was unafraid. Below me the hills and valleys were thick with humans, and the moon swung low that I might see what they did.

"Who are they?" I asked the Shining One. For I was unafraid. And the Shining One made answer: "They are the Sons of God and the Daughters of God."

I looked again, and saw that they beat and trampled each other. Sometimes they seemed not to know that the fellow-creature they pushed from their path fell under their feet. But sometimes they looked as he fell and kicked him brutally.

And I said to the Shining One: "Are they ALL the Sons and Daughters of God?"

And the Shining One said: "ALL."

As I leaned and watched them, it grew clear to me that each was frantically seeking something, and that it was because they sought what they sought with such singleness of purpose that they were so inhuman to all who hindered them.

And I said to the Shining One: "What do they seek?"

And the Shining One made answer: "Happiness."

"Are they all seeking Happiness?"

"All."

"Have any of them found it?"

"None of those have found it."

"Do they ever think they have found it?"

"Sometimes they think they have found it."

My eyes filled, for at that moment I caught a glimpse of a woman with a babe at her breast, and I saw the babe torn from her and the woman cast into a deep pit by a man with his eyes fixed on a shining lump that he believed to be (or perchance to contain, I know not) Happiness.

And I turned to the Shining One, my eyes blinded.

"Will they ever find it?"

And He said: "They will find it."

"All of them?"

"All of them."

"Those who are trampled?"

"Those who are trampled."

"And those who trample?"

"And those who trample."

I looked again, a long time, at what they were doing on the hills and in the valleys, and again my eyes went blind with tears, and I sobbed out to the Shining One:

"Is it God's will, or the work of the Devil, that men seek Happiness?"

"It is God's will."

"And it looks so like the work of the Devil!"

The Shining One smiled inscrutably.

"It does look like the work of the Devil."

When I had looked a little longer, I cried out, protesting: "Why has he put them down there to seek Happiness and to cause each other such immeasurable misery?"

Again the Shining One smiled inscrutably: "They are learning."

"What are they learning?"

"They are learning Life. And they are learning Love."

I said nothing. One man in the herd below held me breathless, fascinated. He walked proudly, and others ran and laid the bound, struggling bodies of living men before him that he might tread upon them and never touch foot to earth. But suddenly a whirlwind seized him and tore his purple from him and set him down, naked among strangers. And they fell upon him and maltreated him sorely.

I clapped my hands.

"Good! Good!" I cried, exultantly. "He got what he deserved."

Then I looked up suddenly, and saw again the inscrutable smile of the Shining One.

And the Shining One spoke quietly. "They all get what they deserve."

"And no worse?"

"And no worse."

And no better?"

"How can there be any better?" They each deserve whatever shall teach them the true way to Happiness."

I was silenced.

And still the people went on seeking, and trampling each other in their eagerness to find. And I perceived what I had not fully grasped before, that the whirlwind caught them up from time to time and set them down elsewhere to continue the Search.

And I said to the Shining One: "Does the whirlwind always set them down again on these hills and in these valleys?"

And the Shining One made answer: "Not always on these hills or in these valleys."

"Where then?"

"Look above you."

And I looked up. Above me stretched the Milky Way and gleamed the stars.

And I breathed "Oh" and fell silent, awed by what was given to me to comprehend.

Below me they still trampled each other.

And I asked the Shining One.

"But no matter where the Whirlwind sets them down, they go on seeking Happiness?"

"They go on seeking happiness."

And the Whirlwind makes no mistakes?"

"The Whirlwind makes no mistakes."

"It puts them sooner or later, where they will get what they deserve?"

"It puts them sooner or later, where they will get what they deserve."

Then the load crushing my heart lightened, and I found I could look at the brutal cruelties that went on below me with pity for the cruel. And the longer I looked the stronger the compassion grew.

And I said to the Shining One:

"They act like men goaded."

"They are goaded."

"What goads them?"

"The name of the goad is Desire."

Then, when I had looked a little longer, I cried out passionately: "Desire is an evil thing."

But the face of the Shining One grew stern and his voice rang out, dismaying me.

"Desire is not an evil thing."

I trembled and thought withdrew herself into the innermost chamber of my heart. Till at last I said: "It is Desire that nerves men on to learn the lessons God has set."

"It is Desire that nerves them."

"The lessons of Life and Love?"

"The lessons of Life and Love!"

Then I could no longer see that they were cruel. I could only see that they were learning. I watched them with deep love and compassion, as one by one the whirlwind carried them out of sight."

* * * * * * * * * * *

What happened after that lecture was even more eventful! As was her custom at astrology conferences, word spread that anyone who wanted to join us at the close of the day for a group meditation was invited to our room. It was packed!

The meditation was uplifting, as always. Afterwards, as people lingered to socialize, Issie came to me and whispered that she had to leave for a while, and that I should stay, say goodnight as folks left, and then lock the door after everyone was gone. I agreed, of course, not thinking to question her instructions or where she was planning to go at such a late hour. I was still high from the meditation.

Issie must have had second thoughts or her guidance changed, as a moment later she began abruptly shooing everyone out of our room, took me by the hand and said, *"Come on, you're coming with us!"* Glad to be included, I had no idea that I was in for a late-night mystery tour and a fantastic adventure that would open many new inner doors!

Our driver was a woman who had attended Issie's lecture and her meditation that night. She had privately told Issie that she knew a man in Miami who regressed people to see their past lives, and that if Issie wanted to meet him, she would arrange it! Of course, Issie did! He was William Swygard, author of *The Awareness Techniques* of past life regression and multi-plane awareness. It was an evening that changed all of our lives forever, and thousands more. Mr. Swygard gave us a simple tool for reviewing our past lives, to understand and resolve our karma and access new planes of consciousness.

This energized those of us in Boston, who believed as Issie did, that *"we do not come unbound into this livingness"* and that our natal charts reveal what our souls carry over from past lives. I spent a year exploring The Awareness Techniques with my good friend, Priscilla Mueller; we loved sharing our results with Issie, who explored these realms with us on occasion. Each inner insight calls upon us to *live it* in the outer world, a lifetime undertaking.

In the next thirty years, I witnessed so many effective results using these techniques, they became an integral part of my practice whenever astrology clients wanted to explore beyond what the chart alone could show them. More and more, clients urged me to write a book about past life therapy, and when my inner guidance said the same, I finally wrote *One Sex To The Other: Reincarnation and the Dual Gender Soul* (see NewAgeSages.com), drawing on much of what I learned from Issie, Bill Swygard and my own experiences.

One memorable example of the healing power of the Awareness Techniques is a case that arose after I had published my book on the subject, so I share it here to illustrate what I mean by 'going beyond the chart.' A few years ago, I was asked to do individual one-hour astrology consults for a group of 10-12 women who were gathering for an annual weekend retreat. This sounded like a fine way to stimulate spiritual growth for them, so I agreed to do it, and prepared for the adventure.

What I didn't anticipate was that one gal had another agenda When it was her turn for a consult, she said she didn't want to hear about her chart, She'd had other astrologers interpret her chart and wanted to be regressed to a past life, to uncover why she struggled so much with her parents. Using the Awareness Techniques, a dramatic story unfolded that showed her a past life in which she caused her present parents enormous suffering. After that, she could forgive them for the suffering they had caused her in this life, and understood why she became a healer in this life. This was a powerful example of what Issie taught, that we meet ourselves on the path of life; others show us how we were in a past life, to help us understand how we impacted others, so that we could really learn the lesson.

My belief in reincarnation, and guiding others to review and gain awareness of their soul records on a conscious plane has been both challenging and rewarding for me, as it was for Issie. It has taken our Western culture a long time to see reincarnation as credible belief, although it is a core tenet of numerous religions and philosophers.

One echo of the struggle of reincarnation to be accepted as valid and misperceptions surrounding 'karma' came in 1992, in the form of a syndicated newspaper cartoon.[13] It has been on my office bulletin ever since, as a reminder that knowing about karma is not the same as

---

[13] *"Non Sequitur"* by Wiley, March 31, 1992: gocomics.com/nonsequitur/1992/03/31.

seeking *grace* to resolve it! Issie understood this well. The cartoon is of a man pointing into an open grave, saying: *"since you're the one who believes in reincarnation, don't think this argument is over!"*

While many astrologers were seeking scientific validation for astrology, Issie's focus on being a channel for healing was valued by her clients, students and likeminded astrologers. This path kept *ego* at bay and was also a lot of fun.

Among the letters I'd received were two from August 1972, *four years after the AFA convention that I had attended,* from attendees of another AFA conference. They were postmarked from Texas and Colorado, but written on the same hotel stationary, so the writers must have written soon after being with Isabel that evening…

"I must tell you how much your talks and meditations have meant to me. I know I'll never be the same kind of astrologer again nor the same person. You have given me so much with your mere presence that I don't think I could absorb it all if I knew you intimately. The understanding you have given me of myself as well as my past self, though your Cosmic Science is more than I have absorbed in the past four years (it's a different kind of peace I supposed). I have gone to sleep the past two nights with the tapes of your meditation. I am going to try the self-awareness technique and hope it can open a few doors for me. I have always been sure that God does relate to each one of us and answers our prayers. Now I must learn to listen for his instructions and pray with all my heart that he'll find me worthy enough to serve him in some way. Thank you so much for having us up in your room that night. You asked me if Astrology was lonely sometimes when you have no one to talk to – I said "Yes." But now it will never be lonely again 'cause I am going into partnership with my God. I am sure the transit of Uranus through my first house will bring many things directly related to what I've learned from you. May you always have an Angel on your shoulder."

Another astrologer praised Issie for how she handled an upsetting situation that had occurred at the conference …

"Before leaving Dallas, I want to write a note to you. You and your guidance were the highlight of the convention for me and obviously (to me now) the reason I felt so strongly to attend. You provided the important balance that has been missing in conventions before. We decided to follow your example after our classes at each week. Although nothing was said on the subject, I sensed that it took a big dose of courage to do what you did. I know your personal convictions made it worth the effort. It is never entirely easy to do what we feel and know is right, in the face of opposition. It is a pity that others feel fear and are threatened. Even though I believe in traditional and scientific astrology – I know there is much more to be done. We are spiritual counselors whether we realize it or not. So your efforts will bear much fruit, not only with those of more experience but especially with newer astrologers. The important thing is that you were a shining light of love. Your sister in spirit, [Name], Denver, CO / August, 1972"

This next letter, also praising Issie for her response to what happened at the conference, spoke to a growing divide among astrologers:

"Dear Isabel, This is a belated thank you. Having never attended an AFA convention I was unsure what lay in store. I imagined 5 days of highbrow academia, which I could immerse myself in and assimilate as much as possible. As it evolved, the whole experience turned my head around and I found myself in an atmosphere of rich spiritual energy. For this I thank you.

As a recently accepted member of the AFA, I would like to apologize for unkind remarks made about you in the text of the banquet presentation. It was my feeling as well as those whom I became acquainted with during the convention that such remarks were uncalled for, least of all to be directed at you, a most talented and generous lady. There is definitely a split within the AFA and I can see that if we (the spiritually oriented) become irate with those who are academically oriented because of their failure to recognize the spirit, then we have defeated our purpose and fulfilled theirs. We must love and forgive them *"for they know not what they do."*

Someday, in some higher incarnation they will know and understand. In the meantime be thankful that you have the understanding not to be shattered by such cruelties and know that many, many souls who love you; I am one. I have heard, from my teacher that you hold a spiritual retreat in New England every year at the end of May. I realize it's a bit early to be inquiring but I'm told that it fills up quite fast and I don't want to miss the boat. Keep me posted on the May retreat as I would like to see and hear you again and take care. Thank you again for all that you showed me in San Francisco. Sincerely yours, [Name], Kailua, HI"

Issie was not alone in caring about the spiritual side of astrology. One astrologer wrote to Issie that she had voiced her concern about what happened, directly to the President of the AFA:

"Dear Isabelle, I was grateful for the opportunity to meet you, take your hand and listen to you several times at the recent AFA convention. After your meditation... the next morning I awoke after a sound sleep, no sign of an ache or pain. ... I enjoyed the remainder of the week to the fullest. I have just written to Robert Cooper and failing to have put in a carbon for you I will repeat paragraph 2 of my letter: *"My main concern today is the reaction at the convention to the response toward that wonderful embodiment of love, Isabelle Hickey. How can one separate the individual's consciousness from astrology? Is it possible that the London Philosophical Society (Alan Leo), the Los Angeles Philosophical Society (Manley Hall), Zain, Rosicrucian Fellowship (Max Heindel) and others have done all of us a disservice? What kind of philosophy tells us that meditation or love is bad for us? It is not required that everyone participate."* ... Love as always, [Name], Woodland Hills, CA, August, 1974"

The AFA Fiasco, as it became known in Issie's circle, stirred many ripple effects as this letter from Alberta, Canada shows:

"In the Libra issue of *The Rising Sign*, one reporter covered the last AFA Convention at which you were a lecturer. Congratulations on your decision not to change the content of your lectures. You can be sure this action has won the admiration and respect of a great many people."

Many astrologers were on the same wavelength with Issie, as this next writer, who spoke on her own and on Issie's behalf:

"Dear Isabel: I attended the convention in San Francisco with hesitation and fear. I've been studying Astrology two years, the first with no help of anyone ... When you spoke, I listened to your voice, heard your words and recognition and happiness filled me. You said all the things I feel about life in general and Astrology ... I attended each of your sessions and taped another in its entirety. ... I shall forever be grateful to see and hear you. I have both of your books and have used them. But until I heard you, I don't believe I really understood them. ... Thank you for being a beautiful channel for wisdom. ...I am so grateful for having been at the convention and having been privileged to sit at your feet and listen. ... life was filled with struggle, hardship, hunger, death and everything a human can suffer. I wondered why I had to go through so much. When I hear others agonizing over something ... and find myself feeling for them – now I KNOW why. You said it; *How can you help another, understand or sympathize unless you have gone through it yourself?* ...Since early childhood, I have had flashes of another life. Now I feel at the threshold of a new life. I am filled with doubt as to my ability and HOW (not why) God wants to use me. Isabel I want you to know, I love you. If I can become a channel for some wisdom to come through that will help others, it will be partly because of you. I will always see you up there in the church, hear your soft, melodious voice and feel the love you spread throughout that building, over those of us sitting there. And if I learn anything, it will be because I am determined to use the talents God has given me (as shown me through your book) and perhaps I can pass on that knowledge to others. May God always be with you.

I hope one day you will write an autobiography. I thought you might like to know something I heard outside the banquet room that last night when I was on my way back from the restroom. Two young fellows in their very early 20's, I'd guess, met in the lobby outside the banquet room. One stopped the other and asked, *"Have you seen Isabel Hickey?"* The other replied, *"Yeah, Man. She's a real flash!"* Apparently the first one didn't understand the jargon because you could see him bristle. *"Flash? What's that supposed to mean?"* *"Oh, you know. She's electric. She's beautiful. She's one great lady."* And at that, the other beamed, and they both excitedly began to tell the other what they felt about you and your sessions. So you see, you reach all ages, all levels. If only I can be able to do that in some small degree, in some way, in whatever way God means for me to do it ... Go in God's Love, [Name], Sacramento, CA / Sept. 1974"

Issie rarely discussed herself, so the above letter may have nudged her to write her autobiography, recognizing the need redress misperceptions of her, which others had projected onto her. Who else besides Isabel could set the record straight, about who she was and why she became an astrologer?

Mr. Cooper must have regretted what transpired at the AFA convention, as he wrote to Issie a letter that was not in the collection. What was in the collection was a copy of a letter by Helen Hickey to Mr. Cooper in August 1980, after Issie's passing. A few excerpts of Helen's letter to him will suffice:

"Issie was hurt by [Name]'s supposedly humorous comments. She was embarrassed because he had her stand up before the entire audience so he could deliver his "put down" remarks. She was humiliated. ... She bore this hurt a long time, as did several of her friends in AFA who resigned over that particular incident. ... Why, why could you not just say: we are sorry you were hurt, we regret that this unpleasant experience happened at an AFA event. Do you realize what that kind of letter would have meant to Issie and those who knew of the situation? ... Issie would not let me write this letter to you shortly after the incident, but I am free to do so now. Sincerely, Helen K. Hickey"

For this one disturbing event under Mr. Cooper's watch in the AFA, there were no doubt countless moments to his credit on behalf of astrologers, including Issie, who spoke for the AFA many times. When Mr. Cooper passed in 2008, perhaps Issie welcomed him on the other side, saying, "never mind the past." Issie *turned the other cheek* to critics, following a Bible passage that she often quoted: *"If needs be, offense comes, but woe unto him through whom it comes,"*

To my dismay in 2005, while Helen's body was failing, a well-known astrologer wrote crass remarks in *The Mountain Astrologer* that were insulting to Issie *and her students!* Rather than burden Helen, I sent a letter to the magazine which they published with an Editor's note, affirming their respect for Issie. In my long message were these excerpts:

"Many astrologers appreciated Isabel Hickey, and thousands were helped by her spiritual leanings ... Isabel long ago graduated from this plane... I was fortunate to study with Isabel for about five

years. ... our lives improved enormously by spending time with her. Was she perfect? Not at all, and she was the first to admit it. ... – Amy Shapiro, M. Ed., Gloucester, MA"

To omit any reference to insults or offenses directed at Issie by other astrologers, would be a disservice to the fact that in *turning the other cheek,* Issie lived what she taught, and forgave. *May we each find the grace to forgive* and remember that forgiveness – a Piscean Age gift – still has value in the Aquarian Age! As Issie reminded us, *don't throw the baby out with the bathwater!*

Five years after the AFA upset, a year before her passing, Issie's papers show a wonderful turn in 1979. Among them was a saved program for a National Council for Geocosmic Research conference, listing Issie as giving an *Opening Meditation* and *A Journey into Self Discovery – who are you? Where did you come from? Where are you going? A discussion of techniques that can be used to discover who you really are.* Being a featured speaker for this *science-focused* group was evidence that spiritually oriented astrology was becoming more accepted and respected, as this letter shows:

"Dear Isabel Hickey, Thank you for contributing your time and energy to make the NCGR conference in NY such a success. The people who attended were all saying how inspiring you were – how much they enjoyed you – and your wonderful energy proved there is a definite need for spiritual growth and insight in this city. People were raving – "hanging off the rafters" to hear what you had to say, and I was so pleased to see the response. Thank you for the energy you sent my way as you were leaving! Love, [Name], Astrology Metaphysics, NYC, NY / May, 1979"

The importance of that NCGR invitation and the response Issie got from participating in that conference goes beyond the healing it must have brought to Issie among her astrology peers. It was also a true milestone in the astrological community, in publicly accepting and respecting her philosophy, as the above letter shows.

* * * * * * * * * * * *

In 1973, after years of observing and meditating on the meaning of Pluto, Issie published her much-awaited *Minerva/Pluto: The*

Choice is Yours, which has since been combined with ACS. This writer may have been referring to the newly released Pluto book:

"Dear Isabel: I have spent weeks with you by way of your book, discovering understanding; I finally discern the difference in *serve* without the martyrdom of *suffer*. Your book is astounding and I feel your concern and cautions deeply. The more I understand, the more I realize you've been there, anticipated my need and laid the way to an answer. I have encountered several guides in my life; you are an important one. Your love and depth of commitment are beautiful. I hope you accept my sincere admiration for your integrity, talent and knowledge; the least I can do is thank you and promise to pass it on. With love, [Name], St. Petersburg, FL / March, 1973"

Issie attracted many artists, whom she urged to use their gifts to serve the greater good, including musician Jonathan Richman, who often played guitar and sang at Issie's Friday evening meditations. One Friday meditator (perhaps Jonathan; the note was unsigned, and came with this photo) wrote from New York...

"How are you? Fine I hope. I'm sorry I couldn't come up in the fall. I've got my band together and we've been playing at lots of places. I've learned a lot of things since I've been traveling with the band. I have concentrated and meditated on you, and I thank you for all the light you have sent us."

People often turn to astrologers during crises, and Issie brought many souls back from the edge of despair. She gave clients hope as a vehicle for transforming grace and taught that if an astrologer says something that scares a client, that astrologer bears the karma for the results. I took that to heart, and still do, in all of my communications. Issie credited her keen psychic sensitivity to her consistency in practicing meditation and urged people to meditate to develop their psychic gifts safely, as this excerpt from a letter to her shows:

"I have just listened to the tapes of your inspirational presentation at the Psychic Conference in Milwaukee in October. As I listened, bells of joy rang inside me because you have the great gift – cosmic truth and understanding and service. It gave me hope.

Thank you! The core of my being feels shaken [states her problem] Please look at our horoscopes, tune in and suggest what I can do. [Name], Wauwatosa, WI. Jan, 1974"

The *Awareness Techniques,* is as Issie described, is a simple and effective tool to help people uncover past lives as this letter shows:

"Dear Isabel, I am the guy who you took back to a past life in India at the Fellowship of the Inner Light Church in Virginia Beach. I wish to thank you for that transformative experience ... showing the light. May peace be with you. Om Shanti, [Name], San Angelo, TX, 1974"

Issie was sensitive to *earth-bound* souls, as this writer shows:

"Dear Issie, A tape I heard on which your fantastic voice revealed some "astrological tidbits" said you were concerned about *earth-bound* spirits and hoped to write a book on this in the near future. Have you done this, or are you in the process of doing it? ... Someday I hope to come for a *"fix"* on Friday or participate in your Monday classes. While my interests cover the gamut of the esoteric sciences, Astrology is close to my heart. Three teachers play a vital role in my study and practice ... Isabel Hickey, Dane Rudhyar and Marc Edmund Jones ... inspirational teachers who ask of the student and native the Highest he or she has to offer. Each sings the Celestial Song of Love that draws froth from the astrological Mandala the divinity from within and THAT my wonderful teacher is what I believe astrology is all about. ... I hope to someday have the pleasure of meeting you. ... Thank you for being so thoughtful and proving the True Masters are those who serve all people. In fellowship, [Name], Dayton, OH / March, 1974"

Invitations for Issie to speak also came from academia, as this New Hampshire writer shows:

"I want to thank you and tell you how much I enjoyed your inspiring lecture at William Patterson College last month. I was thrilled to have the pleasure and honor of hearing such a spiritual person speak. I "tuned you in" as I am a meditator myself ™ and an Astrology student. It was too bad we were not able to talk ... I was anxious to tell you what a beautiful person you are – talk about mind and body becoming one! You are the one person in my lifetime whom I really feel has it all together. Someday I hope to visit you. I have read your book on Pluto and hope to read and study more of what you have written. You are truly my spiritual friend. Thank you so much for giving me such pleasure and peace. God Bless You"

The following brief note from a writer in Virginia Beach, FL, shows that Issie did not shy away from helping people to face hard realities, and showing them a better way:

"Thank you so much for coming to speak to us. As a psychic person you sensed so much the problem in our organization ... I appreciate any words of wisdom. Your friend [Name]"

So touched were those who heard Issie speak, it was common for her to receive a note of gratitude from her host, as this officer of an astrological organization:

"Dear Isabel – There are no words to express the appreciation we feel from having you visit us Saturday, at the workshop ... I knew what it was like to see someone who truly allows Our Father to lead and direct. I realized I had only, partially, allowed Him to enter in. You had words for all, and many of them received it. ... Thank you for coming, dear Isabel. Love from all of us, [Name], Virginia Beach, VA / June, 1974"

Issie also urged astrologers to develop empathy and study the principles of counseling, as this note from a Michigan client shows:

"Bless you! And thank you for your wonderful help with my chart! Words cannot fully express my appreciation! I am trying to follow your advice – I would like to develop healing power and the inspirational writing that you saw in my chart. To be truly a channel for good in this world in whatever way I can serve would make me supremely happy! I am so grateful for your kindness and guidance! It would be a great privilege and pleasure to meet you! With love and blessings"

Issie urged students to always picture a robe of light around any vehicle we were in, as mentioned by this grateful lecture attendee from New York:

"Your talk in Long Island was a highlight of the two years that I've been studying astrology. I, too, have been fortunate in seeing the Blessed Mother one time. She is indeed beautiful and loving. Thank you for the Cosmic Blessings you inscribed in my book. On my way home Saturday another car ran a stop sign coming at us broadside. How I maneuvered the car in that split second is a miracle and mystery to me but my friend and I came thru without a scratch. I didn't even stop to get out to bawl Hell out of the person who ran the stop sign, which I normally would have done. Many Thanks and God Bless!"

STAR ROVERS AND ASTRAL ANGELS

Under Issie's leadership, on June 12th, 1967 at 7:15 PM in Cambridge, MA, a new group, *The Star Rovers,* was born. Its chart showed a lot of positive energy available to rise to its challenges.

The logo we designed for Star Rovers was a yin-yang symbol in an upward-pointing pentacle, in a starry sky, conveying harmony in the heavens and reminding us that as we align with our Higher Selves, we can achieve balance between the inner and outer realms.

Our By-Laws stated a three-part purpose:

> To stimulate interest in the understanding of astrology, its study, and the application of its principles to daily living.

> To bring together in brotherhood those interested in Self-Unfoldment through knowledge of the Cosmic Laws.

> To benefit the public by informing them of the value and significance of astrological insights.

The organization grew to be a special part of Issie's life and was an equally special part of my life from the start. Only in hindsight decades later, can I understand all that Star Rovers gave me and how it impacted the rest of my life in numerous ways.

Issie and I, and dozens more astrologers spoke for Star Rovers: Robert Pelletier, Marcia Moore Douglas, Regina Russell, Priscilla Mueller, Marjorie Marquis, Reese Scott, Jan Brink, Marcia Stark, Frances McEvoy, Bruce Nevin, Diana Rosenberg, Pam Pacelli, Louise Fimlaid, Capel McDutcheon Jane Graham and many more whose names elude me, as I only saved a handful of our newsletters, which have jogged my memory.

We were a fun-loving group, which was contagious. By 1977, we reached seventy-four members. We enjoyed finding ways to be together and serve others. Besides monthly astrology lectures, we held an annual banquet to celebrate the year and changing governing board and met at Harmony Hill for an annual summer picnic.

One fond memory is of our *Read-Ins* where the public could come to have brief horoscope interpretations. The phrase *Read-In* was a wordplay on the youth culture trends of *love-ins*, *sit-ins* and *be-ins*. One year our Read-In raised $300 to help fund physical therapy for children at the Protestant Guild for the Blind. That may have been my first effort in charitable giving, a wonderful feeling.

Revisiting old Star Rovers Newsletters for this book brought me back to that time and happy thoughts of the friends I made, thanks to Issie. Long before I became Star Rovers' VP, then its President, I worked on our newsletter with Priscilla Mueller. I loved developing articles and graphics for it, and Issie's encouragement of my interest in publishing that newsletter opened a new door to my future.

Through Star Rovers newsletter, I wrote many serious pieces like, *'Researching Progressions – Astronomy Embodies Astrology'* monthly *'Lunation Cycle'* reports, an article on the New Year's chart for Boston, announcements of upcoming speakers, etc. I also had a lot of fun with our newsletter as this quote shows:

> *"Our February meeting was super meeting attendance-wise; the room was literally overflowing! Our speaker, Regina Russell, delivered a talk on retrograde planets and their implications for past life experiences. Once again, we stayed so late after the lecture, having fun and refreshments, we literally got locked in by the Midtown! With Star Rovers' Sun in Gemini and Sagittarius rising, we just can't seem to shut up!! Happy star roving 'til we meet again!"*

Issie gave me a lot of creative leeway. I published a fictional horoscope *for Santa Claus* in our December 1974 newsletter, with this commentary, in a piece entitled, *"From the Elves"* ...

"We were terrifically lucky to get this copy of Saint Nick's horoscope. As you can see, his grand trine in fire makes ol' Santa a spirited guy. With Sag rising and a stellium of benefics on the Ascendant, it's safe to say that Santa brings blessings and gifts to the world. Uranus in the 5th shows his particular fondness of surprising children with his rather individualistic personality.

Neptune in Leo in the 9th describes the rather colorful way in which Santa has been known to travel as well as his boundless faith in humanity. Mars in Capricorn in the 2nd house shows what a busy guy he is, pushing his work to meet the season's deadline, and the trine to Saturn in the 10th indicates Santa's discriminating (Virgo) faculties (we hear that he's quite a list-maker).

As in all great men, there are flaws. For Santa, his Cardinal T-square including the Moon shows the unfortunate circumstances of his marital status, as is common knowledge, Saint Nick has been known to leave his wife, Mrs. Claus, during the cold winter nights in order to fulfill his work obligations. With the Moon in Libra, sextile Neptune and his Sag planets, we're sure that Mrs. Claus is sympathetic.

Pluto in the 13th house??? Don't ask us – we only work here."

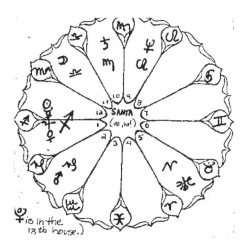

Issie inspired fun, good humor and word plays. The design of the wheel was one I had developed, and used for many charts in the newsletter, including Star Rovers' chart, below. Its planetary placements show an emphasis in Fire, with a Moon-Venus-Jupiter conjunction, trine to Saturn and the Ascendant, conveying warmth and spiritual aspirations. It is a good example of an elective chart whose hard and soft aspects are balanced, giving the tools to manage necessary challenges.

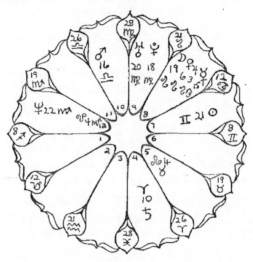

Star Rovers Astrological Association Founding Chart
June 12, 1967 at 7:15 PM in Cambridge, MA[14]

The following transcription is of an interview of Issie on April 21, 1971, excerpts of which ran in Star Rovers' newsletter. With me were two other astrology students, Priscilla Mueller and Howard Kilby. We had so many questions in our excitement, we often talked over each other, leaving some thoughts dangling! It was fun to find this interview again while preparing this book, as another glimpse into Issie's personal story and her work.

Issie: "It all began way back when I first came to Boston to do my work. And that was 1946. There was no activity whatsoever of astrology in Boston."

Where did you live before you came to Boston?

---

[14] Thanks to Peter Kubaska, a fellow student of Issie's, an error was found in 2020 that is corrected here. The prior data was 1 day and 1 hour off from this chart.

Issie: "I lived right here at Maple Street. But, it came along that I was offered a studio at the hotel Brunswick and it was quite a surprise to me because I had a chance to walk around 300 rooms and decide which one I wanted. And the woman who owned the place said for me to make my own price for my rent. She didn't care if I paid anything or I paid something but, she knew that I should come to Boston and get astrological activity going in Boston."

Was she sort of a client of yours?

Issie: "She was a friend and we met in a very strange and unusual way.

So there wasn't hardly any activity in Boston?

Issie: "There was none whatsoever, none whatsoever. There was a little old lady called Mrs. McIntosh and she was the dearest, sweetest thing and she gave me some private lessons. And she was next to the Pierce Building, which is now part of the Pike. And she made a very interesting statement when I was studying with her, she said, *"Isabel, we've done 25 years of the hardest spade work in Boston that's ever been done. Boston has never accepted Astrology and we have had a very difficult time. But you're coming along now and it's going to be different in your time. You're going to have it very much easier. Because of the hardy pioneers that came before you that have now passed on"* – most of them – she was the only one left. And she was so right because there was no acceptance of Astrology as anything scientific, legitimate or even inspirational at that time. So, it was completely a new idea to Boston. I had to laugh at Marc Jones. He called me *"Boston's Spiritual Sparkplug"* because I got the Marc Jones group going and I got the Kerpal Sing group going. I got them all going but I said to them, *"I'll get you going but I won't stay on with you, 'cause I knew I had work in Astrology to do."*

Did you do your own studying in Boston or were you studying with someone?

Issie: "There were no classes. I found a teacher down in Weymouth and I used to go down to her and study with her one day a week. And we would spend about three hours of an afternoon together. And then I did a great deal of studying on my own. I remember her saying to me when I first studied that I had had this all before in a previous life and that I would pick it up very quickly and in three months I'd be doing charts. And I said, Lady you're out of your mind! It's going to take me three years to learn the mathematics! Because I was struggling with the math at that time and to me it was just as clear as mud."

Well, you certainly got it down now!

Issie: "Well, I have it down by rote now. But, don't ask me all the ins and outs and whys!"

So, for the first few years, you had a place at the Brunswick and what happened?

Issie: "Yes, I had a lovely suite at the Brunswick. Right over a big sign that said BAR!"

And now you've got the Rovers and you have the Inn right underneath it. It followed you around!

Issie: "I can't get away from it!"

Now it's a PUB.

Issie: "Now it's a PUB. Yes, that's right! So, we had our regular Wednesday night Astral Angels there and we had a class in astrology."

Was the Astral Angels a meditation group? How did they start?

Issie: "Well, that went way back. That started in 1930."

Before the astrology work?

Issie: "Yes, before I went to Boston, I was doing Astrology here at home for awhile. No charge for it 'cause I had no rent to pay and I didn't care. But the Astral Angels started way back in 1931 or 1932. And that was a bunch of about ten or twelve of us, crazy as coots but we had an awful lot of fun. Like you kids now. We'd get together and we'd go places and we would go to all the meetings with the Theosophical. They didn't like our high spirits there because they were a bunch of old maids. And, so, we saw we weren't wanted and so one night sitting in Walton's, we said, *"Why don't we get our own organization going?"* Only they didn't say *organization*, they said, *"Why don't we get our own thing going?"* I said, *"Why not!"* I looked at them and I said, *"The Astral Angels are born! We aren't good enough to be real ones but we're trying!"* And as casual as that we got together. We had an awful lot of fun because we didn't know anything about meditation and nobody in Boston was teaching meditation. We'd get together on a Sunday afternoon in the office of a realtor who said we could use his place – he was a client of mine. I had helped him a great deal, and so he'd let us use it. And we'd sit down there, and we'd try to meditate, and someone would get a fit of laughing and the next minute we'd all get in gales of laughter. Seymour Swetzoff was the only one that really ..."

Was he part of the group?

Issie: "Sure, Seymour Swetzoff."

[Howard:] *I know Seymour Swetzoff! I've known him for a long time.*

Issie: "Sure, sure, he was part of our first group. He was only twenty."

[Howard:] *When I first came to Cambridge, he was one of the people I made the first connection with, quite by accident.*

Issie: "Is that so?"

[Howard:] *Yes, I was wandering by and I happened to wander in his shop.*

Issie: "You know who else? Hymie Bloom."

[Priscilla:] *No kidding?*

Issie: "Yes, these were all the original Astral Angels."

[Priscilla:] *You're kidding – that's amazing!*

Issie: "No it isn't, they were part of our group."

[Priscilla] *That's amazing. He's one of the most inspired artists in Boston!*

Issie: "Well, sure. And Alan Hovhaness[15] became a very famous composer. And Alan used to play his music for us at the place. There was a piano there. Oh yes, they were the original Astral Angels. Jerry Cooper was another ..."

It would be interesting to compare all the charts to see ...

Issie: "I never did."

---

[15] My transcribed notes read "Alan Hoganist(?)"– Issie had not spelled the name. It was likely Alan Hovhaness, who was indeed a very famous composer of that era.

How did you find each other? Do you feel it was an inner kind of ...

Issie: "I don't know how we found each other. We just got together. Someone would tell somebody else and then they'd come."

Just a kind of spirit there that just drew you together.

Issie: "Yes, drew us together. That was it."

[Amy] *When you first started meditating had you read any philosophies on it?*

Issie: "We had done reading but none of us knew anything and there wasn't a meditation group in Boston. Nowhere. And it was nothing like it is today, you can't imagine. The only thing was the Theosophical Society and that was run by a bunch of old people that didn't' want any youth around. So, we just finally started, and we never had any organization or any dues or anything. We just got together, and we'd go out into along the ocean and meditate there and had a lot of fun. We didn't know what we were doing but we explored everything."

That sounds just like us!

Issie: "Yes, well it is."

[Amy] *Compare that to today when Karma and Reincarnation are household words.*

Issie: "Yeah."

[Priscilla:] *We're all drawn; someone says this is happening and then we all go this way and then we all go that way ... and in a group too.*

Issie: "Well, that's the way we began. And the funniest part of it is that I had some of them come to me on the inner planes before I met them outwardly. And my mouth would open, and I'd look, and I'd say, *"Oh, well, here he comes!"*

[Priscilla:] *That's what I was wondering, if there was an inner – sort of a soul group.*

Issie: "It was a soul group kind of thing."

Oh, this is fascinating!

Issie: "Anyone would hear of anything, we'd all troop together."

Did you start teaching after you had been into meditation for a while?

Issie: "Well, you see the thing is, that at the beginning when I lived in Waltham, I met a group of girls one night and they asked me – I hadn't been a year in the thing – studying, and they asked me – there was a meeting and this was [name not transcribed[16]], and somebody told me about her, that she had a class. So, of course, I was dying to get into her class because it's awfully hard studying by yourself; I had to do all my own studying and had no one to talk this over with. So, anyway, I went to this class, and I saw something in the chart, and I said, boom-boom-boom, isn't this so? And the teacher said, *"Absolutely not!"* And the woman who owned the chart said, *"Yes, it is so. She's absolutely right!"* So, they followed me out, and they wanted to know who I was and who I studied with and I said, *"Well, I haven't studied very much."* Well, we had coffee at the Waldorf, and they tried to talk me into giving them some lessons. And I said, *"Look, I don't know anything."*

You had come to take a class!

Issie: "Yeah, and they said, well, let us come over to your house and ask questions, and we'll talk it over there. And I said, *"so, if you want to do that, alright."* So that's how my first Astrological class got started. One of the things that I think is terribly important to know is that if you are tuned in and you're willing to do anything that God wants you to do, He'll send everybody that you need to do it through to you."

You don't have to go looking.

Issie: "You don't have to look for a thing."

That's a good point.

Issie: "That's a very good point, because I never looked for the place in town, I never looked for a client, I never looked for a class, and so it's always been right. And that way – you see – you don't decide what you want to do. When I was told in meditation, I was to be an Astrologer, I almost flipped. And you'd have to be back in those days to know what this was going to call for."

---

[16] If memory serves, Issie gave the astrologer's name, and said not to include it in the interview, so I omitted it, and don't recall who the astrologer was in this story.

How did that come to you?

Issie: "I was meditating – *"Be an Astrologer!"* And then I went to a psychic healer, a friend of mind who was a masseuse in Newton, and within 48 hours she said to me, *"Isabel, you have to be an Astrologer."* I said, *"I don't want to be an Astrologer."* And she said, *"Well, you have to be."* I knew it was the double-check that I always ask for. Well, it took me eight months to say yes, before I was willing. You knew you were going to be spurned by everybody. You were a crackpot. And my Protestant mother – family, my Catholic husband were going to be absolutely horrified. And it took guts. That's the only thing I can consider a virtue because that's been tested so many times. That's the only thing I can truthfully say I have and that's courage, because I always needed it. And it's come through when I needed it. But I don't lay claim to any other virtue but that one. That I know!"

So, you had a class and these people wanted you to teach them.

Issie: "Yes, yes, they came over to the house and we had one night a week. And they were from Arlington and Stoneham, but that's how it all began."

So, it kind of began informally.

Issie: "Yes, very informally. Everything that has ever happened has been informal. I can't be formal about anything. To me it's stultifying. It has got to flow, 'cuz life is a flowing thing.

So, when did you consider yourself a professional Astrologer?

Issie: "I'm not sure I'm one yet! (Laughter) Well, I don't know, people started coming and I would help them, and it went on that way. This was at home that they would come. And this was before I moved into town. And for a long time, I worked for nothing. And then it came to me in meditation that it wasn't fair. That they had to give something, and they weren't paying attention to what you said. And then I had to start charging, and so I charged a dollar! (*laughter*) And then when I went into town it was three dollars. And it was only within the last few years that I made it ten. And interesting, the reason I did is because people would talk and talk and then at the last minute, they'd say now tell me something. So, I figured if I cut down the time and they had to pay they were going to pay attention and not spend the time conversing about every other thing but what they came for."

That's a good point.

Issie: "Yeah, because I had to do it. Because they would do that."

Do you remember the first chart you ever did?

Issie: "Yes, the first chart I ever did, I didn't see the people. I was asked to do a written chart for two people, a fellow and a girl who were involved with each other. And I got the biggest kick out of it because the girl had all her planets in masculine signs and the man had all his planets in feminine signs. And I realized that the man should have been the girl and the girl should have been the man. So, I did the chart anyway and about a couple of months later, I went to a dance where they were supposed to be there, and they were looking forward to meeting me because they thought the chart had been quite accurate. The charts HAD been accurate, and I saw this great big Amazon woman coming in with this very feminine looking pipsqueak! (*laughter*) And I knew right off it was the couple I'd done the charts for, and sure enough, it was. It really was. It was one of the funny experiences. Then after that chart another fellow called up and wanted a chart and I did it. I didn't know who he was, but I did the chart and sent it to him. And he called up and said it was wrong. And I said why is it wrong? Well, he had Saturn in the first house for the time he had gave me and he said. *"I had a wonderful childhood."* And I said then if that's so, your time is wrong. No, I'm absolutely sure it's right. I said, *"Sir, there's one thing I do know – it can't be right, because nobody ever had a beautiful childhood with Saturn in the first house."* He said his aunt had given it to him. I said, you check. He checked and found out instead of eight o'clock in the morning, it was three o'clock in the afternoon. He apologized. And said he was glad to know because that was the one thing in the chart that he was absolutely sure was wrong. So, knowing your astrological indications is a very big help when you don't see the person you're doing the chart for."

Do you have any idea of how many people you have done charts for?

Issie: "I have absolutely no idea."

Couldn't you make a guess?

Issie: "No I couldn't, I really couldn't. I wouldn't have any idea at all."

One thing I'm curious about – how many of the people, say on average, come back to you steadily?

Issie: "A great many of them."

Do you encourage them?

Issie: "I wouldn't encourage anything. If they want to come back, they come. They ask me, can I come back? It's up to you. I'll say, put to work what I've given you now and then come back. But the thing that makes me laugh and you must have this too, I tell them things – completely forget it – 'cuz I have learned to cross my mind out – and then they come back and tell me what I've said. And I feel like saying, did I say that? (*Laughter*) Because some of them said it's accurate right to the day. And I say, then your time must be right because if their time isn't right your timing will be off. The events will happen, but they will either be before or after. And sometimes this helps you to know the time is off. So …"

Could you pick out anything – say the most outstanding experience – as an Astrologer?

Issie: "Now this you can't print – you haven't got room in the newsletter for all this. You know you don't. "

We have three pages devoted to this article.

Issie: "Oh no!"

Oh yes! (Laughter) This is beautiful, Isabel.

Issie: "You know I hate this kind of thing." (*Laughter*).

That's just your Scorpio Ascendant. (Laughter).

Issie: "It's also my Moon conjunct Neptune and Mercury in Virgo. I'm not half as wanting to have myself talked about."

Issie, nobody has written an article in a publication about you that you were happy about. Right? And some people see you two or three times a week, people practically live around you. And everyone wants to know you as a person too, just as you know us, and well, it won't be an over balanced –

Issie: "I'll tell you right now, it always bothers me."

Isabel, this is beautiful. It's really beautiful.

Issie: "It's not beautiful. It's ego bits."

"It's not. It's like personal ... Three of us can sit here and hold a conversation with you because the room can hold the three of us and that works. But there are others who would like to be sitting here just chatting with you, and this is a way for others to sit and chat with you too. Right?

Issie: "I don't see it ..."

It's a beautiful personal history. After it's written up you'll have veto power over it.

Issie: "Well, I'm not going to put this one on tape."

"Just put it on and we won't put anything in without you looking at it first.

Issie: "Well, the funniest thing that ever happened to me was when a girl called me up one day and she said she wanted an appointment, but she didn't want her chart done. And I said, then, what do you want? She said, well I do the same thing you do, only I do it with sand. Of course, that intrigued me. *(laughter)* How can you do stars with sand? *(laughter)*.

This has to go in now!

Issie: "No it won't, once you hear the whole thing. So she said, can I come in? So at any rate, she made an appointment for three days later. And when I came in – uh – I was at the very corner, my suite was at the very corner of the Brunswick and you came up the back stairs if you wanted a quick entrance to it, otherwise you went around up through the second floor, and came up through the elevator. And she was sitting on the bottom of the steps that were right outside my suite and she looked to be a very heavy woman about forty-five and looked foreign. So, in she came, and she had this huge book under her arm – of course, I am curious about books and I took a look at it and it was the Book of Black Magic by Arthur Wade. So, she came in and sat down and she wanted to know when the Moon would be conjunct Venus in Pisces. So this was the conversation:

(Issie:) "Why do you want to know?"
(Client:) *"'Cuz I want to get my lover back."*

(Issie:) "How are you going to get your lover back with the Moon conjunct Venus in Pisces?"
(Client:) *"Well, if I make a charm, at that time, I'll have him in my bed in three days."* (*Laughter*).
(Issie:) "Well, you called him your lover. Has he been in your life before?"
(Client:) *"Oh, yes."*
(Issie:) I said, "Why did he leave you?"
(Client:) *"He got angry at me."*
(Issie) "Why did he get angry at you?" All the time she's talking and I'm talking, I'm looking at the book. (*laughter*), finding out that all the devils have names and you make pentagrams and you call on these particular devils and then they come. So, anyway, she said:
(Client:) *"Well, I took him to court."*
(Issie:) "What did you take him to court for?"
(Client:) *"'Cuz he wouldn't marry me."* And she said, *"I was pregnant, and he wouldn't marry me, so I took him to court. Now he's very angry at me. But I still love him. I learned this business about making charms from my aunt in the old country. She was Italian."*
(Issie:) And I said, "Well, don't you know this is very dangerous? Did you ever see your Aunt do any of these things?"
(Client:) *"Yes, she lived up in the mountains – the hills of Italy and everyone said she had the evil eye. But people used to go up there and have her make charms. She'd make charms to get rid of a lover, to get rid of a husband or a wife, to get them drawn to you."* "Oh" she said, *"lots of things she'd make charms about."*
(Issie:) I said, "Did you ever see her work?"
(Client:) *"Yes"* she said, *"Once I went up and she said that she could bring back my cousin who died at sixteen in a fire."*
(Issie:) "Did she do it?"
(Client:) *"Yes, she did. She did some charms and I was sitting there and Marie* (that was the name of the cousin) *came right up in the middle of the floor. Maria is what she called her. And I got so frightened because Maria looked at her aunt and said, "Auntie, why don't you leave me alone?"*
(Issie:) "Then what happened?"

(Client:) *"I fainted."*
(Issie:) And I said, remembering all the stories I had read, and evil eyes and things and I said, "What kind of death did she die?"
(Client:) And she said: *"Well, we had to bring her back down to the house because she had no one to take care of her and she yelled and screamed for three weeks before she died."*
(Issie:) "What was she yelling?"
(Client:) *"She said that devils were sitting all around her waiting to get her and she couldn't die and she yelled and hollered and she screamed and she finally died and we made arrangements for a mass for her and when the casket went into the church every candle in the church went out and the priest refused to say mass."*
(Issie:) And I said to her, *"Well, knowing this, why do you fool around with BLACK MAGIC?"*
(Client:) *Oh,"* she said, *"It's ok if you do it for love."*
I never saw her again so I don't ... it was going to be about seven months anyway before the Moon would be conjunct Venus in Pisces.

That's a really far-out story!

Issie: "It really – I mean, that was amazing. It really was."

Did she tell you about the sand?

Issie: "No, she didn't, 'cuz I was so intrigued by the fact that she thought black magic could be used for love.

Isabel, what branch of astrology do you most enjoy?

Issie: "I think the thing I most enjoy is the natal chart because it shows the character and you can help them change what is manifesting negatively. I've been intrigued by Horary Astrology but only use it occasionally. And of course, Medical Astrology is always interesting, because I've had a number of doctors I've worked with in the earlier years and I got a great many charts from them."

What has impressed you the most about people who you have counseled?

Issie: "I don't quite know what you mean about that question."

Did anything impress you more than anything else in dealing with people?

Issie: "Well, the thing that has impressed me the most not only in Astrology, but in all of my work as counseling – 'cuz I do work besides Astrological counseling, is the recognition of people's needs to feel worthwhile. Because so many people sell themselves down the river by not recognizing how really beautiful they are inside. And I think this is very very important for every astrologer to recognize the uniqueness and the worthwhileness of everybody you talk to, because it's true. And I don't think any astrologer will ever get anywhere if they sit in judgment or they are critical. But if they meet the client as though they are having a tremendous privilege of touching the soul, their attitude's going to be right."

How have you seen astrology grow – say, in Boston and nationally?

Issie: "No one could have told me it would grow the way it has, because I went right through the whole thing from the beginning. And it's only within the last five years that it's really gone like wildfire."

[Amy] *I remember when I started studying with you there were hardly any books out on Astrology. Now you have to wade through them."*

Issie: "I know it – you have to use discrimination in what you study because you can get terribly mixed up if you don't."

How much of the business in the last five years do you think is a fad or a passing interest or something that is a real change of direction?

Issie: "I think it depends on the kind of people teaching astrology. And the kind of astrologers they become. Because with some people it is a using of Astrology for their own ends. And with other people it is a real dedication. I think the astrology is going to last, but not all the astrologers."

Isn't Uranus in Libra bringing a lot of this out?

Issie: "I think so, Uranus in Libra, yes. I think it's since Uranus went into Libra – remember Uranus is the esoteric ruler of Libra. So, there is an awakening, a tremendous awakening that's only just begun. But, I think like everything else you get your negatives and your positives. I know people who have studied astrology three months and they set themselves up as an astrologer. And you see, if people go to them and are not fed[17] rightly, they are going to blame astrology and say, oh, that's … and if there's enough quackery in it the state will crack down on it. Already in Canada you cannot practice astrology."

Oh, really?

Issie: "Yes, oh really. Yes, in Canada they consider it a …"

Is this recent?

Issie: "Yes, recently. Somebody just told me recently that they passed a bill that no one can practice astrology in Canada."

I just got the heebie-jeebies.

Issie: "I think it's necessary to eventually have some restriction on this. In other words, set up a test. The time will have to come when there will be a board that will determine whether a person is legitimately an astrologer or not."

That's what will save it.

Issie: "It will have to be that way. But it has to be a fair legislature and not something that was a rigged thing as the other one was."

Like the bar exam for lawyers, or medical board …

Issie: "Yes, it has got to come to that, because otherwise quackery in it is going to harm astrology."

I have some questions about the Star Rovers now. How did you elect the time for the chart? What were you looking for in determining the chart for the Star Rovers?

Issie: "I wanted a chart that would have a great deal of love in it. Because this was the thing I missed in the New England Astrological Association. As long as we function as souls and love each other there is a great deal of harmony. We've had three years of board meetings and have never had a cross word. Never an unpleasantness, everybody was for everybody else. And when the power-ridden individuals got into the New England – it wrecked it, so we withdrew. There was about ten or twelve of us, and we withdrew from that and I waited 7 years before I started the Star Rovers. And then so many people were on my neck saying, *"Isabel, why don't we have an organization?"*

---

[17] In 2020 while re-editing this book, "read" seems to fit better here than "fed."

And I especially was thinking of the young people because I knew they were going to be the ones who carry the ball when I dropped it. And I thought they should have a way to get together and to discuss this. So, when it came to me in meditation to start it, I did. I used to hope that the New England would clean itself up, but it didn't. So … I …"

How did you pick the name STAR ROVERS?

Issie: "That came to me just as I awoke. Just the way everything has come to me. I came to me when we were given that big home on Marlboro Street and I wondered what to call it. Just as I was awakening, I heard a very sweet voice say FELLOWSHIP HOUSE and I knew that was going to be the name of it. And then the STAR ROVERS came just as I was awakening. I think that's a cute title, STAR ROVERS."

Can you talk about what Star Rovers chart shows for the potential of the organization?

Issie: "Well, you know why I picked the Sagittarian Ascendant, because that ties in with the higher side of our philosophy. And another thing, it's friendly and easy flowing; it's not sticky, a little bit crazy, just like I am! (Laughter). And I wanted that Sagittarian Ascendant with Uranus up in the Midheaven or as near to it as I could get it because that does rule astrology. And I think the Sun in Gemini is the power to communicate. And the trine to Mars in Libra where it's in its fall … there wasn't going to be too much fighting I would hope. (Laughter). It would be harmonious. And it would also be very active. And then because Venus and Jupiter were in Leo and the Moon was in Leo, I had to have a – you now you can never pick a chart that hasn't got some bad aspects. The bad aspect here is the Moon square to Neptune but Neptune's in its own house and the Moon is on the hidden side of the 9th house, so if you're picking a chart, you want to pick a chart with those aspects more in the cadent houses. Of course, Venus and Jupiter together is very, very beautiful, and with it trine Saturn, it makes a very strong loving relationship, and a regenerative process with four planets in the 8th house of regeneration. The opposition of Mars to Saturn – Mars has already gone six degrees by it – some people were bothered by Saturn in the sign of its fall and Mars in the sign of its fall. But, the opposition with Mars 6 degrees by it, I thought, gave it power because Saturn is the sustaining force and Mars is the energy to drive it forward. And Mars rules the 5th house, which has to do with young people; and it's trine to the Sun in Gemini, which is another youthful sign … and I knew we would have many, many young people in this organization. Now, Mercury, ruler of the inner side of the chart – see Jupiter rules the personal self of the chart of the group, and Jupiter is conjunct Venus. Now, Mercury rules the solar part of the chart or the soul part of the chart and Mercury is in Cancer trine to Neptune. So, you see I think it's an excellently good chart for the things we have to do. Now, the Sun does square – it's one degree past the square to Uranus, and I waited a day to have that so that it would be passed it. The Sun is one degree passed but that Sun square to Uranus, to me, would mean that there would be no allowing any power play. And this is one of the things, that in an organization everybody has to work together and no power bit. This is what wrecked the New England, which I founded way back in the fifties. And it will wreck any organization if one person tries to usurp in any way the power of the group. And this is why I wanted to be sure that that wouldn't be a prominent fault of this entity – because this is really an entity."

That's well said!

Issie: "You see Neptune rules the end of the matter and Neptune trine to Mercury, the soul ruler, it seemed to me that this was a very good chart. See what people don't understand is that when you are really dedicated to serving God, when anything needs doing you get the direction, either in sleep or as you wake, or as you go to sleep, or in meditation, to do things. And I've always tried to follow that guidance. Not always to my liking, sometimes very much to my liking. Where I got stuck is when it was something I'd like and I'd say, that can't be God. (Laughter). And I remember once hearing a voice in my head: WHY NEED YE THINK EVERYTHING IS TO BE PUNISHMENT? (Laughter). Now what else?"

Are most of the members local or are there a lot of out of town members?

Issie: "There are quite a few out of town members. There are three astrologers in New York who pay their dues every year. And I'm going to try to get hold of them to come to the annual dinner too. I'm going to write Murray. But, they're mostly of course local, that can get to meetings."

How old is Star Rovers?

Issie: "We're going into the fifth year – it's a very young baby so far. We started in June of '67 with a dinner at the Midget Restaurant in Cambridge. And we had a big group the first meeting and every time we've had an annual dinner since, we've had a very good crowd. And I hope we do this year. It's interesting, that last year, with Saturn square Venus and Jupiter, we went through a rather difficult time and it's not to be surprised at – Dottie tried to do a good job as President, but she was sick the whole year. And things just didn't go the way they should. But they're beginning to now. It takes five years – this is an important thing to stress. It takes five years to integrate a group so that it can function as a growing, living organism. And people do not understand that, who haven't been in group work. We have to build a foundation of five to seven years and then if it's well built then it carries on, on its own. It's a very important thing to realize. It's going to take a 5-year period, and I found out in my own meditations, that it took me five years to really center in to really know what meditation is all about. And the ones that go quicker than that are people that have had it in other lifetimes and are just picking up. But, that's the length of time it takes you to get oriented spiritually, so that is the most important thing."

Do you have any idea why it's five years?

Issie: "No, I haven't. You'd think it would be seven."[18]

[Amy:] Is that a Jupiter cycle or something?[19]

Issie: "No, Jupiter's a 6-year and 12-year cycle; I really don't know, but I know it's true."

A lot of people who don't make it to the meetings don't know that we start all our meetings with the Great Invocation.

Issie: "Well, the Great Invocation is in every language in the world practically now, and it's being used all over the planet, because if we

---

[18] In astrology, 5 is associated with Leo (5th sign) and the 5th house of *creativity* and *children*, our greatest creations.
[19] Five years from the date of a chart, Jupiter by transit trines its natal point.

don't ask, we cannot receive. And if we ask the light and love and power of God to come down, it can come down. And the Invocation is a very important thing and for those who are not of the Christian faith, they need not be disturbed by the word Christ, because this is not historically a person. Let Christ return to Earth means let the principle of the highest part of me come back to the personality. Return to Earth – Earth is the personality. And, in a planetary way, let that principle of love and light combine as it is represented through the Christ consciousness, which means anointed by the High Self – the word Christ means anointed – let that principle pervade the Earth."

Do you know where the Invocation comes from?

Issie: "Yes, it came from out of the Arcane school. Alice Bailey's master, D.K., I can't remember just how you say the name. But it came to her through him, and he said, "if this were said by enough people, it would bring the hierarchy into close communion with the planet and they could help the planet in the crises that lie ahead." This started back in the thirties, and you know the crisis is on its way in full force right now. And the first thing, *FROM THE POINT OF LIGHT* has to do with the Buddha who represents the wisdom of God. The *POINT OF LOVE WITHIN THE HEART OF GOD* is the Christ. And the Christ and the Buddha are brothers; brothers of compassion working together. And then *FROM THE CENTER WHERE THE WILL OF GOD IS KNOWN* is the planetary hierarchy stemming out of Shamballa, which is over the city of Jerusalem on the Etheric levels. And that's the center of the forces of Light. And you can see the gathering in Jerusalem right now of these opposing forces. Yet, in spite of all the fighting there, Jerusalem has not been destroyed. And remember in Saint John's Revelations he said, I saw the New Jerusalem that will not pass away. And they put it into the Easter Cantata."

Well, that covers most everything except what do you feel or foresee for the future of the Star Rovers?

Issie: "Well, Uranus is coming up to trine the Sun of the Star Rovers chart and it rules the third hose as you can see, I think there's going to be a great deal of activity, and I think the important thing for all of us is to work together and to really love each other. Not to see the negatives in each other, but to see the positives, because with Venus trine to Saturn and Jupiter trine to Saturn, we've got plenty to work with that is very, very good. And I'm going to become a spectator beginning next year, and I'm looking forward to sitting in the audience and letting someone else run the show. And there are many who are going to be very capable of doing it, so I leave it in good hands when I step out. But I knew that I should take this year because we aren't quite jelled as an entity yet. Anything else?"

That seems to complete it.

Issie: "You asked me when the seminars started. Well, at the very beginning of the New England Astrological Association, we started having seminars at the Hill in Nottingham, New Hampshire, and they've continued. And I think they've done a tremendous amount to get people knowing each other and being relaxed with each other and informal with each other. And every summer we have a seminar and it never has rained yet. It's looked like it. It rained in-between one year. It stopped the minute we had to go outdoors for our lectures. And it's an outdoor affair one Sunday out of every year in August. But, the workshops, the teas and the seminars have been means of helping us to know each other. In a little bit more intimate way than you do in just coming to a meeting. And I do feel very strongly that breaking bread is a form of communion and this is what we have in the teas, and we haven't had anything but super teas every one this year. We just started this last year, and every one has been a delight to all those who come. That is of course for the members only. ... Now you can use what part of this you want. God Bless, Issie."

* * * * * * * * * * * *

Star Rovers held a memorial tribute to Issie at Harmony Hill on August 10th, 1980, two months after she left the body. When we were all gathered, I read parts of our interview aloud, and although I had prepared some remarks on Star Rovers' chart, I heard Issie's voice within say ***"never mind"*** so I scrapped the idea. Rediscovering these texts while working on Issie's *NEVER MIND* book 30 years later makes me wonder now, if her message held another meaning! Below are a few of those undelivered notes of my observations, to underscore how unique Star Rovers was as an organization that Issie had created and nurtured:

"The chart, with Saturn as the handle of a bucket showed the weight of each member's personal life and our collective need to temper our egos, a call to discipleship. The Gemini Sun truly did reflect how much fun we had, with hundreds of stimulating and educational experiences and speakers we enjoyed bringing to the public. The good will of the group was shown in many ways, including a Sun-Saturn quintile (71^0). The Sagittarius rising was a wonderfully spiritually expansive choice for the ascendant and made each of our gatherings an adventure.

At the time of Issie's passing, transiting Uranus exactly conjunct Star Rover's Neptune, 22 degrees, 15 minutes of Scorpio; an abrupt unexpected cutting of a psychic chord. That transit also reminded us; our foundation was spiritual unfoldment through astrology. Also, transiting Neptune at 21 Sagittarius opposing Star Rovers' Sun called upon us to *"let go and let God"* as Issie taught, in faith that she lived on in our hearts and that we could hear her beautiful voice sing with us by being quiet and connecting with our High Selves. Other transits were meaningful too."

The story that I did share that day was a personal one, about the *Mountain and Spirituality*. In my first years with Issie, she would often warn that of all the ambitions, *spiritual ambition* was the most dangerous, and that humility was the last spiritual lesson. I prayed to understand what she meant, as I felt impatient in my desire for enlightenment, and this confused me.

One night my prayer was answered. During a time when just a few TV channels existed and broadcasting ended late at night with a blank screen, on this night, the image at the close of broadcasting was a climber on a mountain trail. The voice speaking cautioned that it is essential for the climber ascend at a pace that will allow him to adjust to the changes in air pressure, and that if one were to jump from the bottom to the mountain peak all at once, the person would die from the shock to the system of the sudden pressure change. That was my answer: that each effort and small progress is vital and lets us adjust to new "air" at each higher elevation.

This *message* resonated with something else that Issie would say: just as consciousness is reality, a person whose consciousness dwells on higher planes *breathes different air than everyone else!* Is it a coincidence that spiritual seekers through the ages are told to *breathe mindfully?*

When Issie began Star Rovers, she dedicated it to the forces of Light, for it to be a channel in the world through astrology. It was a gift to young people, in whom Issie always saw the light, and communicated through love, reflecting her forever-young Spirit.

In combing through saved Star Rovers newsletters, two more messages by Issie surfaced. The first was in the December 1971 Star Rovers newsletter, an article entitled *"More Psychological Insights ... From ISSIE"* in which she elaborates on the astrologer as a counselor. She emphasized that an astrologer can only interpret a life and a destiny at the level at which he or she functions; thus, ongoing self-development is essential:

"To be a good astrological counselor it is necessary to understand the psychology of the individual, whether that individual is "you" or the "other" out there. For me, the two greats in the field of psychology have been Carl Jung and Carl Rogers. Read Carl Rogers' *"On Becoming a Person."* It's in paperback. Rogers is the one who has practical client-centered therapy. If the counselor (and that's what the role of an astrologer is) does not relate to the client, how can he help? If he accepts the client, he will help him accept himself. In this acceptance it is not only the client who is changed, the counselor also changes. It cannot be otherwise. If the counselor can help the other fellow be what he is – and enable him to accept what he is without sitting in any judgment on that "isness" – then the client (and the counselor) can move on to a greater "isness."

"It is only when we accept ourselves as we are that we can change. We cannot move away from what we are until we thoroughly accept what we are. Then change seems to come about almost unnoticed."

"It is not helpful in relationships to maintain a façade – to act in one way on the surface while experiencing something different underneath. Carl Rogers makes an interesting comment on this: *'Most of the times in which I fail to be of help to other individuals can be accounted for in terms of the fact that I have, for some defense reason, felt in one way at a surface level, while in reality my feelings run in a contrary direction."*

"This means being one's self. If the counselor can accept himself as the decidedly imperfect person he is, who by no means functions at all times in the way he wishes to function, then it is very much easier to accept the other person as he is, and a relationship is born. If we don't relate to another, we cannot help them. And if we don't accept the "as is" at any moment we cannot change."

"Doesn't it all mean that by our own attitudes we help the other fellow to feel safe and secure, and when we accept him as he is, he can accept himself. Another quote from Carl Rogers has great meaning to me:

"I have found that truly to accept another person and his feelings is by no means an easy thing, anymore than is understanding. Can I really permit another person to feel hostile toward me? Can I accept his anger as a real and legitimate part of himself? Can I accept him when he views life and his problems in a way quite different from mine? Can I accept him when he feels very positive toward me, admiring me (Pedestal pushing) and wants to model himself after me? All this is involved in acceptance and it doesn't come easy. We find it hard to allow others to feel differently than we do. Yet it has come to seem to me that this separateness of individuals, the right of each individual to utilize his experience in his own way and to discover his meanings in it – this is one of the most priceless potentialities of life. Each person is an island unto himself in a very real sense; and he can only build bridges to other islands if he is first of all willing to be himself and permitted to be himself. So I find that when I can accept another person, which means accepting the feelings and attitudes and beliefs that he has as a real and vital part of him, I am assisting him to become a person and there is great value in this. To the degree that each one of us is willing to be himself, then he finds not only himself changing but he finds other people to whom he relates also changing."

"I feel very strongly that if the people we counsel professionally aren't better for the contact, then we have failed as good astrologers. Healing comes when a person is accepted as he is (and as he can be) without any judgments. Loving acceptance and a recognition of the divine potentials in each person we counsel sets them free and, in a strange sort of way, sets us free too. It is experience that is the teacher for each of us; but healing is Love set free to do its own work, often unrecognized but always life-giving and attitude-changing."

"There are so many people unconscious of their real worth. It is up to us to make them feel worthy; for everyone is dear and preciously worthwhile to the Divine in them. It isn't a matter of saying it – it is a matter of feeling it (and the feeling can't be simulated) – then the other fellow feels it too. It makes him secure and unafraid when he can accept his own divinity and know his own capacity to be and become. More next month, God willing, Issie."

Star Rovers continued until in 1984, when a conflict forced the decision to dissolve the group. We donated Star Rovers' remaining funds to the *Astrologers' Newsletter*, and wrote the following letter to members signed by all five presidents who had served since 1974:

"... The reasons for our decision are too complex to describe here, and in the final analysis we basically agree that Star Rovers has lived its natural life and it is time to let go. ... May we each hold and nourish within our lives the light which brought us all to Star Rovers. As we allow this light within us to make new connections, may the friendships, acquaintances, and professional relationships founded through Star Rovers continue to bless our lives."

What's in a name? Those close to Issie knew that her inspiration for Star Rovers' *name* was the classic novel *The Star Rover* by Jack London. It was about a man, who foiled his prison torturers by leaving his body, and in so doing, roamed the stars freely and discovered many of his past lives! A few of we Star Rovers knew each other in past lives, too!

Several years after the organization dissolved, when my sons were old enough, my husband and I were given a boat by my father, so we could enjoy exploring our island community on the water. We took navigation safety lessons by the Coast Guard and looked forward to many happy family times on the Atlantic under the stars.

When it was time to register the boat, I knew what it to call it!

Ironically, the boat was too expensive for us to maintain, with never-ending repairs. In hindsight, some lessons that *our Star Rover* let us pass along to our sons were similar to lessons I learned in Star Rovers Astrological Association. Fulfilling a dream requires real investment and sacrifice, and the times that our family enjoyed on the ocean made us forget the sacrifices and to feel that it was all worthwhile. Another lesson is to know when to cut your losses and let it go, when you have done all you can. Few things in life ever are fully in our control and this was no exception.

These lessons can take a lifetime (or more) to learn, and I am sure that Issie realized this when naming our Boston astrology group *Star Rover!* We gathered for a time, made many sacrifices to keep it going, and when the burdens grew too great, let it go.

To be a *Star Rover* one does not need a group at all, as its true meaning is to let go of all material attachment in order to roam freely among the star-filled heavens. Issie would know a lot about that!

IT IS ALL RIGHT ... AND IT WAS!

More and more people sought Issie's guidance and insights, and in September 1976, she published her third book: *It Is All Right*. She loved repeating it four times, emphasizing each word to bring home another point: **IT** is all right, it **IS** all right, it is **ALL** right, it is all **RIGHT!** This simple mantra can restore calm and peace.

I consider *It Is ALL Right* a balm for weary souls who want to understand the enigmas of life and learn to apply the wisdom of Eastern mysticism to Western culture. In 2020, I was delighted to publish it in a paperback edition.

Issie dedicated the book to Helen, *"a disciple of Light, who chose to come through me as my daughter. Her sustaining help, not only with this book, but in my life has made the journey of life worthwhile."*

Its chapter titles hint at its gems:

> Prologue – The Fool; The Journey
> Why We Are Where We Are
> Going God's Way
> Our Father Who Art in Heaven
> Through Christ A Thousand Times
> Prayer and Meditation
> Explaining God and Life to Children
> And a Little Child
> The Mating Game
> Healing vs Dis-ease
> The Dis-ease Called Alcoholism
> Death – The Other Side of Life
> Earthbounds – Here and After Here
> Letters from a Son to His Mother
> Protection Against Psychic Forces
> Astrology, Its Place in the Plan
> The Magic Secret – Huna
> Thoughts Along The Way
> Prayers and Mantrams That Have Helped
> "WHY"

This wonderful book is still available and helping seekers of all ages. On June 17, 1980, four years after publishing *It Is All Right,* Issie fulfilled her prophecy, took her last breath and left her body. Having Issie's It Is ALL Right was a good reminder not to bury ourselves in grief at her passing but to celebrate her life and her '*graduation.*' Issie often said, *"It's no coincidence that when a baby is born, the baby cries while everyone else rejoices, and when a person leaves the body, everyone else cries while the soul rejoices."* Issie had a fine graduation, indeed!

Days later, Helen wrote on Issie's Fellowship House letterhead to someone who had written to Issie and was waiting for a response:
"To Whom it May Concern:

Isabel Hickey quietly slipped away from her body on June 17 at Harmony Hill in Nottingham, New Hampshire. For the past several months she had been having breathing problems due to her angina. She cancelled her proposed trip to Hawaii, conducted a three-hour astrology workshop on Saturday, June 14 and spent the weekend surrounded by friends. We laid her body to rest in the cemetery at the Hill, and conducted a memorial service for her on Sunday, at the Marsh Chapel at Boston University, with testimonials from friends from all facets of her life, and with the hymns and songs she dearly loved. The Chapel was thronged as we celebrated her graduation. She left only verbal instructions about her books, etc. and it will be awhile before legal matters are arranged. She had not deposited the enclosed check before her death. It would be helpful, meanwhile, if you would replace the enclosed check with one made out to me. It should be sent to me at [address]. This would facilitate matters as I will be the administrator of her estate. Thank you for your attention to this request. Soon we will be sending out a letter outlining the sequence of events and will be in contact with you at that time. We celebrate Issie's life, her courage, her giving heart and her loving nature.
Sincerely,
Helen K. Hickey / June 26, 1980"

Letters kept arriving as news spread of Issie's passing. Helen saved the next two. The first is notable for a few reasons; the word play of a bell image was common among those whose consciousness Isabel had raised. I have often heard a bell ring in a dream or meditation, and knew it was a message from Issie. Also, Issie taught the importance of protecting the body from negative psychic attachments and *leaky auras*, and emphasized right attitude, the power of positive praying and creative visualization, themes in these letters.

"Dear Ms. Hickey.

When I was in America recently, I visited the metaphysical bookshop in Bethlehem, PA … of course I know that chance is the part of God's Plan, which we do not see. The lady there showed me a copy of your book, It Is All Right, just plucked it from the shelves and said, "Have you seen this" so I bought it, a spiritual gift is not to be denied even if one pays oneself! What a gift! I must say it rang bells in my soul. So much of what I teach in England and USA was there before my eyes, eloquent and simply written. I always say "A wise many speaks with simple words." You are obviously a very wise woman. ... I found the method of sealing the aura at the neck very useful in my own healing work; needless to say the means was presented to me via your book only days before it would be needed. Truly "Where God Guides he provides!" and I have never been let down. I return to P.A. in the autumn to undertake spiritual work. Perhaps one day I may have the pleasure of meeting you. God Bless you and your work. Many thanks for a book that is all a book should be. Light and love, Regards, [Name], England / October, 1980"

On August 4, 1980, a New York psychiatrist wrote to praise Issie for It Is All Right, as *"spiritually elevating and beautiful, giving me strength and much to think about."* Helen wrote the following long reply, revealing that Issie had been writing a last book!

"Dear Friend,

Issie slipped quietly from her body on June 17. She had been experiencing some degree of discomfort and inability to breathe due to angina over the past several months. We buried her body in the cemetery of her beloved Harmony Hilltop. On Sunday, June 22, we had a memorial service for her at the Marsh Chapel of Boston University. There were testimonials from friends of various facets of her life, plus the hymns and songs she dearly loved. The Chapel was thronged, and the service was lovely. We miss her physical presence sorely, but her essence is everywhere.

I am resorting to this mechanical means of communicating with you because of the large volume of daily mail which comes to Issie, and which I am trying to stay abreast of.

I am pleased that you enjoyed "It is All Right." The numbers of persons who have written about the book are simply amazing. It has come into their lives at the right time, and it has changed their perceptions of themselves, their environment and their relationships with others.

Issie was working on her fourth book (6 Chapters are completed) which was largely autobiographical. I am contemplating continuing the manuscript through various phases of her life through oral and written interviews with people who were important to her at various stages of her life. At the moment I have a full time job so the concentrated time needed for such a task is not abundant, but I believe appropriate organization can make the task feasible. I have decided to get through August and September first (there is much to be done to clear up Issie's estate, get the book orders organized and handle correspondence) and then decide how best to take on the completion of the book. It is to be entitled, "Never Mind." Issie's premise was that the only way we could bring order out of chaos on the planet, and the only way we could master our personalities, and develop right relationships with others was through the heart: through love. She attested we could never make it through the mind.

Your Self-Esteem Therapy approach is fascinating. How I'd like to be able to attend one of your courses. I'm going to try for the Oct. 25th one, as I have a friend in New York (I worked there for 16 years) with whom I can stay over the weekend. That date seems feasible, at this point in time. My work as an Associate Dean in a College of Allied Health Professions involves my doing a considerable amount of counseling, and practically all of the students with whom I interact are folks who have no feelings of self-worth. It is amazing how many times this is what is at the bottom of their problems: whether they are academic, personal, social or combinations of these. Thus it is important to me to investigate many approaches to better understanding of myself, so that I can be of greater assistance to others. As the devout and faithful say, "I'll hold the thought" – that I can attend one of your workshops, that is.

Under separate cover I have sent you a copy of "It Is All Right" – you really should have your own copy! There is much to be gained by rereading parts of it when the spirit strikes you. And, also, it might be helpful for some of your patients.

Thank you for sharing your materials – I regret that Issie did not physically read your praise for her book. Writing was not easy for her – it was a struggle, and she had to discipline herself to do it. And, as you can imagine, although she wanted me to do the editing, it was difficult for her to surrender her rough draft to me – I recognized these difficulties, and assured her over and over that I would be gentle with her "baby" and that I wanted it to be as healthy, viable, and well cared for as she did. We had a wonderful friendship as well as being mother and daughter. But it took a lot of heartache and a lot of work to get us to that point. We always loved each other, but we had to work many years to get to understand one another, and to communicate effectively with one another. But, we made it and the energy required along with the discipline were all worthwhile.

Blessings on you and your work. Thanks again for writing.

Love and light, Helen K. Hickey"

ABSENT FROM THE APPEARANCE

Issie had completed six chapters of her fourth book? Imagination took hold: where was it? Among the papers from Helen, a manila folder was labeled: <u>ISSIE'S BOOK "NEVER MIND."</u> Whispers echoed in my head, of Issie saying she might write a book called *Never Mind*.

Much later a more vivid memory returned, of a day at Harmony Hill in 1971. I had just returned from a summer in Holland, where I had met Jo Onvlee, from whom I'd learned a *short form* of T'ai Chi – a *meditation in motion* – and a *free-form* style of T'ai Chi. At the time, T'ai Chi was not yet a mainstream exercise. Jo had made me promise that when I returned to America, I would show to Issie this free style channeling Spirit *in motion*. The weather was a bit dank, so we were all in the living room, by the fireplace. I summoned the courage to tell Issie that I had something that I **had** to show her.

Issie loved surprises and new ideas. I explained that through movement, Spirit would channel a message, and she asked me to ask Spirit to channel a message *for her,* so she could see if it confirmed her intuition about *writing a fourth book*. Spirit-in-motion showed energy pouring from above my head, into my body, from my heart to her. At the time, it seemed too simple to be significant, but Issie smiled and said *"Good, that's enough."*

It was the confirmation she sought. Looking back, it has much more meaning to me now but at the time, I was just relieved to get through the demonstration and that Issie liked it. (It didn't occur to me to ask her to elaborate! Ah, never mind!) Issie often taught that when something is right, we will receive multiple signs that *it's a go;* and when it's wrong, we're apt to feel only doubt. This freestyle T'ai Chi demonstration was surely just one of many signs that Issie had received. Some months later, Issie began to study T'ai Chi also.

Issie had a knack for saying what you needed to hear, to wake you up to an *unlit* situation. Once in a soft, compassionate tone, Issie said to me, about a relationship problem I was experiencing: *"Oh well, we all need to feel needed."* That simple but profound truism helped me to see that being *needed* was not a reason to endure a bad situation and helped me to take a brighter way forward.

Issie taught that just as we are vibratorily connected to everyone in our lives, we can attract the people who are right for us, if we feed a positive image in our creative minds of the qualities we want in a person. This is like making a mental shopping list of character traits, and then affirming in gratitude that the person was "out there" and on his way. Time and time again, I have seen this principle work, for myself and for others.

Years later in 1978, I worked for a publisher of metaphysical books. I loved the dynamics of publishing, developing manuscripts with worthy authors. I didn't know Issie was writing her last book, or I would have approached her to publish it then, but Issie knew that she would not publish it during her lifetime.

After Issie's passing in 1980, my friendship with Helen grew. She cheered me on each time I showed her one of my manuscripts and as each was published. Helen asked me to oversee the combining of *Astrology: A Cosmic Science* with *Minerva / Pluto: The Choice is Yours,* and we collaborated to adapt ACS into a computer generated *"Isabel Hickey Natal Report."* So, it was odd to me that Helen had saved Issie's manuscript for 25 years without asking me to work on it with her. As it turns out, that wasn't quite true.

After reviewing the contents of the folder, I thought I understood Helen's silence. It was mainly disjointed notes and thoughts. Some pages were typed, others handwritten; some had titles; others were missing pages, leaving thoughts dangling. At times the voice was unfamiliar as if it was notes from a course. *Never Mind,* I thought! I'll type them up, add a few footnotes, and offer it to a publisher.

I did just that.

Not surprising, the publisher found most of the material to be uninspiring, yet they felt that my footnotes were intriguing, and asked me to expand them with stories of knowing Issie in my youth. So, I revised the manuscript with memories of my years with Issie.

So, I did just that.

The writing zipped along until another puzzle arose and I could go no further until it was solved. Happily, in a few months, my search led to Issie's grandson Jay, who had the missing puzzle piece! Words cannot convey my joy in learning that Issie *had given Jay NEVER MIND before her passing!*

Ha! So Helen had only given me *remnants* that Issie had *rejected but not discarded* when Issie gave the book to Jay! Or was there more to the story? Why did Issie save the rest of the papers that Helen passed along to me? Would I ever know?

Never mind, I could hear Issie say, *it is all right* for me and Jay to decide what more to include, which brings us to the third phase of this magical journey – its *wings.* Whether the disjointed notes were by Issie or uncited sources, *it all inspired her,* which makes it worth sharing, and so Jay and I decided to do just that in the next chapter.

In closing my memoirs, I'd like to share two poems with you. One, I wrote in 2008, after contemplating the contents of Issie's papers, some years before realizing that what I thought I had was not what I had at all, which still makes me laugh when I think about it.

The other poem came in 1986, when I was taking a seminar called *"Cakes for the Queen of Heaven."* One assignment was to pray to a *feminine* Divinity. I asked in meditation how best to do that and heard *'Her Prayer.'* It is based on an idea Issie also taught, that if we invoke a maternal Divinity, we will find peace and more spiritual balance. It is meant to compliment *The Lord's Prayer.*

ODE TO *ISSIE* ... WHO *IS!*

There once was a woman named Isabel ...
Isabel, Isabel Hickey.
She walked on this planet some 76 years
And her friends all knew her as "Issie."
Now Issie chose a rugged road;
One that very few could follow.
She pioneered a path of cheer,

Filling hearts with hope from heaven above,
Feeding souls with boundless motherly love.

Issie offered herself as a channel of light
At the age of thirty-three.
In no time at all God had answered her call
And set her to work to teach you and me.
As healer and astrologer, we came to learn
The karmic law of energy returning;
We found forgiveness in our hearts
With a hunger that was yearning
Oh, Isabel ...
We loved you oh so well.
You are listening ... even now,
Yes ... we can tell.

HER PRAYER

Our Mother Who Art in Nature
Fruitful is They Womb
Thy Rhythms Come
Thy Will is One
In Our Hearts And In Our Deeds.
Give Us Your Sanctuary In Times of Darkness
Blessing and Protecting Us
So That We May Bless And Protect Others.
Help Us Learn From Our Experiences
So That We May Be Wise In Our Ways
For Thine Is The Ultimate Source
Of Healing Grace and Highest Love, Forever.
And So It Is.

MORE FROM ISSIE

On May 9, 1942 at 2 AM, Issie drew a horary chart for a *"Vision of Divine Mother."* Issie urged us to *invite the Divine Feminine* into our consciousness to counterbalance male-dominant ideologies that led to an oppressive spirituality. Thirty-seven years after her "Vision" Issie wrote about this vision, one year before leaving her body. It was prophetic of her *graduation*.

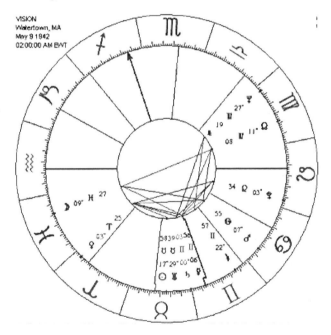

THE WOUNDED MASTER

With my last struggling breath, I reached the last step before the plateau on the top of the mountain. Blood, scars, and torn skin showed the long hard journey up the steep, rugged mountain. The deep lines, forever etched in my face, mirrored the worried thoughts and deep emotional battles that I had to overcome during my perilous journey.

Ahead of me was freedom, peace, rest, and fulfillment, but I needed superhuman strength to make the last grueling effort to lift my body onto the resting plateau nestled in the top of the mountain.

Praying, pleading for the Master to reach out and take my extended hand, I waited for strength to make the last lunge to freedom. It had taken many years to reach these heights. Many years spent in the darkness of the valley below, followed by many years at the foot of the mountain, in preparation for the climb. Then, the long, lonely years of my ascent. Inch by inch I had groped my way. I had weathered the worst of storms that Mother Nature and human nature had thrown at me. Now at the end of the climb, or so very near the end, I could not remain where I was, nor return to where I had been. I had to move forward – just one more gigantic leap and I would be home. I closed my eyes and, leaning my haggard face against the cold, hard mountain, I prayed.

Opening my tear-filled eyes, I looked up and ahead. There, reaching out to me with a glow of love and light was the healing hand of my Master. His hand reached and grasped mine. A surge of healing energy entered my body. With this new force I lunged up and ahead, and landed face down on the resting plateau on the top of the mountain.

My body was racked with pain and I could not control the tears mixed with anguish and joy. They welled up from the very root of my being, making rivers of emotion that drowned me. After a long time, the bottomless well of tears ran dry and a peace started to settle down on me. My thoughts started to clear as I remembered that the peaceful state was not mine, but was the peace of my Master at whose feet I was laying. I reached out and embraced His feet not daring to look up at Him. I lay there waiting for the courage to come so that I could speak. After a time I felt that I was ready. I asked, *"Master, may I look up and see your beloved face, face to face?"* Taking His time, the Master in His deep peaceful voice answered, *"Yes, my child, yes you may, but be prepared, it is not what you expect."*

This answer put a cold hand of fear on my heart. What could my beloved Master mean? How could he be anything but beauty in its most perfect expression? I could wait no longer. Gathering all my courage, I raised my head and allowed my eyes to gaze upon my beloved Master.

Oh, he is so very beau ----. Oh no, oh my God, my Master has been cruelly wounded! I could not bear to look upon the ugliness! My head fell to the ground as once again the tears started to flow, and I was lost in the waters of grief. My wounded Master was silent. His silence was a healing one. Soon I was able to collect myself and once again I spoke. *"Master, do I ever have to go down the mountain again?"*

"No, my child, you have attained, and you <u>never</u> have to go down again."

"Then, Master, I can stay with you. I will nurse your wounded face. What can I do to help you heal this ugly wound? One side of your face is so very beautiful and the other side is ----."

"My child, because you did not see my face before, you do not know, but you have added your gift of healing to it. After you arrived another small patch of the wound became healed. As others attain and arrive as you, and contribute their gift of healing love, more and more my face will be healed and will become beautiful once more."

"Master, how did this happen?"

"Ages ago, my child, I too went down the mountain into the valley. While I was in the valley, I tried to teach others about my Master. I was both myself and my Master, for I had traveled to the top of the mountain and had attained as you have done. But, while I was down in the valley, something went wrong. The others thought that I was only Light and that there was no dark side to me. They thought there never was a dark side of me and that this made them different from me. They did not understand that the dark shadow gives the Light its splendor. With this deeply ingrained in their thoughts, they thought I was to carry them up the mountain. They thought all they had to do was ask me, hold on to me, and then I would do all the work. They would not listen when I asked them, 'Why do you call me good, only GOD is good?' I could not make them understand, even when I told them, 'Greater things that I do, ye shall do.' I knew I had to leave them in the valley and return to the mountain top. This I did. When I returned, I knew I could never turn my back on them. Somehow they would have to learn that everyone has to prepare and climb the rugged, steep mountain with their own inner light guiding their ascent. I then decided to recreate my darkness. One side of my face to show the darkness that I was; the other side to show the perfection that I had become. My own darkness would only be healed by little

ones like you who attain. So here I have stayed, silently meditating, sending out healing rays of Love and Light and courage to all, especially those who are at the foot of the mountain preparing to climb, and to those who are at various points in their journey upward. My silent meditations are magnetic, so when anyone is ready to climb they will feel the strong pull from my loving thoughts. No one could ever arrive on their own power alone."

My wounded Master rested now. This was the longest I had ever heard Him speak. I needed silence to understand and absorb the lesson my Master had taught. But more questions were forming in my mind. I knew I had to speak again.

"Master, what of all the others that I worked with while I was in the valley, and climbing the mountain? I, too, talked about you, and a few accepted you and now they, too, are climbing. Does that work add to the healing?"

"No, my little one. A space is reserved on my wounds for their final healing touch. Their name is written on the space, but only they can heal it by attaining."

In the silence that followed, I began to become frightened. I was afraid because of the thought that was forming in my head. Yes, if I would acknowledge the Light side of me I knew what I had to do – then the small patch of darkness that was left tried to control me. In the silence I knew my Master could hear my struggle. I knew He would not interfere. The choice was always mine. The forces of darkness and light within me were having their final battle. I waited to see the outcome. Finally, triumphantly the Forces of Light absorbed the Forces of Darkness within me. I opened my mouth and spoke.

"Master, allow me to rest here with you for the night and tomorrow morning I will go back down the mountain to work. Again I will try to tell others about you, and the work they need to do on themselves to become like you. But allow me to rest with you, because this last battle had taken all my strength." The Master was silent. The one tear that caressed His beautiful face was my answer. Embracing His feet, I lay down to sleep.

With the rising sun, I gathered myself together. I needed one last reassurance from my Master before I started my bleak journey. Slowly, I spoke, *"Master, am I your disciple forever? I need your answer before I can start out again."*

My Master took both my hands and raised me up. He placed both hands on my shoulders and looked into my eyes. Slowly, deeply, He spoke ----

"*My child, you are not my disciple. You are my savior. YOU are my CHRIST.*" (Dated February 3, 1979)

THE VOICE WITHIN

Beloved, when every man has learned that within himself is a spark of the Great Brightness, through which guidance can come from the Source of All, there will be no more need of Incarnate Teachers. Teach mankind how each can unfold that spark of divine Selfhood, that it may become a glowing flame to illumine his days and guide his life. To not a one is guidance lacking. It doth but sleep in some, awaiting his vibrant call to come forth and lead the way, through paths of darkness and illusion.

When first the Voice of conscience leads a man to do that which he doth not desire, or to forego that for which he longs, he has dimly awakened to the possibility of that daily guidance. But alas! Man doth follow fitfully, and doth combat that Inner Voice with intellect grown worldly-wise, and steeped in the ways of illusion. There are not two ways, Beloved – there is the One Way, and the *"no way but fruitless wandering."* He who will but follow blindly, trustingly, the Voice of God as it speaks within himself, will be securely led into paths of peace and righteousness. Yet how many among the Earth-children possess this utter trust! They do follow a little way, and then when they see that the path of release doth lead them o'er the hillside's steeps, they turn them back, complaining that they are not led, and lose themselves in the mists and fogs of their own reasoning. Again and again they turn back, just as the path opens broad and straight before them, and say there is no Way, and their guidance false.

Oh My Beloved! When will man cease setting up as god his own little reason, his own little will, and hearken unto My Voice which speaks unceasingly within him! I do not say the pathway is not steep that leads to Truth and Peace. I do not promise they shall not be beset with many illusions on the way, that seem to menace the fearful traveler and turn him back. Yet I do say they shall be led through all confusion, through all attack, and find release, if they but cling in utter trust to My guiding hand, and listen to My Voice within their hearts.

[20]Then you have to wait for the answer, for instruction. I have rarely gotten definite <u>instructions</u> while *in* the Silence. It has been for me an attunement to Power and Wisdom in <u>essence</u>. The direction, the instruction in <u>words</u>, the guidance, comes when I am about some routine task that occupies my <u>conscious</u> mind. Then the answer will often flash into my mind full-formed, without my conscious participation or intrusion. Or my <u>body</u> will be guided to where the solution waits. But in the Silence comes the exaltation, the sense of intimate Peace, the quickening, the enheartening, the realization of Something mighty working through to a right conclusion, a pregnant hush, a stirring, a communion – how can one put it! Perhaps I can illustrate with a personal experience. My four-year-old daughter was stricken with scarlet fever. The doctor had come and gone, the family had retired, and I was sitting up with her. I made my attunement with the infinite, and felt such happiness, such well-being, such freedom from anxiety! I moved about in ease and rhythm, and a warm and happy expectation of Good. It is a tingling aliveness at times – a Peace that is vital and real.

In entering the Silence, I have sometimes had to approach it from the heaviness and gloom of earthly routine and pressure of human living. At such times, I have had to wait until I could lighten the atmosphere in which my mind had been dwelling, and dissipate it.

Sometimes I have had to work through the cold and chill and hardness of mental fog that the "dark forces" throw around one like a mantle, before I could dispel it and enter the warmth and friendliness and expansiveness of the Silence. I do not <u>fight</u> the dark forces or drive them away; I summon compassion and pray for their enlightenment together with my own; and so together we dispel the contracting chill and enter the warm of Infinite Love and Wisdom. I am conscious of astonishment in the dark ones, that I do not assail them or fear them, but open the way for them with me to greater Light. Then there is a pause, a relaxing, and a release of warmth and power from above.

We have to "throw the switch" – we have to open the door – to power and light by our belief that that power is there and available to

---

[20] This paragraph begins a page but it is not clear if it follows the paragraph above it, which ended another page.

us. Not to believe and yet to try, is to tell the subconscious that it is no use to try! "He that is not for Me is against Me." – "A house divided against itself!" The subconscious believes without question whatever you tell it, and if <u>you</u> question, it accepts the questionability of what you are trying to believe or do.

<u>After</u> Meditation, we must <u>use</u> what is given us in the Silence, to meet our daily problems, in the <u>knowledge</u> that all the powers of the universe are at work to meet our needs from the standpoint of omniscience.

MISCELLANEOUS INSPIRATIONS,
MUSINGS & ADVICE TO ASTROLOGERS AND SEEKERS

These next writings were *either* Issie's *or* were her notes by other sources; which was the case was not always evident, as her shorthand notes were often mixed in with the text. Issie advised us: *"don't take my word for it – digest it and test it for yourself; if it works for you, great; if not, toss it out!"*

Fair enough! Choose for yourself what to keep or toss, with Issie's other sage advice: *"don't throw the baby out with the bath water!"* We begin with material that we know was original to Issie.

In the 1970s, Issie continued to lecture while writing <u>It Is All Right</u> and allowed some of her lectures to be recorded on audiotapes.[21] The following quotes are from these recorded talks; I gave them subtitles, based on what she was discussing:

WHY NEVER MIND: "When I say *"Never Mind"* – and you'll never solve the issues of life with your mind – I don't mean that your mind isn't important. The Sun – the Spirit – in Aquarius is like the Sun in February, cold, detached, not at its height of warmth. Leo is too attached to those they love; it's the love sign. They also demand too much of people, until they learn better. Leo's consciousness of love, and the rest of the signs' consciousness of love is different. Now, Aquarius balances that by a detachment or indifference to individuals is often difficult for people around them. When you get the true Uranian Aquarian, it won't be this way at all, and the whole mission of Aquarius, this New Age of Aquarius, is to teach people to be loving

---

[21] These were distributed by Llewellyn for a while, then discontinued.

but not attached. That's what we're learning. Some people are born at the turn of the age who bring into the New Age that which they've learned in past lifetimes, with an understanding of the new, yet not throwing out all of the old, because we're not supposed to. You see, there are certain things in our values and our morals of the past that must not be lost, and will be, after the arc of the covenant coming into the New Age. And so, I believe Aquarius has much to do with the True Mind, not the concrete mind. The Conscious mind is the True Mind, the Thinker. The brain is the instrument the thinker uses. "

YOUR WORTH: "One thing that bothers me most is the lack of recognition in so many people; they don't understand their own worth in the right way, and guilt. If I can help them understand their own worth – and for you too that are astrologers – and remove guilt from them; if you do nothing else, you have helped them tremendously. All of us are working on this. We have to keep reminding ourselves who we are and realizing that, and "let light, let love flow through and get ourselves out of the way."

OUR LAST LESSON: "Humility is the last thing we learn. The great teachers let you do as you please. No forces of light ever put pressure on and say *you have to* do anything. Remember, the pendulum swings; if it swings too far, and you've been too emotional in a past life, you'll come on your next life with your emotional capacity cut off and have to develop your mind. Many things in the chart will prove this."

YOUR TRUE SELF: "The persona is the role we play in life and if you role-play long enough, it gets stuck on you, and you're not being you. You're being the kind of role the other person expects you to be. And a lot of people get stuck in their persona. They're role-playing. It's like clothes are to the body. We have to have clothes, but we can get stuck in our clothes and not realize we're behind it."

DREAMS: "When you become interested in astrology and psychology, you'll begin to have amazing dreams and it will tell you so much. Your dreams will help you understand all these things, if you put a paper beside your bed and a pencil, and say, *I'm going to write down my dreams."*

YOUR INNER BEAST: "One thing I've learned and helped people understand, is when you've hit the highest aspiration you're capable of, there's a corresponding beast in the sub-basement of ourselves that says, "okay, I'm coming up!" It comes up for transmutation. I do retreats and we have 2 or 3 days of completely tuning in, and the last meeting before we break up, I always say, now look, you've been on the mountaintop very high, and you're going into the valley where everyone's going to throw the books at you. You're going into a period where, by hitting the highest in you, you have brought up the lowest, so I want you to be prepared."

OWN YOUR SHADOW: "The shadow is the repository of inhibitions, repressions, fears, suspicions, feeling of guilt or weakness, the Achilles' heel in the armor one wears before the world. One is usually quick to see it in others, and when we cannot face the negatives in ourselves, we project them onto the other fellow and see them in him. So, when you accuse the other fellow of certain quality, be sure you're not projecting that quality that you can't face in yourself."

YOUR DEBT: "Wherever you have Neptune, is where you've got to sacrifice or are obliged to give yourself up in some way, where you owe a debt to the collective whole. Neptune's vibration is not easily understood because it's not of this dimension. If you would touch the real essence of Neptune, you would see such a beautiful energy, unbelievably beautiful. But you have to go in, to find the real thing of Neptune. "

NATURE: "I always make obeisance to Mother Earth, always, and thank her for allowing us to dwell on her surface. You can draw tremendous Earth energy; at the center of the Earth is the Kundalini fire energy of the Earth. The Earth is an organism just as truly as we are, and if you're tired out or you're fatigued, just pull that energy up from the center of the Earth; it enters your solar plexus, which you remember is the drawing down of the Sun force and drawing up the Earth fire to here – this is why the American Indian, when they did their ritual dances, went back, bringing down the Sun force, and then went over and paid obeisance to the Earth fire, and brought it up to the solar plexus and mixed it there. You see, when you know these things, they become very real to you because you realize, the Sun and Moon mix in the solar plexus. You see, we can draw up; that's why our relationship with nature is very, very important. You know that lull that comes just at twilight time, and suddenly everything's kind of quiet? The Day Divas are leaving, and the Night Divas are coming in, and it's a wonderful thing at that time to tune into Mother Nature."

EARTHLINGS: "I've come to the conclusion that there are two kinds of people on Earth. The true Earth children and those who've come from other planets and other systems to learn certain things they need to learn here, or to teach or to help. And I'll tell you the difference. The ones who are the true Earth children are perfectly content on the Earth – they don't want to leave it, they don't even want to talk about death, they don't want to go. But the others have a nostalgia, and a great lonesomeness, and if you ask, what's the matter they'll say, I don't know, I just don't feel comfortable down here, and you'll know those are the children that don't belong to the Earth. They have this loneliness, a cry of the soul for something other than this world."

PROTECT YOUR ENERGY: "If you find yourself having your energy drawn out of you, then just say, inwardly, *"I will not allow my essence to be drawn on; I will give of my overflow."* If you don't give of your overflow, you don't really help them, because there are certain energies you need to maintain your personality."

WHO'S LIVING WHEN? "This matter of consciousness is very interesting. We are not all cut to the same measure – we live in different historical layers. And when people ask you as astrologers, when is the Aquarian Age coming in, for some people it's already in, for some people it's going to be eons of time before it gets here. Some belong in the barbarian civilization and solve their conflicts as they did in those days. Some are on the level of the 13th century Christian treating his shadow as the Devil incarnate. A man who belongs temperamentally and psychologically to the 20th century would have ideas that would never enter the head of our medieval specimen, for the hellfire and brimstone person living psychologically in the 18th century can't accept what is plain to the one living in the 20th century. This is important to understand, for there is no blame where there is understanding. We meet the Puritan and the Prostitute walking the same street. What is the only immediate reality for each depends on where they are walking within themselves psychologically."

SWITCH ON THE LIGHT: "Makes no difference what pathway we take, if it has meaning and validity to us. Only that which acts on me do I recognize as real and actual. We make no progress unless we become acquainted with our own nature. Our subconscious can be our friend or our greatest enemy; either we love it or hate it, and it loves or hates us. Consciousness must confront the unconscious and a balance between them must be found, not possible through logic and reasoning, but through symbols. Integration means facing the darkness in ourselves, turning light on it, and when the darkness becomes light, the personality is permeated with light, and consciousness gains in scope and insight. And you know it ties right in with Saint John: *"The light was in the darkness and the darkness comprehendeth it not ... the light that lighteth every man that cometh into the world."* Where is the darkness when you turn on the switch? If you go in a dark room, do you fight the darkness, or do you turn on the switch and make it light?"

IT'S YOUR CALL: "This planet is a planetary school; we're all here to learn; there are no saints on Earth, except those that have chosen to come back to serve. So we know that no chart is going to be free of what we call *afflictions,* but we have tremendous power in our thinking and our feeling. Thinking creates the thoughtform; feeling is the motor that drives that thoughtform out into action. And if you believe, for instance, that Saturn is malefic, it is malefic for you, whether it's true or not. So, your belief system is just as important as your astrological chart, and if you believe that adverse aspects are challenges that will call forth your resources and your courage and your strength, you're not going to worry too much about them."

HIGHER SELVES: "Many people have come to me scared to death by what astrologers have told them. We are karmically responsible for everything we say as counselors. We not only have to know what we're talking about through technique; we have to know when to say and how to say things that comes from the inner guidance that comes. I stress this because if you are doing counseling, remember, not matter how much you think you know on the downstairs level, you do not know as much as your *Essential Self,* so, before you talk to a client, say, *"Let my High Self and their High Self get together upstairs and give us what we need to know."* Because this way, the wisdom that pours through you, – not from you – will come through and you'll really be a blessing."

HOPE, NOT FEAR: "You have to decide where this person stands on the path of evolution; you don't talk to a kindergartener the same as an 8th grader. It's awfully important *how* you say things. If you look at a Saturn transit and say, *"Oh you're coming to an awful time,"* can you imagine what it does to the person?

But suppose you say, *"When you're going through a Saturn transit, if you'll realize that it's like standing on the shore; the tide is out, and if you launch your boat out into the deep at this particular time, you'll get stuck in the mudflat. Just keep the status quo and wait until this passes."*

Now, I've had people come in and say, *"You know, Issie, you don't know how much you've helped me when you gave me the date that the pressure would be off. When I thought it was going to last forever, I just couldn't take it, but when I knew I only had a certain length of time to be tested by Saturn..."* – and actually the day after Saturn moves off you begin to feel the difference. So tell the person, *"Look, this is the cycle you're in; don't make any changes right now, just hold the status quo, and after this date, the pressure will be off and you can go as far as you want when you want."* Now this way, you don't scare them."

URANUS: "No one can predict how Uranus is going to operate. Don't ever try but say, *"You're coming into a Uranian cycle; this means look for the unexpected."* Sometimes I steal Don Bradley's stuff, and say, because it'll lift them: *"it's the thrill planet; unusual, unexpected things are going to happen to you."* That gives them an entirely different perspective than, *"Oh, you're going to hit over the head with a thunder bolt!"* You say, *"Look, whatever this means – and only God knows, I don't – it's going to change your whole outlook, your attitude, it may blow you out of your present situation if you've been in a rut for a long time, and Uranus comes on and hits the chart, you know everything's going to be new. You're going to make changes you don't expect, but don't worry about it. The only difference between a rut and a grave is the depth, so the rut isn't going to be there anymore, but Uranus never takes anything from you that it doesn't give you something better in its place."*

The keynote of Uranus is *"Behold, I maketh all things new."* Uranus is the only planet in the chart that you cannot control or handle because it always happens through somebody else. And the only thing is, you still can control it by the right attitude to whatever it is. And so, you can say to the person, *"It will work through somebody else, and it is destiny."* It's the only planet that I feel, that destiny is something that was set up before you came in. Uranus will bring something that is destiny but will take it out again. That's destiny in the sense that it's something that we have already put into motion and we bring through. Uranus will always change your point of view, your consciousness."

CONNECTIONS: Why do you suppose some of us feel in tune with each other and recognize each other? I'm not a stranger to some of you; you've seen me *upstairs* on another level. We get together up there before we meet down here, you know. And sometimes you meet somebody and say, *"God, I can't stand them,"* and they haven't done anything to you; you just don't understand that first reaction of repulsion is here's an ancient enemy walking back into your life. You see, it's so connected.

TREE OF LIFE: Jupiter and Venus are outwardly benefic and inwardly corrosive. Mars and Saturn are outwardly corrosive and inwardly benefic. You overdo when it's Jupiter. You're apt to lose your judgment because everything's going so fine.

Did any of us ever grow through 'easy-going'? Every bit of Mars and Saturn, and when I talk about Saturn and Mars, I'm going to talk about the Tree of Life in regard to it, because Mars is very high up in the tree, and Saturn is the 3rd principle down from Kether the Crown, the highest of all. Saturn and Mars are your best friends, and Venus and Jupiter can make you lazy and indulgent.

Remind people if they think they're being picked on; Jupiter goes twice around the zodiac, Saturn only once, so you get twice as much good as what you call not good. Many things we call *not good* are the best things that could happen to us.

GET BUSY: When Mars is active, hitting off your animal nature: do something, tell the person get busy, and do something, even if only scrubbing a floor. You have to use Mars' energy, the adrenaline, to activate it rightly to get out tensions, resentments, and for some people, if Mercury is strong, writing them out helps. If Venus is strong, painting them out helps. There are many techniques to help people handle adverse aspects in their chart if you know how to do it, because you can't repress energy for a long time without becoming physically sick.

LOVE AND DIABETES: We've done a lot of work and research in medical astrology; we found that Cancer was tied up with resentment, long held and held down, probably from more than one lifetime. Diabetes and bitterness go together. Sugar in the body is upset when you have diabetes. Sugar's the symbol of sweetness and bitterness and diabetes are tied together. In cases of low blood sugar, the person will not put themselves first, and take responsibility for their bodies; talk to them about appreciating themselves; they don't love themselves properly.

THE DIVINE THIRD: In any relationship, as long as there's just two, it's an opposition. But those of you that know the Tarot, the Lover Card, that High Self above the two, the man and the woman; if you have that *Divine Third* in the relationship, I don't give a hoot what your chart says, you're safe; that Self will guide the two selves down here. That Lovers card is a great card to meditate on.

ABOUT IT IS ALL RIGHT: it deals with all these laws. There's a chapter on alcoholism to help people understand what it's all about, a chapter on Earth-bounds, a chapter on telling children about God, and all the things people want to know. Affirmations or mantras are extremely helpful; they can help every single one of us, and these things work.

RETROGRADE NATAL PLANETS: *"Retrograde* makes it more subjective; it pushes it in. Energies that are subjective don't come out and work as fast, but sometimes that's very good; sometimes you can release that energy slower and get more out of it. "

PROGRESSIONS: "When a planet goes direct by progression, especially Mercury, it is always a very important year in your life; Mercury rules the consciousness, and consciousness IS the only reality. And with Mercury and Venus coming together, or the year Mercury changes signs, or goes Direct or Retrograde, is always an important year to the consciousness; watch the changes that Mercury brings by Progression. Progressions are changes taking place within you that, when they take place, *will* change out here.

Transits are what happen out here, but you cannot change in consciousness without changing what happens to you out here, maybe not as quickly as transits bring it in, but that's the difference between transits and progressions. Progressions are changes in your consciousness inside, and transits are what are happening from other people and circumstances out here. Now progressions, on the inner side are most important.

TRANSITS: Remember in telling people about cycles: transiting energies work ahead of time. By the time they hit exact, the damage has been done. If you're going to get a blow, the power of that blow builds up; when it hits you it's all done. I always tell people how to handle these cycles ahead of time. The only planet that holds on and goes on beyond what you'd expect is Saturn, but the rest have worked by the time the aspect is exact. When we take our evolution into our own hands, Saturn becomes our friend, not our enemy.

THE COUNSELOR'S PATH: You have to communicate what you've learned, if you're going to play that role in this life, you have to go through many, many experiences. I seldom hear a voice inside me but one day I sat down and I said, *"Look, I couldn't have been that bad, to have all the karma I've had in this lifetime. I couldn't have been."* I heard a lovely, sweet voice say, *"Why needs ye think it is karma? It is education. How do you suppose you can help a broken heart unless yours has been broken? How can you understand if you haven't suffered? You chose this road and that is why all these experiences have been necessary."*

When you stick your neck out as a teacher, you cannot legitimately teach anything that you do not understand from the heart level, so I'll warn you all that are teachers and counselors, you're in for it! It is forced growth, but it is wonderful when you know why. After that I didn't feel so badly.

TWO LOVES: The Seven angels before the thrown of God are the seven angelic forces connected with the Earth, but as we have evolved, other planets have come in. Neptune, as you know is the higher octave of Venus. The difference between Neptune and Venus us: Venus is *you love me, and I'll love you.* Neptune says *I'll love you because it's the nature of our being to love.*

ON HUMOR: Let me tell you, if we have to walk this road of Earth, don't lose your sense of humor, because it makes the road lighter. At home when I see anybody getting heavy, I deliberately act the clown, because if you can see the funny side of yourself and of life, and laugh with people, it makes it so much nicer, doesn't it?

YOUNG PEOPLE: I work with about 300 young people every Friday night in Boston, and we have a ball. They're really scared of the older people, until they see you love them. They've gone through so much – and I know they've been crazy in lots of ways – but they also have something so wonderful. They can look right through us and see whether we're real or not. And if we've sat in judgment, or make judgments against them, they retreat. You think they don't have humor, but it's amazing; it's much more subtle, and many of them are poker faces, and they'll test you to see if you'll understand them. Once they see that you really care about them, you'll see that humor come out.

We have a great many laughs in Boston on Friday nights, but you must take them seriously on one side, and not seriously on the other. I really think, when dealing with young people, it is more a radiation of your approval of them, because there really is much you can approve of. I don't know where these kids come from, every time we get a place, it gets all filled up, and we have to go looking for something else. And we've always got a place and it's never cost us anything, and I never charge them anything. This is a free enterprise and they keep coming and coming and coming. You don't believe the hunger they've got for God until you come in contact with them.

SILENCE HAS POWER: We had the discipline of silence in my training by my teacher, and those of us who talked too much had to shut up, and those who didn't talk at all had to learn to talk. It was a very interesting and wonderful discipline, because we found out many things. You know, we used to have to take at first an hour a day – and we were with people – keep our mouth shut, and yet radiate so much lovingness, that no one would say, *'now what's the matter with you?'* We lost if we did. Then we had to take a whole day. Now this doesn't mean not saying what was necessary to be said, but making it a day of silence. And if you've ever been on a retreat – we have them in New England – and they'll always be about four hours of one day where we're absolutely still. We do no talking, and everyone says they never knew how much energy they could gather by being silent.

THE LAW OF RIGHT RELATIONS: If you break a relationship in a friendly fashion, and there isn't resentment, anger, and fighting, you're through with that karma. No relationship is ended if you don't end it in a loving manner. If you say, *"Well the other person isn't loving"* that's not your business. Your only business is that you hold no resentment, because if you do, you're sowing the seeds of cancer in the physical body, and you're doing yourself a tremendous amount of damage. Here is where astrology needs to point these laws out to people. You can't just know the technical part of astrology, and not understand why we're in situations. Nothing's in our orbit that we haven't ourselves sent out.

A LIVING LIGHT: The light that has to do with the Sun is a yellow gold that is so beautiful. When I say, what you see in meditation often, or you see on the inner levels, it's *living* light – it's light as we don't know it. The light and colors you'll see – and many of you will see – in meditation, is so *living*.

OYSTERS AND PEARLS: I'll tell you one other little incident that will help you in dealing with relationships, because I have a daughter that's a spiritual student. So, we were really trying, and we got a house that we bought, and we turned it over to God. We said, if anybody needed anything we could give, let them come.

The result was, I had to live in my office for three years, 'cuz I couldn't sleep in my own bed, somebody needed it (*laugh*). Anyway, I had a Scorpio aunt who was in her 70's who was a very frustrated person, because she'd never been married, she'd stayed with her parents until one of her parents died at 90, and so forth. And she came and was one of the most morose Scorpios I ever saw. As Helen said, it was just as if a heavy, grey soggy blanket was hanging in the middle of the house.

We did do our very best; we loved her, we prayed for her, we did everything we could to make her happy. She got more and more morose (*laugh*). And finally, I sat down one morning in meditation, and I asked, *"Where are we failing? Something's wrong, because we honestly and sincerely tried."* If she saw me kiss my daughter as she went out – we were a 'kissing kin' – and we'd kiss her. The face would freeze, and she'd look terrible.

I knew what was the matter. She'd never had any real love in her life, and we were trying to give it to her. So, I sat down, and said, *"Look, God, what gives? We've tried, we've done everything."* And I heard this voice say, *"She's the pearl in your oyster."* That really startled me. I'd never thought much about oysters, so I called a friend and asked, hey how are pearls made? She said, irritation gets into the oyster, and in order to protect itself, it puts this very pearly substance all around it.

I got the biggest kick out of that, because I suddenly realized, by our trying, we covered the irritation – *(laugh)* Aunt Lexie – with a substance that would make a beautiful pearl. And it didn't make any difference whether or not she changed, but now our whole group, when anybody's irritating them, they'll say, *"Oh, that's the pearl in my oyster."* And, you know, this helps, because we are going to have pearls in our oyster *(laugh)*. So, I just wanted to share that with you, so the next time someone irritates you, remember about that pearl.

ATTITUDE: When you get a chart, and you're talking to a client, Mercury is very important for you to take a look at before opening your mouth. In an Air sign, it's through their mind you're going to 'hook the fish' for God. In a Water sign, they're going to be emotional in their approach. In an Earth sign, they're going to want to know material things. I laugh sometimes, because some people come in and say, *"I'm not interested in my character, I'm not interested in any of your ideas from the inner side. I just want to know about my financial affairs."*

I'll say, *"Yes."* I start working, and before they've gone out that door, I've convinced them, because this is true, that they can't unhook their financial things out here from the kind of person they are in here. It can't be done, because your attitude toward things, your attitude toward material things are going to depend on what you really are inside. And if you change yourself, you're going to change your finances. It really is true.

LIFE AND DEATH: It depends on where you're standing, which is life and which is death. The person who comes into a body, we say, *"Here they come."* On the other side, they say, *"There they go."* When the time comes to go out, people here say, *"There they go"* and people on the next dimension say, *"Here they come."* Think about that; it's just the other side of the coin, and you can't die no matter how hard you try. Sure, you can take your body off, but you're not dead. Life is forever, and you understand that, you'll know why the baby cries when it comes in, and if you've been any kind of person worthwhile, they cry when you go out.

AQUARIANS: "Remember, there are two very distinct types of Aquarians. Saturn and Uranus are the rulers of Aquarius. If Saturn is stronger in the chart than Uranus, you've got a Saturnian Aquarian, and they'll be very different than your Uranian Aquarian. Not all Aquarians are part of the Aquarian Age, but every single person with Uranus highlighted – angular or close to Sun, Moon or Mercury – no matter what sign he is, is a Uranian.

PISCES: There are 2 types of Pisces. Jupiter and Neptune rule Pisces. Jupiter's the co-reagent of Neptune. It's as though there came a time in the evolutionary process, where *'Way-Up-There'* called a meeting, and said, *"Now look, Jupiter, we're giving you somebody to help you. We're sending Neptune into the Earth system. Neptune is going to help you by taking more and more of the responsibility for the sign Pisces."* But still Jupiter is there; you still find Jupiterean types. They're much more indulgent than your Neptune types. Always think of that – especially in horary astrology – pay attention to the two rulers.

DIGNITIES: Exaltations, detriments, fall and rulerships are terrifically important in telling you the energies you have brought to a high degree of efficiency, and the ones you haven't.

ASPECTS: Your *'bad aspects'*, as the average astrologer calls them, also give you the energy, strength and the courage to work anything out if you will use it.

JUPITER TRANSITS: When I've had a Jupiter transit, and asked that it might increase my wisdom inside, and that I might learn more, understanding, I found out something strange. When I've said, *"It doesn't matter whether I have anything out here or not but do increase my awareness."* Well, if it does that, it has to come down through, so I got the blessing on the outside, even though I wasn't looking for it.

SATURN VS URANUS: Saturn is the status quo, everything that's been established, crystallized. Uranus is the explosive thing that comes in, cracks and breaks it up. If Uranus goes over Saturn, some long status quo business or something that's been a weight is suddenly gone and the person feels a great sense of freedom. When Saturn goes over Uranus more responsibility and restriction confines or restricts in some way. Uranus works through other people, so someone in the family might be sick and need more attention, there might be more demands on you through other people. Remember, Uranus always works through other people in your personal chart. It's the only planet that you can't act on but can react to.

The rest of the planets you can change how you use that energy. The energy is pure, but it's how we have used it in the past. Always go back to the chart and see the Birthchart indication between two planets before you tell anybody how it's going to work. If you have a trine at birth, and a square comes up, hitting it off as a square, it will release the good way you have used that energy in the past. Supposing you have Uranus trine the Sun. When Uranus comes to that Sun, it will give you tremendous impetus forward. But suppose you have Uranus square the Sun at birth, or opposition, and Uranus comes to that Sun; you will say to the person, *'Look, you're going to have sudden very unpredictable impulses, or something's going to happen through someone else. Don't use your self-will; let it go, accept what comes, but don't bring your will up, or you'll be in trouble."* I've seen people break up a marriage under that, and I say, *"you're very foolish, because when that Uranus gets by that square at birth, you're going to be sorry you did it."*

And when Saturn is strong in the chart, you just say, *"Cool it, kid"* and explain Saturn this way, because so many people have been scared about Saturn: *"You are coming to a time where you're standing on a beach, symbolically. The tide is out; you're going to want to launch your boat out into the ocean, and if you do it right now, you're going to get stuck in the mudflat. Wait until the tide turns and hold the status quo. Whether you like it or not, the place on which you stand is holy ground, even if it looks like Hell right at the moment. Just hold still; don't make any changes."* And give them the exact day when Saturn walks off, and believe me, they'll come back and bless you, because I've had so many of them say to me: *"Issie, when you told me it was only going to last this long, I could stand it, but when I thought it was going on forever, I just was ready to just cop out completely on it."* When you discipline yourself, you take the constructive side of Saturn. Saturn is strict and undeviating justice, and if you try, Saturn works with you.

URANUS TRANSITS: I think, ahead of time, those of us that meditate, knowing what those energies mean, should sort of *talk* to Uranus, and ask that it might – because it's our High Self – ask that that energy may be used constructively in healing. Your High Self will never say "No" if you offer to be a healer, because it's always looking to help people down here. It can't say no. That's what we're about on this planet, is healing each other. Not "*we*" doing it, but letting the energies through us do it.

THE ASTROLOGERS' JOB: "The personal unconscious is the total of all the personality patterns of the past, and has no light of its own. Of course, this is intimately tied with the shadow, which is Saturn. Our job as astrologers and counselors is to help people understand their basic drives, needs and how best to fulfill them constructively. One must understand his unconscious forces and the shadow. Every one of us has a dark side, a shadow, and the only time you don't cast a shadow out in the world is when the Sun is directly overhead. Now the Sun is symbol of the real Self, and when you're completely aligned with your real Self, letting that put the Sunshine down through, you do not cast a shadow. But the minute we step out then the shadow shows. Now remember, that the shadow is not real, but it can cause a tremendous amount of trouble. The shadow is the dark side of ourselves. If we recognize that dark side, we can do something about our faults."

These next morsels from Issie's papers mostly seem to be notes of lectures she attended or books she had read; their sources are unknown. Issie spoke of a *Universal Mind*, from where all truth and wisdom springs, yet we would have liked to acknowledge the good folks who channeled such truths as our source.

ATOMS respond to different vibrational rates when the soul awakens to a higher conscious reality.

REINCARNATION: How in our newly born egos forgets their Source; at the end of one's incarnation "the Ego snaps the silver cord that binds him to the mortal form, and withdraws himself along the thread of light."

JESUS ON CHILDREN: "… The essence of wonder and delight is an intrinsic quality of the Spirit, and abides within … this spark of Self-realization is the contact which the subconscious has to the Superconscious in which lie all the potentialities of divinity … observing the wonders and the beauties of Nature, our souls expand in delight. ... so we preserve our priceless youth; so we grow in grace and in our knowledge of divinity.

MEMORY AND PERSONALITY: Memory is the exclusive faculty of the Subconscious, the custodian of all that has passed through the conscious mind from infancy to the present. The Subconscious records not only event, circumstance, physical and emotional conditions and surroundings, but <u>our mental and emotional reactions to them</u>, compounded into our personalities as <u>the sum of all our past</u>. ... the past is in our hands as truly as the present and future, if we observe our actions and attitudes, and give wiser instructions that will change our personalities in line with greater wisdom and experience. Through Memory, we develop habit, which becomes the Self.

MASS CONSCIOUSNESS: A family group, a tribe, and a nation, or a race, react as a composite whole to conditions they are called upon by circumstance or choice to undergo; and build up their own collective repressions and inhibitions, making a collective subconsciousness ... "mass-consciousness." The more one is in contact with humanity, the more one is at the mercy of impinging thoughts and emotions, which one either ignores and thus leaves unmastered, or accepts or rejects by dealing with them consciously. ... choose your thoughts ... "A little knowledge is dangerous; drink deep or taste not the Pierian spring." We should seek causes, think clearly, and not accept so unreasoningly the conclusions of this impinging consciousness.

Thinking and aspiring men and women often retire to monasteries and convents, to be free from the contaminating influence of mass-consciousness, and thus develop strong selves that would transcend personality and be able to make an impress on mass thought through "auric contact" – through prayer and blessings, through radiation. We must note the arising of unsought thoughts and feelings within the deeps of our own selves, and take action upon them: consciously approve or reject, and reinstruct our own subconsciousness; and transmute a bit of mass-consciousness which has reached us, and redirect it.

SUPERCONSCIOUS - HAPPINESS ... the State of Being of the Superconscious is a permeating Radiance like the sun, never ceasing to shine despite clouds and storms that may enwrap the Earth. Contact the Superconscious to abide in this ever-present light of Happiness, and to shine within, despite the clouds below, and eventually to dispel them and bring sunshine into the life of the self and of others.

DIRECT PERCEPTION: the Superconscious does not have to reason – it KNOWS because it exists in Reality, and has the faculty of instantaneous perception. Although this contact is made by the Conscious Mind in its earnest search for Light, it is the Subconscious which makes use of the memory-patterns of ideas which the Conscious Mind has implanted, in order to translate the Truth desired into terms which will be familiar to him. For the Superconscious does not think in terms, or words – it perceives, and it realizes comprehensively. To contact the Superconscious, relax and leave the other Mind alone to do its work without impatience or interference from the Conscious Mind. Sometimes this revelation from Superconscious to Conscious strikes with startling suddenness and an almost spectacular realization, like a flash of light that comes when pole is brought close to pole in electrical contact.

PROPHETS AND TEACHERS: God has ever revealed Himself through Prophets and Teachers. Light we seek, that our Light may shine out and someone who still depends upon the outer light may be guided toward that day when he too will seek and find the Light Within.

DIVINE GUIDANCE: I wish I could sufficiently impress upon the aspirant the necessity for utter and unquestioning obedience to the Voice Within. When the Master seeks to use a human vehicle, He must be able to depend upon it. It must not fail Him. Our Lord cannot always stop to explain His Plan to you. In the first place, to do so would be to expose it to the opposition of those forces which ignorantly oppose the Light (and it must be obvious to the aspirant that such indeed there are!) Then again, His Plan would often be utterly incomprehensible to the human personality, who at most sees but a few of the countless threads that are being used to weave a wondrous garment. It matters not that the direction which our Master gives you is not comprehensible to you; your path lies in trusting obedience. Many who are great in the eyes of the world are used by the Master whenever they will respond, but too often they are too much concerned about some excellent scheme of their own to heed the Master's Voice when its purport is not understood. Such people may do much for man and for themselves, but they cannot be <u>depended upon</u> to do the Master's work.

OBEDIENCE: must be instant and unequivocal. At first it is hard to listen and catch the Master's Voice; but the facility grows with practice. One must seek guidance not once or twice a day, but constantly. It doth not avail to ask God to keep you from mistake, unless you listen constantly for His Voice. At first you wander oft, and have to return repeatedly, and seek guidance anew. But through constant, quiet vigilance there comes a time when you walk with the Master as a constant Presence.

It is not to be assumed that you will always infallibly interpret the Master's Voice. Much of the human enters in to distort, especially in the early stages of your endeavor. Yet you may be sure that if you have erred in any vital matter, in bringing through your direction, the Master will quickly correct, if you but let Him.

The tests of obedience and responsiveness are very subtle. You must be proven unfailingly reliable, if the Master is to depend on you for any very vital work. Many are willing, many are able, many are faithful, but so few are yet dependable. You would be astounded could you see upon how slight a thread the greatest decisions often hang.

When you ask for guidance, reach up to the very Highest Being, and let Him guide you however He may wish, through your own Higher Self. Listen closely, for the answer is often dim at first because your mind so quickly intrudes. Often one is confused between two impressions. In such a case, it is usually wisest to <u>write</u> your request for guidance. In fact it is always wisest to ask for your guidance in writing until such time as the awareness of the Master's Presence has grown into an abiding consciousness. Writing occupies the intellect, focuses the attention, and clears the mind for the direction to be more definitely received. Write whatever comes, even if it be but a word at a time. Constantly listening clears the channel. There is no better way. The student must learn to trust his own Inner Voice. Often false humility leads one virtually to say, *"Nothing can come through <u>me</u>. I know you made me, God, but You can't do anything with me!"* This attitude is not only a self-betrayal, but a betrayal of the Father Himself, Who seeks to manifest through you and through all His children. Do not fight this Inner Voice, but trust and listen until clear grows the Voice and plain the Way and the Mighty Plan.

Sometimes you can look back and see the significance of a direction you have blindly followed. But most often you cannot see, and only know that by your obedience you have been serving, even though you know not how or why. You will very soon find proof abundant that your guidance thus sought is unfailing and divine. But the proof comes when you seek it not. You cannot ask for it. Utter faith is the first requisite of discipleship.

It may seem at first a trying path to follow; but it soon reveals itself as the only sure and happy way, and really the easiest way of all. Utter release of the self-will, and listening obedience, brings a tranquillity and freedom from struggle and doubt, that cannot be measured; and no self-choice could bear a fraction of the interest of a life so dedicated. One daily watches a drama unfold in which one is both action and spectator. And the rhythm of one's life becomes secure.

COSMIC CURRENTS: Just as there are tides and currents in the ocean and in the air, so are there in the realm of the Superconscious. Power, vibration, currents of thought, of feeling, of vitality, of well-being, of capacity to achieve, sweep rhythmically through the others, cognate, motivated, and impelled by Superconscious activity. By proper and sustained attunement with the Superconscious, one can become sensitively aware of these currents, these tides, and let them sweep through him and carry him on to his own fulfillments. We speak casually of "luck"; but what so often appears to be "good luck" is the result of a person's consciously or unconsciously putting himself in line with Cosmic currents and letting them sweep him on to victory or success. Or, conversely, "bad luck" is due to lack of attunement, lack of sensitivity, which prevents proper synchronization with the Cosmic Currents and makes him miss his timing and be too hasty or too slow to take the currents as they sweep by and through him; or too stubborn or self-willed, so that he opposes them instead of being carried onward by them.

SUBCONSCIOUS AND EVIL: We have warned the student that emphasis on evil, or on the negative, serves only to reinforce it. That is why "denial" is psychologically an incorrect method. To say, "I am not afraid," <u>impresses</u> the subconscious with the idea of "afraid." A positive statement is always wisest, because it presents the ideal instead of the unideal. To feel, "I have Confidence, Courage, Strength, etc." is to impress the Subconscious constructively.

In eliminating faults of character, one should begin by building in the concepts of the ideal, until they become a part of the self, and can be depended upon to a considerable extent. When one becomes aware of the unideal, one does not <u>deny</u> it, but immediately, by the method of substitution, turns his thoughts and feelings to the opposite virtue. This results in a type of "re-polarization."

It is, however, a mistake to think that the substitution of good for evil is all that is necessary. It is only a temporary expedient, a first step, however valuable it may be. The Subconscious <u>always remembers</u>, and substitution alone is not enough. We are likely to be caught unawares by the subconscious memory of evil, or of a bad habit, unless we consciously transmute the very roots of that evil. Not denial, but <u>transmutation</u> of evil is the ultimate aim; so that when, in the future the Subconscious remembers evil, it will remember transmutation and redemption in connection with that evil. It is a mistake to ignore; it is a mistake to deny; but to build in the good and to consciously redeem the evil leads to Personality Mastery on the Path of Purification.

SUBCONSCIOUS AND GUILT: The contact of the personal self to the Superconscious is by way of the Subconscious. Mental aspiration becomes <u>empowered</u> by the emotional aspect of the Subconscious and thereby contacts the "Higher Self." Under certain circumstances, however, the Subconscious fails to make that contact. The Subconscious has a strong sense of worthiness and unworthiness, impressed upon it by moral principles inculcated in youth by relatives and teachers, and by Conscious Mind acceptance of moral values through hearing, reading, and reasoning upon them. There is probably no one who does not hold in his own Subconscious a certain degree of "guilt consciousness," due to his own failure to live up to the principles impressed as aforesaid upon the Subconscious. Many of these formerly accepted "precepts" we have outgrown, or changed our minds about; but that does not eradicate them from Subconscious memory unless we deal with them consciously. That is why it is well to uncover them, reason upon them, deal with them consciously, and teach the Subconscious our new attitude about them.

The wise student will train himself to become alert to the least stirrings of "guilt feelings": of shame, embarrassment, and humiliation. He should not ignore them, nor discount them, but should face them with conscious kindness to the human self; and console the shrinking Subconscious, encouraging it to bring such feelings to the surface and be enlightened. If it is possible to make amends, he should do so, in some form or other. He should seek to understand the things that brought about the failure to adhere to a principle, recognize the humanness of temptation and failure, and resolve to be increasingly true to the principles he still holds dear. Guild, shame, embarrassment, and humiliation are <u>negative</u> emotions, and should not be encouraged; they should be supplanted by true humility and contrition, and the assured determination to become increasingly true to all one values. That is all that can be expected of anyone; and one should not hold oneself more exactingly to a standard than he would another; nor hold another more rigidly to a standard than he would hold himself. "To err is human," and one must be wise and compassionate in dealing with the Self's self, and with the self of every other Self.

MAKING AMENDS: One further demand the Subconscious makes on the conscious self, before it will consider it worthy to contact the Superconscious; and that is, that it make amends for the wrongs that it has committed, consciously or unconsciously. The Subconscious is imbued with a strong sense of Justice. Whenever the Subconscious brings to the threshold of consciousness a wrong we have done another, we should acknowledge it and see in what way, if any, we can make amends. The Subconscious does not demand perfection; but it does demand righteous intent and the carrying out into action of every possible means of restitution or adjustment.

It is true that many of these past misguided actions of ours have passed beyond the bounds of possible restitution or recompense. What procedure then will satisfy the Subconscious? First, what the Church would call a sincere "act of contrition" followed by "penance." Remembering that the Subconscious is strongly impressed by "symbol," which is its means of communicating with the Superconscious, we should, at some personal <u>sacrifice</u> (to show our sincerity), consciously repay to another or to mankind as a whole, for the wrong inflicted on someone we cannot now repay. This beneficence should not be done to glorify self for generosity but should be a humble attempt to make amends for wrongs once done; to balance the account as well as may be, and to assure the Subconscious of the sincerity of one's intent.

Deeds of kindness, words of compassion and hope, also assure the Subconscious that one is worthy of the gifts of Divine Beneficence. An attitude of "I have in ignorance and self-will done so much that was harmful to my brothers, that all I can do to help them is no more than is required of an aspiring son of God," will open the Threshold to the Superconscious by the joyous acquiesence of the Subconscious.

ASSOCIATION: One of the foremost activities of the Subconscious Mind is "association." Every impression that comes to the Conscious Mind stirs the Subconscious to immediate association of that impression with others that in one way or another have a relation to it. This is one way in which the Subconscious records it for future memory, and it is the way in which it recalls it to the Conscious Mind. Association is a manifestation of the Law of Attraction; and it is this attraction of ideas one to another which holds together all the concepts which form part of our "mind-entity" that gives to each individual the character that is his. But this activity of the Subconscious is far more dominant than most of us are aware. It is important that we become conscious of this, for the fact is that our conscious thinking occupies a very small part of our thinking. We are ruled and activated by the Subconscious most of the time.

I advise the aspirant to watch his thinking and discover the Subconscious activities for himself. It is with the utmost difficulty that a Conscious Mind maintains concentration. It is said that 15 seconds is the longest time the ordinary person can concentrate his attention on a single idea before intruding factors enter in – in other words, before the Subconscious interposes some of its associated picturing and ideas, and we say "the mind wanders." In point of fact, by far the greatest part of our thinking is dominated by Subconscious meanderings, consciously or unconsciously permitted.

It is good practice to sit down quietly and take any idea you choose – not just one that comes to mind from the Subconscious, but one that you consciously select – and try to concentrate upon it; and watch the association process of the Subconscious thrust itself upon you. Do not fight it – note it, and discover if you can how the connections are made. Then turn quietly but determinedly back to your original thought again. Follow this process until you can more and more check the undesired chains of association. The Conscious Mind must learn to rule the Subconscious and use it wisely and constructively; and not be at the mercy of an undirected "stream of consciousness". Realize that this faculty of the Subconscious is the key to Memory and to the infinity of knowledge. Use the Subconscious as fully as you can, but do not let it choose what you shall think and feel; for the Conscious Mind is the seat of Will, of conscious choice, and the Subconscious should not be allowed to usurp its prerogative. Your true individuality is dependent on your conscious choices. Use the Subconscious, depend upon it, but be the Master of your own intent and action.

HUMOR: Humor is one of the qualities belonging to the true Subconscious, as distinct from the purely instinctive consciousness of animal man. It was the latest developed of all the human qualities. In fact, it is a purely human characteristic, not found in other realms and evolutions, because its existence was not called for. But Humor was called forth by the sheer bitterness and anguish of human living. It was a blessing of alleviation, given to relieve the tensions of suffering humanity. In the ancient myth of Pandora, after she had loosed all the negative qualities upon the Earth, she opened the box once more, and released "Hope" to relieve the sufferings of the human heart. Yet I tell you, my brothers, Hope has not a fraction of the remedial power that Humor can impart. For Hope is but a looking-forward to better conditions in the future – the expectation of ultimate Good. But Humor releases tensions, it pricks the bubble of pompousness and pride, and views everything in proper proportion; it changes the atmosphere of pessimism and despair, and enables one to meet the present conditions with more freedom and joy. In a word, Humor is a change of mental attitude that can make the present ills fall into proper place in the overall picture. Yes, Humor, true humor, is one of the most blessed gifts presented unto mortal man.

By Humor, I do not mean sarcasm, nor barbed or ribald wit, but the ability to get and give genuine amusement at the incongruities which human acts and attitudes present. Humor should begin with self, for unless one can laugh at oneself in his ludicrous cavorting, he is not humble enough to exercise true Humor. Humor should always be laughing with, and never at; as we have oft been told. Humor makes a mock of undue solemnity, undue worry and fear; at overvaluing of non-essentials, of self-importance and self-consciousness. It is an attempt to put everything in its proper place in the infinite and eternal. Humor makes much of little, and makes little of the unessential much.

Humor is a sense of order, of propriety, of balance, that is quick to see and point out lack of order, balance and fitness, and make of them a joyous mock that will restore a normal attitude and quicken right activity.

Through the Subconscious capacity to make links between objects and ideas, the quality of Humor can manifest. It is through "association of ideas" in incongruous relations or degrees of value, that we evidence Humor. It is viewing things in unusual or ludicrous relationships, or observing with amusement the unusual or ludicrous relationships which present themselves in situation or attitude. Any deviation from common sense or from the norm is an object of humorous observation. To note the humorous, reinforces the normal and restores balance.

Show me the person who has no true sense of Humor and I will reveal to you a person who overvalues self, and is given to placing undue emphasis on less important things; who tends to bigotry and narrow-mindedness, and unjust criticism of his fellow men.

But because Humor, like the divinely potent spark of Self-Realization, lies innately in the Subconscious Mind of every man, it is possible for all to awaken it, and bring it forth to alleviate and soothe the ills of mortal existence, and make man's state more loving, more joyous and more free. Cultivate Humor, my brothers: even "assume a virtue if you have it not." If Humor comes hard at first, its manifestation may be labored and may bring you scorn. Laugh then at the <u>scorn</u> – find humor in the very clumsiness of your fumbling efforts. Say, "I was trying to be funny – and look what a mess I made of it!" Every <u>beginning</u> is inept, my friends, – shall we refrain because we make a sorry spectacle of ourselves in our first attempts! Humor, true Humor, is based on Humility and on Sincerity. If you cannot achieve it, it is possible you are consumed with pride, and with a posing for effect! Face, then, these flaws ere you proceed anew with Humor.

GUIDING THE SUBCONSCIOUS: It is the responsibility of the Conscious Mind to determine what shall enter the Subconscious. And it is the responsibility of the Conscious Mind to correct anything wrongful or incorrect which the Subconscious presents from the past into present consciousness. This is done by "suggestion" or "command." By "command" I do not mean a tense or violent effort of will, but a firm and kindly determination expressed clearly to the Subconscious.

"Suggestion" is a term too familiar to all my readers, I am sure, to need any amplification. It is well for the student, however, to realize that suggestion, which approaches the Subconscious of yourself or of another by indirection, is often more effective than direct command. Suggestion leaves the will free to arrive at the desired conclusion or acceptance of the idea, without arousing opposition.

The aspirant should watch carefully for any sign of resistance in the Subconscious to the given suggestion or command. If such sign is felt, and time permits, it is well to explore the matter thoroughly and correct the cause of the resistance by wise and kindly teaching and guidance of the Subconscious. Through practice, and by sympathetic and patient and patient comprehension, the Subconscious can be persuaded to give up its secrets and reveal its inhibitions and reluctances. If action is urgent, the command or suggestion must be given firmly; but you should not be surprised if there is resistance in the Subconscious that will hinder the full unfoldment of your intent.

Substitution is always preferable to conflict within the Subconscious. Provide it with an acceptable idea rather than clamp the lid on an undesirable urge or concept. Do not antagonize the Subconscious, or it will retire with its idea into secrecy and by devious ways that you will not be aware of, force it into conscious activity to your embarrassment at some future time.

When you have given a suggestion or command to the Subconscious, do not intrude upon it in its work. Provide it with all available information and give it direction. Remove all obstacles in so far as you can. And picture perfection and ideality and right conclusions. Then leave it alone, to work the problem out in its own unique and fulsome way.

CONSCIOUS TRAINING AND USE OF SUBCONSCIOUS MIND – OCCULT RETROSPECTION: There is a principle of retrospection which is used in many, if not most, occult groups, and which will be most valuable for the student to practice during his study and mastery of the negative subconscious mind within himself. The student is undertaking to analyze all his negative reactions, tracing them to their source in the race subconscious, and to watch for them and transmute them as they recur. He is doing this in two ways: by general observation and transmutation of ANY negative tendency he observes, and special observation and transmutation of some specific quality. The student is now requested, before retiring, to align with his Higher Self and review all the events, thoughts, and emotions of the day, and examine himself honestly and carefully as to how he met these situations.

There should be no remorse, no self-condemnation, but rather a self-confessional followed by a reinforcing of the idea, and a resolution to improve constantly through discriminate thought and action. Having completed this self-examination (which may very profitably be carried on in bed, before closing the eyes in sleep), greet the All-Highest One, and ask Him to aid you with these problems with which you are working.

Now there are two ways of carrying on this retrospection. One is to start with the last event of the day, tracing its cause in events, thoughts, and emotions which preceded it, and going backward over the day to the time of waking in the morning. This is the method most frequently used in occult groups, since it traces events back to their causes, thus teaching a valuable lesson: and also because it leads to a tracing back still further into past lives. Sometimes this tracing is done consciously, and sometimes memories of long-past lives flash unexpectedly in upon the unprepared mind.

Such a method has its advantages, but it also has grave dangers. Modern psychoanalysis has shown us clearly the dangers of this practice; and those of you who have assimilated the lessons so far given in this Subconscious series will readily perceive them. Psychoanalysis which follows this particular retrospective process does not always stop with causes which eventuated in this life; it often strikes back into past lives, with emotions and thoughts long ago outgrown, and impresses them upon the mind of today's patient with profound shock and revulsion. More than this, it may break the bounds of man's individual past and strike directly into the mass-memory with all its horrors and perversions of the Real. The disadvantages of such a method are too obvious to enumerate in this article – but I ask each student to think out for himself these disadvantages.

The other method makes use of the opposite process, and is the one which we recommend to our students. According to this method, the student in his retrospection begins with HIS FIRST WAKING MOMENTS, and traces thoughts, emotions and acts, comments on his attitude toward them; makes fresh resolves as he contemplate them in retrospection; and sees emotions, thoughts and actions as causes shaping into other emotions, thoughts and actions as surely as by the other method. The former method leads to dangers of involution, while the latter follows cause in its resultant evolution. Let the student be faithful in following out this principle of retrospection, and he will find himself DURING THE DAY noting the causes and effects, and applying at once the corrective principle.

THE SPIRAL: Let me call your attention to two phenomena in Nature: One is the whirlpool – a sectional vortex in which water swirls over a larger surface, drawing any floating objects closer and closer in a constricting spiral till they reach the downward swirl that pulls them around the circumference of a descending cone, into the depths which are focused in a central point.

The other is the waterspout on water, and the tornado on land. This is the reverse of the whirlpool: for it starts from a central point and spirals <u>upward</u>, widening as the spiral increases, and carrying upward with it water or surface objects that lie in its path.

These are negative manifestations of a spiral motion and power. The wise student can learn to make use of a spiral power in his own unfoldment. There are those who say that "life" itself is movement, <u>spiral</u> movement in and through appropriate types of matter. Mass consciousness is a matter of sectional spiral movement by which the un-individualized mind and emotional nature is swept in negatively to its own undoing. Every conscious being should avoid being swept into mass emotions over which he has no control – and equally into mass ideas that pass for true ideals, but are far from being what they purport to be. On the physical plane we can see these sectional vortices; in mass-consciousness, we can <u>feel</u> them.

The first step in the rightful use of spiral movement is to gain sufficient self-control to enable oneself to keep away from negative vortices of thought and emotion. Mastery of the subconscious is vital to this achievement. The next step is based on powerful idealism. The concentration in faith, humility, and aspiration on a laudable and practical ideal forms a center of power. That center of power begins to swirl emotionally and draw to it in a spiraling movement from far to nearer and nearer, all the elements needful to make a full and true manifestation of that idea. This should not be done through <u>will</u> – except as 'will" is realized as quiet and assured persistence – but through valuing the ideal with warm and rich emotional power, and realizing without any doubt its possibility of manifesting. "Through the power of the Infinite, this can be in material and human manifestation." One waits then, in confidence and watches the spiral power assemble the elements appropriate to its full and ideal expression. One does not limit, one does not define the manner of fulfillment; one concentrates on valuing the ideal with full confidence that it can be made manifest in rightfulness. This is the method of Creative Imagination.

There is another phase of spiritual manifestation of the spiral, which is the reverse of "precipitation," even as negatively the waterspout and tornado are the reverse of the whirlpool. There is a spiraling upward of the life, the soul, the mind, the environment by which that is lesser, limited, confined, expands and becomes more rich, more full, more universal, more spiritually powerful. In using this phase of a spiral motion consciously, one conceives the self, the environment, etc., as a potent focus of the spiral movement of life and consciousness. One knows the Infinite with all its potency is focused in the self and the environment in which he finds himself, and he visualizes a spiraling outward and upward to include within the consciousness and the environment more and more of the vast expanse of the Good, the True, and the Beautiful. This focused power is the power of Impersonal Love. The self does not move, but the consciousness is felt to be expanding through the power of Love and Aspiration, in a spiral, to include more and more of the utterly true and desirable. One feels the self to grow in trust, and beauty, and worthiness, to thus expand in spiral consciousness.

THE SOUL SPEAKS: Long have you gone your way alone down the road of deafness and blind eyes and pain; not the way I would have led you, though perfectly right, for it was an education. The blindness and the darkness of it has taught us what not to do therefore we know the path.

Ours were not object lessons; always we have learned through opposites. To learn the great lesson of listening we talked too much. We told others of the path they should take long before we thought of following our own. We hated all things to learn how to love; we took all to ourselves to learn how to give. We did the things of death to learn life truly. We have suffered great pain to know the secret source of the everlasting joy. We feared, in order that we may become fearless and know the mystery of the dark. We chose the road of separation to feel the ecstasy of oneness and completion at last. We entered the terrible sphere of time and space in order to transcend both and be free. We took upon ourselves pounds of tiresome flesh to make of it a golden symbol of the great spiritual beauty and freedom. We asked for everything at first through our desiring and through brooding we learned the most wonderful lesson of all; wanting nothing but to give.

Long have I sat mute and silent in the darkness. Now we have learned the lesson. The circle of separateness is complete. We are ready to enter a new globe now, a globe much larger than the one we have known, much more wonderful. In it there are greater tests than we ever had before. But the new tests instead of being painful are joyous; not separateness is ahead but oneness; union in all things. The path gleams before us that leads to Wisdom, Love and Understanding.

ON LOVE: Those who are kept apart who overcome great obstacles, who learn the greatest thing of all – to wait – who touch the upper reaches of splendor in love of man and woman and thus prepare themselves for the greater union and the higher questing which is the love of God together. In the big expansions of life, in moments of great happiness, or hard driven by pain – most of us have realized that the higher we rise in human consciousness, the nearer we get to the All.

There is always wrecking work before a new and wider circle is entered upon. Hold to nothing in matter. It is slavery. Give yourself laughingly to your daily bread without thought of result. That which we think we want today will look as absurd tomorrow as the hopelessness of a child over a plaything broken. Separation is as essential as companionship for the real Romance.

NOTES FROM ALICE BAILEY'S BOOKS

The source of these next notes seem, at least partly, from the teachings of Alice Bailey, whom Issie greatly admired. Some of the above notes may also have come from Alice Bailey's books.

ON SPEECH: "We must learn silence in face of that which is evil; silence where suffering of world is concerned yet withal, speaking where encouragement is necessary using tongue for constructive ends. … He was a server because he had no ends of his own to serve and from him goes out no vibration, which can beguile him from his chosen path.

ETHERIC BODY: Energy centers coming from 7 planes or areas of consciousness. Etheric vitalizes and energizes the physical body and integrates it into the energy of the Earth and solar system. Web of energy streams, of lines of Love and Light – Along these lines cosmic forces flow as the blood flows thru veins and arteries. ... expressing essential unity of all life ... centers awaken by Character Building, Right Motive, Service, Meditation, Knowledge of the Centers, Breathing exercises must not concentrate on centers – must purify bodies in which the centers are found. Seclusion needed to work directly on centers and none of us have that opportunity.

If disciple serves, loves, works and disciplines himself – they will develop safely. Why it's dangerous: Aura is essentially a radiator. Let the emotional aura be exchanged for the soul one – High thinking, Right Living, Loving Activity, Living Light, Criticism must go.

ENERGY: Your body is a dynamo – the more you use it the more energy is supplied from the Infinite source. If you don't use it there is no need for any new supply. Be more active and you will have more energy – be less active and you will lose energy. Use it and from the source more energy becomes available. Love more and you will have more love to give – if you want to become an infinite source of love show as much love as you can.

Use More and You Have More is the law of life. Only misers love energy, don't be a miser. Anything that comes into the process of time becomes old. The moment it enters time it starts to get old. But your center is always fresh – eternally young. Once in contact with it, love is an every-moment discovery.

You are so afraid of allowing anything to happen – lose your fear and let things happen. The river is flowing – don't push it. There is no need – it is flowing by itself – be on the bank and let it be – if you are courageous enough drop yourself in the river and float with it – don't swim – that means fighting. Just float.

BELIEF, EMOTIONS AND IMAGINATION CREATE YOUR WORLD – No perfection on earth – Spirit is always in a state of becoming – perfection would mean completion – cannot be ... use your mind to discriminate among the thoughts you want to form into your system of beliefs. All kinds of thoughts – good and bad – come in – chose what you want to entertain … Brain is the physical counterpart of the mind … through its functions the soul and intellect are connected with the body …When your ideas about yourself change, so does your experience. … You are you but which one – each of us creates our own world – Belief makes it.

FATHER RIZZO

Issie loved Father Rizzo. In her notes from one of his lectures in 1977, she wrote:

TOTAL LOVE ELIMINATES ALL KARMA … the magnetic attractive power of higher atoms draw atoms of higher frequency, take place of those of lower vibrations … the teacher's job to increase the mental equipment (not stuffing facts into the mind but understanding) … emotions and feelings need to be controlled by the mind … detachment is so important … personality reactions are based upon emotion – attachment to externals … clear seeing leads to wise action. … Our goal in evolution is full awareness – functioning as souls, not personalities … the unevolved emits no light, flickers at intervals during life of average man … becomes a shining light in the disciple.

SECRET DOCTRINES: Matter is the vehicle for the manifestation of Soul on this plane of existence (we live in our forms – we are not it). Soul is the vehicle on a higher plane for the manifestation of Spirit; these 3 are a trinity synthesized by Life, which pervades them all.

OCCULT FUNDAMENTALS BY MURIEL SANATSAN

These quotes from Issie's papers convey a lot about her work:

THE AURA: "Through attunement with the One God, and the use of one's body as a channel of the Healing and Harmonizing Light, subtle emanations issue forth and surround the body in a magnetic sphere." "The outermost sphere of the aura on any plane is that to which occult students refer as "the ring-pass-not" – the limit of the individual's sphere of influence on that plane. "… Through service, one's aura, or field of influence, becomes enlarged."

VIBRATION: "Thought is the great form-producer, and is in itself vibration of a certain order, tending to clothe itself in matter that is responsive to that vibration." ... "Sound and motion are also creators of form." ... "Not only do physical objects vibrate, but emotions and thoughts vibrate and respond to vibration." ... "Vibration presupposes an interplay of matter and life."

INCARNATION, OVERSHADOWING AND INSPIRATION: The Hierarchy, Angels, Masters, Initiates and Disciples reach mankind by incarnating in a human baby body or taking over the body of another at the time the original occupant leaves it or when a Master or Initiate wishes to use a body temporarily, for specific purposes. He trains an incarnate student to step out of his body and let the Master use it with permission. Overshadowing: the Master or Initiate does not incarnate in the body but uses the student's body on some other plane, so that while the student speaks or acts on this plane, the Master's ideas are presented through direct inspiration, "tuning it" to the Ideals of God. The Master may inspire any attuned vehicle by entering the student's aura, standing beside him, and impressing him mentally, emotionally or spiritually."

GOOD & EVIL: Godhood is the unlimited capacity to realize an idea. It takes two Brothers to establish the Mastery: the Mastery of Light, and the Mastery over Darkness; Mastery of Good, Mastery over (not of) Evil. Emulate one another in that which seemeth good; do not that which displeases you in others; neither criticize, but understand.

CENTERS: The sincere student should lift up his heart in aspiration to his Higher Self, his Master, and his God; and await the coming in good time of his own Supernal Flame.

MASTER'S VEHICLE: When an Angel wishes a garment of flesh, two Angels overshadow 2 humans at the moment of physical uniting. The child born of that union comes bearing a light not of Earth.

AS ONE BOOK CLOSES, ANOTHER OPENS

We close with words *via Issie* that *found me* as I was completing this book. I got the idea to include Issie's original cover design of *Astrology: A Cosmic Science*. I have two copies, one from Helen Hickey. Without a thought, I took that one off the shelf. Upon lifting the cover to scan it, I noticed a handwritten message in Issie's script on the facing page. It is called *"This is Truth about the Self"* or *Pattern on the Trestleboard* by Paul Foster Case.

"All the Power that ever was or will be is here now.

I am a center of expression for the Primal Will to Good that eternally creates and sustains the Universe.

Through me its unfailing Wisdom takes form in thought and word.

Filled with Understanding of its perfect law I am guided moment by moment along the path of liberation.

From the exhaustless riches of its Limitless Substance, I draw all things needful both spiritual and material.

I recognize the manifestation of the Undeviating Justice in all the circumstances of my life.

In all things, great and small, I see the Beauty of the Divine Expression.

Living from that Will, supported by its unfailing Wisdom and Understanding, mine is the Victorious Life.

I look forward with confidence to the perfect realization of the Eternal Splendor of the Limitless Light.

In thought and word and deed, I rest my life, from day to day upon the sure Foundation of Eternal Being.

The Kingdom of God[22] *is embodied in my flesh."*

---

[22] In other sources, *Spirit* or *Heaven* is used where Issie wrote *God*.

INDEX OF ISSIE-ISMS

Many of Issie's sayings or *"Issie-isms"* as we came to call them are below, with where they can be found herein. Countless more of her teachings, mantras, prayers, insights, allegories and stories are in <u>Astrology: A Cosmic Science,</u> <u>It Is All Right,</u> and *Your Cosmic Blueprint: A Seeker's Guide* (Natal Report). You are invited to comment on any of the ones you like at NewAgeSages.com.

ISSIE-ISM:	**PAGE:**
I never let the title of my talk interfere with what I'm going to say!	i
We are vibratorily connected to everything	73, 120, 168
Absent from the appearance is present with the power	77, 93, 98
We do not come unbound into this livingness	4, 73, 87, 117, 124
We do not start here or stop here; infinity goes in both directions.	73
Discipline is Disciple-In	80
If we knew better, we would do better	73, 103
Consciousness IS Reality	87, 110, 158, 184
Act as if	89
The spiritual life is never dull!	95
Love never dies; it only changes form	96
The Pearl in Your Oyster	105, 187-188
Put it on the inner altar and ask for guidance	77
Let go and let God	49, 78, 95, 109, 118, 158

The following "Issie-isms" although not discussed in this book, are words of wisdom that Isabel often passed along ...

Love anyone enough and you'll never lose them; hate anyone enough and they'll never leave you. (This is from a reincarnation perspective.)

God has 3 answers to prayers; yes, no and wait, I've got something better. (Most relevant during Saturn transits, which require patience.)

All my Ways are Pleasant Ways – All my Paths are Peace (An affirmation to help calm the mind and refocus on gratitude)

Is it Loving? Will it hurt anyone? (Ask yourself if facing a hard decision.)

Alone-ness is All-One-Ness (An affirmation that we are never really alone.)

ABOUT THE AUTHORS

Jay Hickey   **Amy Shapiro**

Jay lives in Epsom, New Hampshire, where he runs a Tree Farm with his wife Patricia, and works closely with Town government. Jay served in the United States Army as a Medic, stationed at the Military Hospital in Munich Germany; he worked for many years in construction with his brothers, and served on the Rescue Squad. He works with the Federal Emergency Management Agency (FEMA) to help homeowners and the Board of Selectmen with flood plain regulations, planning, zoning compliance, public ordinances, and wetland concerns. Jay has served as Town Project Manager, Acquisitions Manager, and Chairman of the Board of Selectmen.

Amy has served as President of Star Rovers, and Boston's NCGR. She was Editor for Para Research, consultant for Astral Research, writer for Horoscope Magazine, Dell, New Age Retailer, Cosmic Communications, founded *Cape Ann School of Astrology* and produced *Good Heavens!* radio and cable shows. Amy has taught T'ai Chi, is a Past Life Therapist, Nutrition Consultant, Author and Publisher. She earned her BA at Curry College, M Ed at Boston College, trained at Harvard's Mind/Body Institute and New England Society for Clinical Hypnosis. Amy lives in Gloucester MA with husband Ed Kaznocha, where they raised two sons and enjoy the ocean and gardening. She may be reached at NewAgeSages.com.

OTHER *NEW AGE SAGES* BOOKS:

Before This Song Ends: *A Timeless Romance* by Amy Shapiro

The Critique of Pure Music*,* by Dr. Oskar Adler

The DIS-Appointment Book: *A Humor Therapy Guide to Conquering Disappointments,* by Amy Shapiro

Dr. Oskar Adler: *A Complete Man*, by Amy Shapiro

Forces At Work: Astrology and Career, by Amy Shapiro

The Gift of the Tortoise: *New Insights Into the I Ching,* by Jo Onvlee and Amy Shapiro

Inviting Eris To The Party: *Our Provocateur In Unfair Affairs,* by Amy Shapiro

It Is ALL Right: by Isabel Hickey

One Sex To The Other: *Reincarnation and the Dual-Gender Soul* By Amy Shapiro

Over The Mountains, by Johan Onvlee and Amy Shapiro

Questioning The Oracle: *The I Ching,* by Jo Onvlee and Amy Shapiro

The Sparrow's Tale: *T'ai Chi Stories to Inspire,* by Johan Onvlee and Amy Shapiro

The Testament of Astrology (7 Volumes) by Dr. Oskar Adler

For these or ***Your Cosmic Blueprint***, visit NewAgeSages.com

Printed in France by Amazon
Brétigny-sur-Orge, FR